# THE IMAGE OF GOD IN MAN

ACCORDING TO

## CYRIL OF ALEXANDRIA

# THE IMAGE OF GOD IN MAN

ACCORDING TO

## CYRIL OF ALEXANDRIA

By

WALTER J. BURGHARDT, S.J.

*Professor of Patrology and Patristic Theology*
*Woodstock College*

WIPF & STOCK · Eugene, Oregon

Wipf and Stock Publishers
199 W 8th Ave, Suite 3
Eugene, OR 97401

The Image of God in Man According to Cyril of Alexandria
By Burghardt, Walter J.
ISBN 13: 978-1-60608-395-6
Publication date 01/07/2009
Previously published by Woodstock College Press, 1957

IMPRIMI POTEST:

> GULIELMUS F. MALONEY, S.J.
> *Praepositus Provinciae Marylandiae*
> Datum Baltimorensi die 20 decembris, 1956

NIHIL OBSTAT:

> EDUARDUS A. CERNY, S.S., D.D.
> *Censor Librorum*

IMPRIMATUR:

> ✝FRANCISCUS P. KEOUGH, D.D.
> *Archiepiscopus Baltimorensis*
> Datum Baltimorensi die 28 ianuarii, 1957

TO MY MOTHER
AND
TO THE MEMORY OF
MY FATHER AND BROTHER

# TABLE OF CONTENTS

# INTRODUCTION

The patristic conception of the image of God in man is of uncommon significance for historical theology, because it enters so intimately into —in fact, sometimes commands—the anthropology of the Fathers, their vision of man as privileged in paradise, as disfigured by sin, as restored through Christ. This is especially true of the Greek Fathers, with their emphasis on divinization, their insistence that God became man to make men gods. Several of the early authors who comprise Cyril of Alexandria's intellectual background have been carefully studied from this point of view: Irenaeus, for example, by A. Struker and E. Peterson; Clement of Alexandria by A. Mayer; Origen by H. Crouzel; Athanasius by R. Bernard; Gregory of Nyssa by J. B. Schoemann, R. Leys, and H. Merki among many.

Cyril's theology of the image has not been overlooked; but, to the present, it has been incorporated into Cyrillan studies simply as part of some broader framework, such as dogma,[1] spirituality,[2] sanctification,[3] divinization,[4] soteriology.[5] Such an approach is justified by the teleology of the individual monograph; it is even imperative if Cyril's image is not to lie in theological isolation; but inevitably the consequence is abbreviation, fragmentation, simplification, and with these the peril of distortion. The chronic danger that lurks in any compression, in any synthesis, becomes acute in the present instance, because the work of

[1] This is true of H. du Manoir, *Dogme et spiritualité chez saint Cyrille d'Alexandrie* (Paris, 1944). In this splendid study references to the image of God in man are frequent and the importance of the concept is recognized; but there is no effort to organize the disparate elements.

[2] Cf., for example, H. du Manoir, "Cyrille d'Alexandrie (saint)," *Dictionnaire de spiritualité* 2 (1953) 2672-83. Several columns (2676-78) are devoted to Cyril's concept of God's image in man; the concept is recognized as focal; but the treatment is understandably specialized and compendious.

[3] Thus, J. Mahé, "La sanctification d'après saint Cyrille d'Alexandrie," *Revue d'histoire ecclésiastique* 10 (1909) 30-40, 469-92. Image and likeness are mentioned (e.g., p. 33) but are quite lost in a profusion of other details.

[4] J. Gross has consecrated a chapter to Cyril in his *La divinisation du chrétien d'après les Pères grecs* (Paris, 1938) pp. 277-97; but he seems preoccupied with ἀφθαρσία and ἀθανασία, to the detriment of other aspects of the image.

[5] E. Weigl, *Die Heilslehre des hl. Cyrill von Alexandrien* (Mainz, 1905), is not unaware of the role of divine resemblance in Cyril's theology (cf. p. 16 ff., 46-47), but his subject is so comprehensive that it does not permit development of the image doctrine as such.

detail, of analysis, has not yet been achieved. It is to remedy this deficiency that our investigation has been undertaken.

In the light of the above, a full-length study of Cyril's conception of God's image in man does not call for apology; it is a felt need of theology. But what might well prove a theological burden assumes unusual allure in the perspective of Cyril's own declaration that "conformity and likeness to God is the creature's supreme adornment,"[6] his conviction that "our whole happiness consists in this, that we have been made to God's likeness."[7]

The first two chapters of this monograph are, in a sense, introductory; they simplify our quest by a process of clarification and limitation. Image and likeness are discovered to be not disparate but synonymous concepts, and the resemblance of man to his God is found focused not in the body but in the soul. Chapters 3-8, the heart of the matter, consider the content of Cyril's image. Six facets have been distinguished: reason, freedom, dominion, sanctification, incorruptibility, and sonship. Because of Cyril's ambivalent attitude towards woman, chapter 9 pauses briefly to include the female of the species expressly in his theology of the image. The last two chapters trace the fate of the image from Adam through sin to Christ.

It would be ungracious not to acknowledge publicly the debt I owe to Rev. Dr. Johannes Quasten, of the Catholic University of America, for scholarly counsel in the preparation of this monograph.

[6] *De sancta et consubstantiali trinitate* dial. 2 (*PG* 75, 740).
[7] *Ibid.*, dial. 3 (*PG* 75, 808).

# WORKS OF CYRIL[1]

---

[1] For problems of authenticity and dating cf. O. Bardenhewer, *Geschichte der altkirchlichen Literatur* 4 (Freiburg, 1924) 28–70; J. Mahé, "Cyrille (saint), patriarche d'Alexandrie," *DTC* 3, 2483–2501; H. du Manoir, *Dogme et spiritualité chez saint Cyrille d'Alexandrie* (Paris, 1944) pp. 53–60; G. Jouassard, "L'Activité littéraire de saint Cyrille d'Alexandrie jusqu'à 428: Essai de chronologie et de synthèse," in *Mélanges E. Podechard* (Lyons, 1945) pp. 159–74. On *John* cf. J. Mahé, "La date du Commentaire de saint Cyrille d'Alexandrie sur l'Evangile selon saint Jean," *Bulletin de littérature ecclésiastique* 8 (1907) 41–45; on the *Thesaurus* cf. N. Charlier, "Le 'Thesaurus de trinitate' de s. Cyrille d'Alexandrie: Questions de critique littéraire," *Revue d'histoire ecclésiastique* 45 (1950) 25–81.

[2] Where more than one edition is mentioned, the first named is the edition used in this study. As a general rule, where a choice of editions was possible, we have preferred Pusey to *PG*, and *ACO* to both.

[3] R. Devreesse has pointed out that these fragments demand a careful scrutiny before they can be used with confidence; cf. "Chaînes exégétiques grecques," *Dictionnaire de la Bible, Supplément* 1 (Paris, 1928) 1134.

*Commentarius in Isaiam prophetam* (*PG* 70, 9–1450).
*Commentarius in duodecim prophetas* (Pusey, *op. cit.*; *PG* 71 and 72, 9–364).[4]
*Commentarius in Matthaeum* (fragments: *PG* 72, 365–474).
*Commentarius in Lucam:*
 *PG* 72, 475–950.
  Payne Smith, R., *S. Cyrilli Alexandriae archiepiscopi commentarii in Lucae evangelium quae supersunt syriace.* Oxford, 1858. English translation: *id., A Commentary upon the Gospel according to St. Luke by St. Cyril, Patriarch of Alexandria.* 2 vols. Oxford, 1859.
  Rücker, A., *Die Lukashomilien des hl. Cyrill von Alexandrien: Ein Beitrag zur Geschichte der Exegese.* Breslau, 1911. Cf. pp. 87–101: unedited fragments in Syriac and German.
  Sickenberger, J., *Fragmente der Homilien des Cyrill von Alexandrien zum Lukasevangelium,* in *Texte und Untersuchungen* 34/1 (Leipzig, 1909) 63–108.
  Chabot, I. B., *S. Cyrilli Alexandrini commentarii in Lucam* 1 (*CSCO* 70, Scriptores syri 27). Paris and Leipzig, 1912. Latin translation: Tonneau, R. M., *S. Cyrilli Alexandrini commentarii in Lucam* 1 (*CSCO* 140, Scriptores syri 70). Louvain, 1953.[5]
*Commentarius in Ioannem* (Pusey, *op. cit.*; *PG* 73 and 74, 9–756).
*Commentarius in epistolam ad Romanos* (fragments: Pusey, *In Ioannem* 3, 173–248; *PG* 74, 773–856).
*Commentarius in epistolam 1 ad Corinthios* (fragments: Pusey, *In Ioannem* 3, 249–319; *PG* 74, 856–916).
*Commentarius in epistolam 2 ad Corinthios* (fragments: Pusey, *In Ioannem* 3, 320–61; *PG* 74, 916–52).
*Commentarius in epistolam ad Hebraeos* (fragments: Pusey, *In Ioannem* 3, 362–440; *PG* 74, 953–1006).[6]
*Thesaurus de sancta et consubstantiali trinitate* (*PG* 75, 9–656).
*De sancta et consubstantiali trinitate* (*PG* 75, 657–1124).
*Quod unus sit Christus* (*PG* 75, 1253–1361; Pusey, *op. cit.*).
*Scholia de incarnatione Unigeniti* (*PG* 75, 1369–1412; Pusey, *op. cit.*).
*Adversus Nestorii blasphemias contradictionum libri quinque* (*ACO* 1, 1, 6, 13–106: Pusey, *op. cit.*; *PG* 76, 9–248).

[4] Inconsiderable fragments of other *OT* commentaries may be found in *PG* 69 and 70.
[5] In citing the *Commentary on Luke,* I have tried as far as possible to restore the Greek catenae-fragments (*PG* 72) to the original homilies as witnessed by the very literal Syriac version edited and translated by Payne Smith and by Chabot.
[6] Inconsiderable fragments of other *NT* commentaries may be found in *PG* 74.

*Adversus nolentes confiteri sanctam virginem esse deiparam* (*ACO* 1, 1, 7, 19–32; *PG* 76, 255–92).

*Explicatio duodecim capitum* (*ACO* 1, 1, 5, 15–25; Pusey, *op. cit.*; *PG* 76, 293–312).

*Apologeticus pro duodecim capitibus adversus orientales episcopos* (*ACO* 1, 1, 7, 33–65; Pusey, *op. cit.*; *PG* 76, 315–85).

*Apologeticus contra Theodoretum pro duodecim capitibus* (*ACO* 1, 1, 6, 107–46; Pusey, *op. cit.*; *PG* 76, 385–452).

*Apologeticus ad imperatorem Theodosium* (*ACO* 1, 1, 3, 75–90; Pusey, *op. cit.*; *PG* 76, 453–88).

*Pro sancta christianorum religione adversus libros athei Iuliani* (*PG* 76, 503–1064).

*Epistola ad Calosyrium* (Pusey, *In Ioannem* 3, 603–607; *PG* 76, 1066–77).

*De dogmatum solutione* (Pusey, *In Ioannem* 3, 547–66).

*Responsiones ad Tiberium diaconum sociosque suos* (Pusey, *In Ioannem* 3, 567–602).

*De recta in dominum nostrum Iesum Christum fide, ad imperatorem Theodosium* (*ACO* 1, 1, 1, 42–72; *PG* 76, 1133–1200).

*De recta fide, ad dominas* (*ACO* 1, 1, 5, 62–118; *PG* 76, 1201–1336).

*De recta fide, ad augustas* (*ACO* 1, 1, 5, 26–61; *PG* 76, 1336–1420).

*Contra Synousiastas* (fragments: Pusey, *In Ioannem* 3, 476–91).

*Epistolae* (*ACO* 1, *passim*; *PG* 77, 9–390).

*Homiliae paschales* (*PG* 77, 401–981).

*Homiliae diversae* (*ACO* 1, *passim*; *PG* 77, 981–1116).[7]

[7] Of these seventeen homilies as reproduced by Migne, du Manoir, *op. cit.*, pp. 58–60, considers 10, 11, and 13 as certainly spurious; he sees 3, 12, and 20 as probably authentic; he insists that the rest must be subjected to serious investigation.

# SELECT BIBLIOGRAPHY

Asselin, D. T., "The Notion of Dominion in Genesis 1–3," *Catholic Biblical Quarterly* 16 (1954) 277–94.

Aubineau, M., "Incorruptibilité et divinisation selon saint Irénée," *Recherches de science religieuse* 44 (1956) 25–52.

Bardenhewer, O., *Geschichte der altkirchlichen Literatur* 4. 2nd ed.; Freiburg, 1924.

Bernard, R., *L'Image de Dieu d'après saint Athanase*. Paris, 1952.

Bouyer, L., *L'Incarnation et l'Eglise-Corps du Christ dans la théologie de saint Athanase*. Paris, 1943.

Camelot, Th., "La théologie de l'image de Dieu," *Revue des sciences philosophiques et théologiques* 40 (1956) 443–71.

Charlier, N., "Le 'Thesaurus de trinitate' de s. Cyrille d'Alexandrie: Questions de critique littéraire," *Revue d'histoire ecclésiastique* 45 (1950) 25–81.

Crouzel, H., *Théologie de l'image de Dieu chez Origène*. Paris, 1956.

Daniélou, J., *Platonisme et théologie mystique: Essai sur la doctrine spirituelle de saint Grégoire de Nysse*. Paris, 1944.

Dörr, F., *Diadochus von Photike und die Messalianer: Ein Kampf zwischen wahrer und falscher Mystik im fünften Jahrhundert*. Freiburg, 1937.

Dubarle, A. M., "Les conditions du salut avant la venue du Sauveur chez saint Cyrille d'Alexandrie," *Revue des sciences philosophiques et théologiques* 32 (1948) 359–62.

du Manoir, H., "Cyrille d'Alexandrie (saint)," *Dictionnaire de spiritualité* 2 (1953) 2672–83.

———, *Dogme et spiritualité chez saint Cyrille d'Alexandrie*. Paris, 1944.

———, "Le problème de Dieu chez Cyrille d'Alexandrie," *Recherches de science religieuse* 27 (1937) 385–407, 549–96.

Gross, J., *La divinisation du chrétien d'après les Pères grecs*. Paris, 1938.

Janssens, L., "Notre filiation divine d'après saint Cyrille d'Alexandrie," *Ephemerides theologicae Lovanienses* 15 (1938) 233–78.

Jouassard, G., "L'Activité littéraire de saint Cyrille d'Alexandrie jusqu'à 428: Essai de chronologie et de synthèse," in *Mélanges E. Podechard* (Lyons, 1945) pp. 159–74.

Kerrigan, A., *St. Cyril of Alexandria, Interpreter of the Old Testament*. Rome, 1952.

Klebba, E., *Die Anthropologie des hl. Irenaeus*. Münster i. W., 1894.

Langevin, G., "Le thème de l'incorruptibilité dans le commentaire de saint Cyrille d'Alexandrie sur l'Evangile selon saint Jean," *Sciences ecclésiastiques* 8 (1956) 295–316.

Leys, R., *L'Image de Dieu chez Grégoire de Nysse*. Brussels and Paris, 1951.

Mahé, J., "Cyrille (saint), patriarche d'Alexandrie," *Dictionnaire de théologie catholique* 3 (1908) 2476–2527.

——, "La date du Commentaire de saint Cyrille d'Alexandrie sur l'Evangile selon saint Jean," *Bulletin de littérature ecclésiastique* 8 (1907) 41–45.

——, "L'Eucharistie d'après saint Cyrille d'Alexandrie," *Revue d'histoire ecclésiastique* 8 (1907) 677–96.

——, "La sanctification d'après saint Cyrille d'Alexandrie," *Revue d'histoire ecclésiastique* 10 (1909) 30–40, 469–92.

Malevez, L., "L'Eglise dans le Christ: Etude de théologie historique et théorique," *Recherches de science religieuse* 25 (1935) 257–91, 418–40.

Mayer, A., *Das Gottesbild im Menschen nach Clemens von Alexandrien*. Rome, 1942.

Merki, H., ΟΜΟΙΩΣΙΣ ΘΕΩ: *Von der platonischen Angleichung an Gott zur Gottähnlichkeit bei Gregor von Nyssa*. Fribourg, 1952.

Montmasson, E., "L'Homme créé à l'image de Dieu d'après Théodoret de Cyr et Procope de Gaza," *Echos d'orient* 14 (1911) 334–39; 15 (1912) 154–62.

Muckle, J. T., "The Doctrine of St. Gregory of Nyssa on Man as the Image of God," *Mediaeval Studies* 7 (1945) 55–84.

Oepke, A., "γυνή," in G. Kittel, *Theologisches Wörterbuch zum Neuen Testament* 1 (1933) 776–90.

Peterson, E., "L'Immagine di Dio in S. Ireneo," *Scuola cattolica* 19 (1941) 3–11.

Philips, G., "La grâce des justes de l'Ancien Testament," *Ephemerides theologicae Lovanienses* 23 (1947) 521–56; 24 (1948) 23–58.

Rahner, H., "Das Menschenbild des Origenes," *Eranos-Jahrbuch* 15 (1947) 197–248.

Sagüés, J., "El Espíritu Santo en la santificación del hombre según la doctrina de S. Cirilo de Alejandría," *Estudios eclesiásticos* 21 (1947) 35–83.

Schmidt, K. L., "Homo imago Dei im Alten und Neuen Testament," *Eranos-Jahrbuch* 15 (1947) 149–95.

Schoemann, J. B., "Gregors von Nyssa theologische Anthropologie als Bildtheologie," *Scholastik* 18 (1943) 31–53, 175–200.

Slomkowski, A., *L'Etat primitif de l'homme dans la tradition de l'église avant saint Augustin*. Paris, 1928.

Struker, A., *Die Gottebenbildlichkeit des Menschen in der christlichen Literatur der ersten zwei Jahrhunderte.* Münster i. W., 1913.

Völker, W., *Das Vollkommenheitsideal des Origenes.* Tübingen, 1931.

————, *Der wahre Gnostiker nach Clemens Alexandrinus.* Berlin and Leipzig, 1952.

von Balthasar, H., *Présence et pensée: Essai sur la philosophie religieuse de Grégoire de Nysse.* Paris, 1942.

von Rad, G., Kittel, G., Kleinknecht, H., "εἰκών," in G. Kittel, *Theologisches Wörterbuch zum Neuen Testament* 2 (1935) 378–96.

Weigl, E., *Die Heilslehre des hl. Cyrill von Alexandrien.* Mainz, 1905.

# SIGLA

## OLD TESTAMENT

| | | | |
|---|---|---|---|
| Gn | Genesis | Lam | Lamentations |
| Ex | Exodus | Ez | Ezekiel |
| Lv | Leviticus | Dn | Daniel |
| Nm | Numbers | Hos | Hosea |
| Dt | Deuteronomy | Jl | Joel |
| Jos | Joshua | Amos | Amos |
| Jg | Judges | Ob | Obadiah |
| Ru | Ruth | Jon | Jonah |
| 1, 2 S | 1, 2 Samuel | Mi | Micah |
| 1, 2 K | 1, 2 Kings | Na | Nahum |
| 1, 2 Chr | 1, 2 Chronicles | Hb | Habakkuk |
| Ezr | Ezra | Zeph | Zephaniah |
| Neh | Nehemiah | Hg | Haggai |
| Est | Esther | Za | Zechariah |
| Jb | Job | Mal | Malachi |
| Ps | Psalms | Bar | Baruch |
| Prv | Proverbs | Tob | Tobit |
| Qoh | Qoheleth | Jud | Judith |
| | (Ecclesiastes) | Wis | Wisdom of Solomon |
| Ct | Song of Songs | Sir | Ben Sira |
| Is | Isaiah | | (Ecclesiasticus) |
| Jer | Jeremiah | 1, 2 Mac | 1, 2 Maccabees |

## NEW TESTAMENT

| | | | |
|---|---|---|---|
| Mt | Matthew | Col | Colossians |
| Mk | Mark | 1, 2 Th | 1, 2 Thessalonians |
| Lk | Luke | 1, 2 Tim | 1, 2 Timothy |
| Jn | John | Tit | Titus |
| Acts | Acts | Phm | Philemon |
| Rom | Romans | Heb | Hebrews |
| 1, 2 Cor | 1, 2 Corinthians | Jas | James |
| Gal | Galatians | 1, 2 Pt | 1, 2 Peter |
| Eph | Ephesians | 1, 2, 3 Jn | 1, 2, 3 John |
| Phil | Philippians | Jude | Jude |
| | Ap | Apocalypse | |

# CHAPTER 1

# IMAGE AND LIKENESS

The patristic concept of the divine image in man has its earliest and its deepest roots in the opening chapter of Genesis. "Then God said, 'Let us make man in our image, after our likeness. . . .' So God created man in His own image; in the image of God He created him; male and female He created them" (Gn 1:26–27). The occurrence of two words, ṣelem and d^emût, εἰκών and ὁμοίωσις, "image" and "likeness," in verse 26, and the omission of d^emût, ὁμοίωσις, "likeness," in verse 27, have complicated beyond measure the ancient Christian understanding of man's resemblance to the divine. Cyril himself could not remain remote from the problem thus raised. What is the relationship between image and likeness in Gn 1:26? More pointedly, are the terms simply synonyms or do they cloak a significant distinction? As far as Cyril is concerned, the question is not premature; in fact, his response will simplify our ultimate quest. But, because Cyril's position is difficult to appreciate in isolation from its ancestry, it is imperative to mark the more important stages in the early Christian tradition on this point.

The extant evidence indicates that a distinction between image and likeness is first to be found in Gnosticism.[1] Current in the Italian school of Valentinian[2] and discoverable in the Oriental school of the same Gnostic[3] is the belief that the demiurge, in creating the world, fashioned the "earthy" man after God's image, the "psychic" man to His likeness. In Gnosticism ὁμοίωσις is a divine seed which forms the essence of the "pneumatic" man; it is a gift of nature and consequently inamissible.[4] For the first two centuries in general, A. Struker's intimate analysis of the problem has issued in the following conclusion:

The division of a double resemblance seems indicated here and there, especially in Ps.-Justin's *Cohortatio ad gentiles* and in the Sibyllines. In the Clementines, where the distinction is formulated explicitly (εἰκών, ὁμοιότης), the meaning of this twin possession, characterized as original, is not quite clarified. Formally

---

[1] Cf. J. Gross, *La divinisation du chrétien d'après les Pères grecs* (Paris, 1938) pp. 158, 130–31.

[2] Cf. Irenaeus, *Adversus haereses* 1, 1, 10 (Harvey 1, 49).

[3] Cf. Clement of Alexandria, *Excerpta ex Theodoto* 54, 2 (*GCS* 17, 125).

[4] Cf. Gross, *op. cit.*, p. 158.

(εἰκών, ὁμοίωσις) and with an explanation full of significance for posterity it is found in ecclesiastical literature in none but Irenaeus, who was stimulated externally by Gnosticism.[5]

The consistency of Irenaeus has been challenged. Sometimes, it is true, he employs image and likeness synonymously, not merely of man's primitive state but of Adam's descendants as well. Nevertheless, it would seem a defensible position that essentially Irenaeus distinguished image from likeness. The former consists of natural gifts, particularly reason and free will, and cannot be lost. The latter is supernatural, characterized by possession of the Word and participation of the Spirit; it was lost in Adam and has been restored through Christ.[6]

In a study of Cyril, however, it is the Alexandrian tradition that is peculiarly pertinent. The Jewish philosopher, Philo, with whose exegetical method the exegesis of Cyril has several points of contact,[7] finds in the Mosaic "likeness" simply a more perfect "image." For, "since images do not always correspond to their archetype and pattern . . . the writer further brought out his meaning by adding 'after the likeness'

[5] A. Struker, *Die Gottebenbildlichkeit des Menschen in der christlichen Literatur der ersten zwei Jahrhunderte* (Münster i. W., 1913) p. 133.

[6] In substance this position is maintained by Struker, *ibid.*; E. Klebba, *Die Anthropologie des hl. Irenaeus* (Münster i. W., 1894) pp. 22–26, 73, 184; J. Hochban, "St. Irenaeus on the Atonement," *Theological Studies* 7 (1946) 528; and, with reservations, by I. Hislop, "The Image of God in Man according to St. Irenaeus," *Life of the Spirit: Blackfriars* 3 (1946) 72. F. Vernet, "Irénée, Saint," *DTC* 7, 2455, asserts that Irenaeus "usually perceives either in the *imago* the resemblance by natural goods and in the *similitudo* the resemblance by supernatural goods, or in the one and the other the image and likeness by grace." Vernet is copied by A. Slomkowski, *L'Etat primitif de l'homme dans la tradition de l'église avant saint Augustin* (Paris, 1928). Gross, *op. cit.*, pp. 145–59, while recognizing that Irenaeus often uses the terms synonymously, submits that there are passages where an opposition is so precise as to be beyond doubt. In such passages man is the image of God, i.e., of the Incarnate Word, by his complete human nature, an inalienable resemblance common to all men; he is God's likeness through a created grace conditioned on possession of the Spirit, a likeness lost by Adam for himself and his posterity. Even F. Tennant, who claims with Wendt and Harnack that Irenaeus' doctrine of divine likeness discloses "incompatible lines," admits that the distinction between image and likeness "embodies the writer's usual conception of man's constitution"; *The Sources of the Doctrines of the Fall and Original Sin* (Cambridge, 1903) p. 285. For a typical passage cf. *Adversus haereses* 5, 6, 1 (Harvey 2, 234): "imaginem quidem habens in plasmate, similitudinem vero non assumens per Spiritum"; cf. *ibid.* 5, 16, 1 (Harvey 2, 367–68).

[7] Cf. A. Kerrigan, *St. Cyril of Alexandria, Interpreter of the Old Testament* (Rome, 1952) pp. 155–67, 195, 205–6, 383 (note 3), 390.

. . . thus showing that an accurate cast, bearing a clear impression, was intended."[8] Clement of Alexandria goes further. He records an opinion held by "some of our own" that the image was received by man immediately upon creation, while the likeness was to be assumed through a gradual process of perfection.[9] It is quite likely that Clement adopted this distinction;[10] for he often discriminates between image and likeness in such fashion as to make the latter more perfect than the former, a progressive actualization within Christianity of man's inalienable aptitude for perfection, an intellectual assimilation to God never completely realized in this life.[11] It is scarcely a surprise, then, to confront much the same distinction in Origen. The phraseology of Gn 1:27 tells him that man received in his initial state the dignity of image, which made it possible for him to acquire by diligent effort, by imitation of God, the perfection of likeness at life's culmination.[12] For the early Christian Alexandrians, we may conclude, image and likeness are related as potency to act.

A turning-point in the Alexandrian orientation is evident soon after Nicaea. As early as the *Contra gentes* and the *De incarnatione* of his twenties, the originality of Athanasius reveals itself in the absence of any distinction between image and likeness, despite the example of Irenaeus, Clement, and Origen.[13] Among the Cappadocians, the same may be said of Gregory of Nazianzus, and even of Basil, if we can discount the promise on the last page of his unfinished *Hexaemeron* to explain, "God

[8] Philo, *De opificio mundi* 71 [23] (Cohn-Wendland 1, 19; tr. *LCL*, Philo 1, 57).

[9] Cf. Clement of Alexandria, *Stromata* 2, 22 (*GCS* 15, 185).

[10] That he did seems obvious to Gross, *op. cit.*, p. 161. Slomkowski is of a different mind: "Without espousing this philosophical exegesis as his own, [Clement] understands the progress of the first man in a more simple fashion and returns to the opinion which puts him in a state of childhood"; *op. cit.*, p. 49.

[11] Cf. Clement of Alexandria, *Protrepticus* 12 (*GCS* 12, 86); *Paedagogus* 1, 12 (*GCS* 12, 148–49). For a documented summary of Clement's doctrine of progressive assimilation to God, cf. A. de la Barre, "Clément d'Alexandrie," *DTC* 3, 171–74.

[12] Cf. Origen, *De principiis* 3, 6, 1 (*GCS* 22, 280); *Contra Celsum* 4, 30 (*GCS* 2, 299); *In epist. ad Rom.* 4, 5 (*PG* 14, 978); *In Ioannem* 20, 22 (*GCS* 10, 355). For a detailed study of the progression from image to likeness in Origen, cf. H. Crouzel, *Théologie de l'image de Dieu chez Origène* (Paris, 1956) pp. 217–45; cf. also the valuable observations on the early patristic outlook by Th. Camelot, "La théologie de l'image de Dieu," *Revue des sciences philosophiques et théologiques* 40 (1956) 443–71, esp. 460–65.

[13] Cf. R. Bernard, *L'Image de Dieu d'après saint Athanase* (Paris, 1952) p. 27, with the reasons there suggested for Athanasius' stand; also Gross, *op. cit.*, pp. 204–5.

willing," wherein man possesses the image and how he lays hold on the likeness.[14] Gregory of Nyssa is more subtle; even so, the investigations of J. Muckle have convinced him that it is impossible to sustain the thesis of scholars like Fr. Hilt that by image Gregory means man's natural gifts, and by likeness his supernatural prerogatives. Gregory "does not distinguish between image and likeness as two distinct things. With him the image is an image because it is like its original. He uses the terms almost interchangeably. . . . "[15]

This aspect of Gregory's image doctrine, however, is the object of a more penetrating and persuasive study on the part of Roger Leys. Leys concedes that in many passages the expression, "to the image and likeness," is hardly more than hendiadys; the two terms in union designate no more than each in isolation. But Leys submits that this is true primarily where Gregory mentions the divine resemblance casually, in passing, without developing the idea. Where he specifies, he seems to distinguish between εἰκών and ὁμοίωσις, not as two different things but as two aspects of one same reality. Εἰκών presents the static aspect, whether original or terminal; ὁμοίωσις is a dynamic notion implying a becoming. Ὁμοίωσις is the acquisition or progressive realization of εἰκών; it is a striving for assimilation, a μίμησις according to the exigencies of εἰκών, which God has deposited in us like some preliminary sketch. The two aspects are not adequately distinct; ὁμοίωσις is εἰκών in process of realization. It is only temporarily that they are in any sense distinct. They coincide in this life for the perfect, and they will coincide for all in heaven after the general resurrection, just as they did in the beginning, when nature made its appearance simultaneously with perfection, and completion went hand in hand with birth. Both terms, εἰκών and ὁμοίωσις, are found in Gregory on the supernatural level.[16]

[14] Cf. Basil, *Homiliae in Hexaemeron* 9, 6 (*PG* 29, 208).

[15] J. T. Muckle, "The Doctrine of St. Gregory of Nyssa on Man as the Image of God," *Mediaeval Studies* 7 (1945) 59. Disagreement with Hilt's thesis is voiced likewise by Slomkowski, *op. cit.*, p. 116, note 1, and by F. Diekamp, *Die Gotteslehre des hl. Gregor von Nyssa* 1 (Münster, 1896) 70–72.

[16] Cf. R. Leys, *L'Image de Dieu chez saint Grégoire de Nysse* (Brussels and Paris, 1951) pp. 116–19. Worth consulting in this connection is H. Merki, ΟΜΟΙΩΣΙΣ ΘΕΩ: *Von der platonischen Angleichung an Gott zur Gottähnlichkeit bei Gregor von Nyssa* (Fribourg, 1952) pp. 138–64. Merki shows that Gregory employs ὁμοίωσις mostly in a static-ontic sense; it is especially when taken in this sense that ὁμοίωσις is identical with εἰκών. Both ideas are applicable to man only; both express a condition of human perfection and total resemblance to God; both were lost, and both must be restored in the same way; both rest on participation in God. To the basically dynamic theme of ὁμοίωσις Gregory has closely allied εἰκών, while into the

Didymus the Blind, whose Trinitarian theology betrays the influence of the Cappadocians, handles the two expressions without awareness of a distinction.[17] On broad lines this attitude expresses rather well the neo-Alexandrian trend (perhaps preformed to some extent by Philo), in contrast to the pre-Nicene development represented by Clement and Origen, and revived by Gregory of Nyssa.

Among the Antiochenes and the more or less independent theologians it is difficult to discern a traditional pattern. Various differentiations between image and likeness emerge from Methodius, Cyril of Jerusalem, and John Chrysostom,[18] while the potency-and-act distinction is resurrected by the unknown author of the two homilies *De hominis structura*[19]

concept that is of itself sheerly ontic-static he breathed a certain dynamism, a capacity for development. From the homogeneity of content in the two themes (Merki concludes) it follows that, if we are to give a complete picture of Gregory's doctrine of resemblance, we must, in treating ὁμοίωσις, look simultaneously at εἰκών; for Gregory's ὁμοίωσις πρὸς τὸ Θεῖον and his εἰκὼν Θεοῦ often serve to express the same condition of perfection and the same religious possession. Cf. also p. 173: When Gregory uses Gn 1:26 as a springboard, κατ' εἰκόνα and καθ' ὁμοίωσιν are always and everywhere "absolutely synonymous"; when he uses ὁμοίωσις (severed from εἰκών) in its dynamic aspect, the springboard is not Gn 1:26 but philosophy.

[17] Cf. Didymus, *De trinitate* 2, 12 (*PG* 39, 680–81).

[18] For Methodius cf. Gross, *op. cit.*, p. 193; also *Symposium* 1, 4–5 (*GCS* 27, 12–13), with which Gross compares *De resurrectione* 1, 35, 2–4 (*GCS* 27, 274–75). Cf. Cyril of Jerusalem, *Catecheses* 14, 10 (*PG* 33, 836–37); Chrysostom, *In cap. 1 Gen. homiliae* 9, 3 (*PG* 53, 78).

[19] Until 1936 the authenticity of the two homilies, *In scripturae verba: Faciamus hominem ad imaginem et similitudinem nostram*, edited in *PG* (44, 257–98) under the name of Gregory of Nyssa, was commonly rejected, primarily on the basis of the distinction therein between εἰκών as nature (reason) and ὁμοίωσις as supernature (grace), a distinction regarded as alien to Gregory's authenticated writings. In the *Byzantinische Zeitschrift* 36 (1936) 46–57, E. von Ivanka argued for their authenticity with a careful investigation of the sources of these two homilies and Gregory's *De opificio hominis*. However, scholars like H. von Balthasar and J. B. Schoemann were not convinced that von Ivanka's arguments outweighed the traditional objections. More recently, Leys has supplemented von Ivanka's research with a study of the εἰκών–ὁμοίωσις difficulty; cf. *op. cit.*, pp. 130–38. His conclusion is that λογικός for Gregory is not necessarily sheer natural reason, and εἰκών is not always grace; and so the εἰκών–ὁμοίωσις distinction in the first of the homilies can be fitted into Gregory's doctrinal pattern. This, and the twenty-one authentically Gregorian themes in the two homilies, as well as von Ivanka's study of the sources, convince Leys that they stem from Gregory. Merki is not impressed; it seems to him "certain that they cannot have Gregory for author"; *op. cit.*, p. 173.—It is this work that has been edited (though the text is not exactly the same) under the title, *De hominis structura*, in *PG* 30, 9–62, among the works ascribed to Basil the Great. Basil's authorship was defended by E. Stephanou in

and by the fifth-century Diadochus of Photike.[20] On the other hand, authors like Hippolytus, Theodore of Mopsuestia, and Theodoret of Cyrus fail to discriminate between the two concepts; whether designedly or not, is hard to say. Of the Latin writers, especially in the fourth century and the early years of the fifth, much the same must be said. Some introduce a distinction, e.g., Gregory of Elvira, Philastrius of Brescia, Paulinus of Nola, and Jerome;[21] others do not, e.g., Hilary of Poitiers, Zeno of Verona, and Ambrose.[22]

At all events, the fact remains that many of the neo-Alexandrians, consistently more conservative than their forefathers, appear to have abandoned the distinction between εἰκών and ὁμοίωσις advocated by

Echos d'orient 31 (1932) 385-98. In a lengthy study in Recherches de science religieuse 33 (1946) 317-58, S. Giet concludes that (a) In verba and De hominis structura are linked in a relationship of dependence, with the latter a later composition than the former; (b) In verba is not the work of Gregory; it goes back probably to a sermon of Basil, but so imperfectly that it must be used with great caution; (c) De hominis structura does not emanate from Basil; it was elaborated in a Gregorian milieu; it must be used with even greater caution.—For the purposes of the present study it is justifiable to consider In verba and De hominis structura as, in any event, part of the fourth-century Alexandrian tradition. Pertinent texts are: De hominis structura 1, 19-21 (PG 30, 29-33); In scripturae verba 1 (PG 44, 273).

[20] Cf. Diadochus, Capita centum gnostica 4; 78; 89 (Sources chrétiennes 5^bis, 86, 135-36, 149-50). Cf. E. des Places, "Diadoque de Photicé," Dictionnaire de spiritualité 3, 826-27. One should likewise consult the splendid analysis of Diadochus' doctrine on the divine image by F. Dörr, Diadochus von Photike und die Messalianer: Ein Kampf zwischen wahrer und falscher Mystik im fünften Jahrhundert (Freiburg, 1937) pp. 64-72. The εἰκών is nothing else than essential holiness, the germ and pledge of ὁμοίωσις, which is itself the unfolding and enrichment of the life of grace given in baptism, demands our cooperation through virtue, and is consummated in perfect charity. Dörr realizes that Diadochus recognizes a natural "image" impressed on our spiritual nature, especially by free will, but he is convinced that for Diadochus man's spirituality is not so much the image itself as far more the matter on which the image is laid or engraved.

[21] Cf. Philastrius, Diversarum hereseon liber 137, 2; 137, 5; 137, 9 (CSEL 38, 107-8); Paulinus, Epistulae 24, 9 (CSEL 29, 209-10); Jerome, In Ezechielem prophetam 9 (PL 25, 282). For Gregory cf. Slomkowski, op. cit., pp. 134-35.

[22] The so-called Epistola seu libellus 5 (PL 10, 737) records the statement that the Father first gave man the gift of the image, intending to bestow the likeness later, if the image were preserved intact. Apropos of this passage J. C. Trombelli wrote a dissertation on the image which may be found in PL 10, 848-78. Unhappily, the Epistola is not the work of Hilary; cf. Bardenhewer, op. cit. 3, 387. However, Hilary's reasoning may be gathered from Contra Constantium imperatorem 21 (PL 10, 596-97). For Zeno cf. Tractatus 2, 19 (PL 11, 456). Slomkowski, op. cit., p. 134, has concluded that a majority of the fourth-century Latin Fathers employed imago and similitudo as synonyms.

Clement and Origen. If this new orientation was at all widespread, it may well have been a contributing factor to the dogmatic, uncompromising solution offered by the last of the eminent Alexandrians, Cyril. His first step is to pose the problem:

> Is there a difference between "according to image" and "according to likeness," or are they identical? For they say that we received the former concurrently with creation, but not the latter; this has been reserved for us in the world to come. That is why, runs the argument, it is written, "When Christ shall appear, we shall be like to Him" (1 Jn 3:2). And again . . . "Let us make man to our image and likeness" (Gn 1:26), and after man's production . . . "And God made man; to His own image He made him" (Gn 1:27), with no mention then of "according to likeness," to show . . . that we had not yet received this, but that it has been reserved for us in that life of blessedness.[23]

Briefly, Cyril is aware of the thesis which held that the image was given man in the world's beginning, while the likeness is reserved for the world's end. The basis of the thesis was scriptural: (a) St. John's assertion that it is at the Second Coming that we shall be like Christ, and (b) the omission of ὁμοίωσις from Gn 1:27. Cyril's answer is unequivocal:

> If they say that "according to image" and "according to likeness" are two different things, let them show the difference! For our mind is that "according to image" means nothing else than "according to likeness," and conversely "according to likeness" means nothing but "according to image": the likeness to God we obtained in our primal constitution, and we are images of God. . . . Now, if the Holy Scripture said somewhere that God made man according to His own image, and did not mention "according to [His] likeness," we should understand that it was sufficient to say "according to [His] image," inasmuch as it meant nothing else than "according to [His] likeness." The fact is, it is useless to say that the latter has been reserved for us for the life to come; for, seeing that God said, "Let us make man according to our image and likeness," who will dare to say that He made man according to His image but not according to His likeness? We shall, it is true, be like to Christ in incorruption . . . [but] even now we are not alien to His likeness, if it is really true that He is formed in us through the Holy Spirit. . . .[24]

Cyril's response, therefore, comes down to this: the two ideas are synonymous, and ὁμοίωσις as well as εἰκών was given man in the beginning. He argues (a) that a difference in meaning is not demonstrable, and

[23] Cyril, *De dogmatum solutione* 3 (Pusey, *In Ioannem* 3, 554).
[24] *Ibid.* (Pusey 3, 555–57).

(b) that God's original decree as expressed in Gn 1:26 can hardly be said to have been frustrated a verse later. The Johannine assurance of an after-life likeness does not militate against a resemblance to God here and now.

For the purposes of the present inquiry the significant fact is that Cyril flatly refuses to distinguish between εἰκών and ὁμοίωσις.[25] It is significant, in the first instance, because it simplifies our study. Cyril is convinced that the two terms are indistinguishable in Genesis, and he proceeds to employ them indiscriminately. On this level he is splendidly consistent. In the relatively few cases where he appears faithless to his principle, it is only to observe that an image necessarily bears a likeness to the object it represents;[26] that is why the Son, who "is" the Father's Image, "has" the Father's likeness.[27]

It is significant, in the second place, because Cyril's stand harmonizes with the best in contemporary exegesis. Many competent exegetes insist that P (= the Priestly Tradition) did not intend to introduce a distinction between ṣelem and dᵉmût in Gn 1:26, that the Hebrew text offers no handle for such discrimination, that we are simply confronted with two synonymous expressions.[28] Even those who discover a distinction do not locate it in any genuine difference of content; it is a matter of synonyms with different emphases or connotations. They see in dᵉmût either a limiting noun which excludes from ṣelem equality between God

[25] The perfect synonymity of εἰκών and ὁμοίωσις in Cyril in upheld by Gross, op. cit., p. 280; H. du Manoir de Juaye, Dogme et spiritualité chez saint Cyrille d'Alexandrie (Paris, 1944) pp. 94–95; E. Weigl, Die Heilslehre des hl. Cyrill von Alexandrien (Mainz, 1905) p. 35. When Petavius claims to have found a distinction in De adoratione 1 (PG 68, 145), he must be judged to have misinterpreted the passage; cf. De trinitate 8, 5, 6 (Dogmata theologica 3 [Paris, 1865] 469–70).

[26] Cf. Cyril, Thesaurus 32 (PG 75, 476); ibid. 4 (PG 75, 52); In psalmos, Ps 113:16 (PG 69, 1268–69); Adversus Nestorii blasphemias 2, 8 (ACO 1, 1, 6, 46; PG 76, 93).

[27] Cf. Cyril, In Aggaeum (Pusey 2, 280; PG 71, 1061). Cf. In Ioannem 9, 1 (Pusey 2, 437; PG 74, 221): perfect likeness, therefore perfect image. On the other hand, the synonymity of the expressions is so much a part of Cyril's ordinary thinking that he can speak of the Incarnate Word as "the Father's Image and Likeness"; In Amos 3 (Pusey 1, 502; PG 71, 537). Again, the perfect εἰκών of the Father is the Son, and the natural ὁμοίωσις of the Son is His Spirit; cf. In Ioannem 11, 11 (Pusey 2, 731; PG 74, 553).

[28] Cf. H. Gunkel, Genesis (Göttingen, 1922) p. 111; P. Heinisch, Das Buch Genesis (Bonn, 1930) p. 101; G. von Rad, s.v. εἰκών, in G. Kittel, Theologisches Wörterbuch zum Neuen Testament 2 (1935) 389: the writer is struggling to express a mystery, and an ancient formula has come to his assistance.

and man,[29] or a more abstract expression which strengthens ṣelem by way of accumulation,[30] or a specifying substantive which reveals that this image, unlike some others, is actually a good likeness of the original.[31]

It is significant, finally, because the thesis of Cyril, the most conspicuous Eastern theologian in the first half of the fifth century, is so much akin to the interpretation favored by his counterpart and contemporary in the West. Writing in 419, Augustine is aware that the absence of "et similitudinem" from Gn 1:27 has led some to believe that the likeness adds something to the image, that it is a gift reserved for man refashioned through the grace of Christ. "But I wonder," he muses, "if [Moses] did not decide in the second instance to mention the image alone for the simple reason that, where there is image, there is necessarily likeness too."[32]

Cyril, therefore, recognizes no need to distinguish image (εἰκών) from likeness (ὁμοίωσις, ὁμοιότης, ὁμοίωμα). With that, our quest is perceptibly simplified. But before proceeding to Cyril's image as it exists in the concrete, it is worth asking whether his general conception of an image, his "theory" of image, his broader principles relative to *Gottebenbildlichkeit*, may be initially illuminating. I would suggest that some rays of light, not dazzling perhaps but surely not negligible, come from two directions.

The first ray of light is a unique effort on Cyril's part to distinguish the different kinds of εἰκών:

One—the first—is the image of natural identity by reason of exactly the same properties; for example, Abel [sprung] from Adam, Isaac from Abraham. A second is the image according to sheer likeness (ἐμφέρειαν) of distinctive features and the exact modeling of the form in relief; thus, a wood carving of the king, or some other manner of artistic representation. Another image has reference to manners and morals and way of life, and one's will in regard to good and evil. In this sense we may say that a person who does good is like Paul, whereas one who does evil is like Cain; for, it is reasonable to suppose, the same activity, good or bad, effects likeness (ὁμοίωσιν) in each, confers it. Another kind of image

[29] So R. de Vaux, *La Genèse* (*La sainte Bible*, ed. L'Ecole biblique de Jérusalem; Paris, 1951) p. 42, note *b*.
[30] So A. Dillmann, *Genesis Critically and Exegetically Expounded*, tr. W. B. Stevenson, Vol. 1 (Edinburgh, 1897) 79–80.
[31] So A. Clamer, *Genèse* (Pirot-Clamer, *La sainte Bible* 1/1; Paris, 1953) pp. 112–13.
[32] Augustine, *Quaestiones in Heptateuchum* 5 (Quaest. de Deut.) 4 (*CSEL* 28/2, 371–72).

is dignity and honor and glory and supremacy; for example, if someone should succeed to another's government and should perform with authority everything that could be fit and proper for his predecessor. An image in another way is according to some other quality or quantity of a thing, some figure or proportion—this is speaking summarily, of necessity.[33]

In brief, one can be an image of another by reason of (a) generation, (b) artistic representation, (c) moral character, (d) dignity, or (e) in some other way. Cyril proceeds to expatiate on the first species of image in the relationship between God the Father and the Image who is His natural Son. He does not apply his categories to the image of God in men; and, as we shall see, the catalog covers only a portion of that image, two relatively minor aspects: man's virtuous activity ("manners and morals and way of life") and his sovereignty over creation ("dignity and honor and glory and supremacy").[34]

The second ray of light is Cyril's insistence that there is a radical distinction between the image of God that is God, and the image of God that is man. Only the Son is a perfect (ἀσινής), identical (ἀπαράλλακτος), utterly accurate and exact (ἀκριβεστάτη) image of the Father.[35] His is a likeness by nature, in essence; for the Father inscribes His whole self on the nature of the Son, impresses Himself substantially.[36] The resemblance is consummate,[37] so much so that the Son has in Himself all the perfections of His Father.[38] There is but one difference: the Father is Father, and the Son is Son.[39] The point is, a natural (φυσική) image and likeness (εἰκὼν καὶ ὁμοίωσις) with reference to the Father can be achieved only by ὁμοιότης in nature, a total resemblance (ἐμφέρεια) which springs from the essence itself.[40]

In creatures, on the other hand, there is nothing which is formed accurately and univocally (ἀκριβῶς καὶ μοναδικῶς) to God's nature and glory.[41] No created thing is substantially and immutably identical with God,[42]

---

[33] In Ioannem 2, 8 (Pusey 1, 339–40).

[34] The first category does not appear applicable to man's generation through spiritual rebirth; it requires exactly the same nature in image and archetype.

[35] Cf. Thesaurus 32 (PG 75, 553); ibid. 33 (PG 75, 572); also In Ioannem 1, 2 (Pusey 1, 25): ἀπαράλλακτον ὁμοιότητα.

[36] Cf. In epistolam 2 ad Corinthios 1, 2 (Pusey, In Ioannem 3, 326–27).

[37] Cf. In Ioannem 9 (Pusey 2, 423); also Thesaurus 13 (PG 75, 225): τὸ τελείως ὅμοιον.

[38] Cf. In Ioannem 6 (Pusey 2, 129).

[39] Cf. ibid. 11, 2 (Pusey 2, 637).

[40] Cf. De sancta et consubstantiali trinitate dial. 5 (PG 75, 949). Such is natural sonship whether among men or in the Trinity; cf. ibid. (PG 75, 953–56).

[41] Cf. ibid. (PG 75, 952).

[42] Cf. Contra Iulianum 8 (PG 76, 909).

naturally and perfectly like God.[43] We do not have total, utter ὁμοιότης to the Father.[44] Our likeness to God is not a likeness of nature (ὁμοίωσις φυσική), such as obtains between angel and angel, between man and man.[45] We are not transformed into the Son's nature; we do not cast off our own.[46] Our imaging of God is a matter of participation,[47] and participation implies difference in nature.[48] We are "mere (ψιλή) image, simply a copy (ἰσοτυπίαν), fashioned to the archetype by adornments from without."[49] The difference is reducible to identity of nature in the one case and participation in nature in the other.[50]

As we shall see, it is the notion of participation, of μέθεξις (in intimate alliance with imitation and grace, μίμησις and χάρις), which, more than any other concept, dominates Cyril's theology of the image of God in man.

[43] Cf. *Thesaurus* 16 (*PG* 75, 304).

[44] Cf. *In Ioannem* 10, 2 (Pusey 2, 547).

[45] Cf. *De sancta et consubstantiali trinitate* dial. 1 (*PG* 75, 676).

[46] Cf. *Thesaurus* 12 (*PG* 75, 200-205).

[47] Cf. *In epistolam 2 ad Corinthios* 1, 2 (Pusey, *In Ioannem* 3, 326): κατὰ μέθεξιν.

[48] Cf. *De sancta et consubstantiali trinitate* dial. 5 (*PG* 75, 956).

[49] *In Ioannem* 11, 2 (Pusey 2, 637).

[50] The Son as Image is a constant theme of the *Thesaurus*; it merits a detailed study in its own right.

# CHAPTER 2

# BODY OR SOUL?

For Cyril of Alexandria, image and likeness are synonymous concepts; he refuses to discriminate. A second preliminary problem will simplify our quest still further: where is this image, this likeness to God? Is it in the whole man or in some constituent part of man? Is it discoverable in the body or must it be restricted to the intangible, the spiritual in man? Can we point to an early Christian pattern of thought, particularly in Alexandria, which may have left its mark on Cyril?

The Alexandrian orientation, not surprisingly, finds its springboard in Philo:

> After all the rest . . . Moses tells us that man was created after the image of God and after His likeness. Right well does he say this, for nothing earth-born is more like God than man. Let no one represent the likeness as one to a bodily form; for neither is God in human form, nor is the human body God-like. No, it is in respect of the Mind, the sovereign element of the soul, that the word "image" is used. . . .[1]

For Philo, therefore, man resembles God not in his bodily structure but in his soul; specifically, in his mind. It may be that Philo is compelled to some such conclusion by the logic of premises stated a bit later; I mean his double-creation theory, his ideal and corporeal man. He sees a "vast difference" between the man formed from clay (Gn 2:7) and "the man that came into existence earlier after the image of God" (Gn 1:27). The man formed from clay is "an object of sense-perception . . . consisting of body and soul, man or woman, by nature mortal"; God's image "was an idea or type or seal, an object of thought (only), incorporeal, neither male nor female, by nature incorruptible."[2]

Clement of Alexandria likewise denies expressly that God's image and likeness reside in the human body: "it is not meet to assimilate

---

[1] Philo, *De opificio mundi* 69 [23] (Cohn-Wendland 1, 18; tr. *LCL*, Philo 1, 55); cf. *De plantatione* 18 [5] (Cohn-Wendland 2, 128; tr. *LCL*, Philo 3, 223).

[2] Philo, *De opificio mundi* 134 [46] (Cohn-Wendland 1, 38; tr. *LCL*, Philo 1, 107). This is the double creation of the sixth day: the ideal man (Gn 1:27) and the corporeal or individual man (Gn 2:7); cf. H. A. Wolfson, *Philo: Foundations of Religious Philosophy in Judaism, Christianity, and Islam* 1 (2nd printing revised; Cambridge, Mass., 1948) 310.

mortal to immortal." Man images God with his mind, with his soul.[3] Origen's language is suspiciously reminiscent of Philo's distinction:

This man who [Scripture] says was made (factum) to God's image we do not take to mean corporeal man. The reason is, it is not the body's formation that contains God's image; and it is not said that man was made (factus) corporeal, but that he was molded (plasmatus) such. . . . Now he who was made (factus) to God's image is our inner man, invisible and incorporeal and incorrupt and immortal. It is in such as these, you see, that God's image is more correctly discerned. If, on the other hand, there is anyone who thinks it is this corporeal man that was made (factus) to God's image and likeness, he gives the impression of representing God Himself as corporeal, in human form—an opinion about God that is obviously irreverent.[4]

The language is Philonian. Origen understands Moses to speak of a double creation, a twofold production; but he has abandoned Philo's ideal and real man for Paul's inner and outer man.[5] Origen insists that the man who was made to God's image is not the material, outward man; that would be to clothe God in human form. As an example of this latter tendency he singles out Melito, then refutes arguments for it drawn from the theophanies and from the fact that Scripture invests God with senses.[6] "It is within you that the image of heaven's King has been set."[7] Consequently, "he who affirms that the 'according to the image' is not in the body but in the rational soul will present an opinion not to be despised, comprehending as he does the soul's capacities."[8]

Following the example of his Alexandrian predecessors, Athanasius leaves no room for a corporeal element in his concept of the image.[9] In his eyes it is through the soul, "immortal and invisible," that men "copy God in the midst of the visible and the mortal."[10]

[3] Clement of Alexandria, Stromata 2, 19 (GCS 15, 169).

[4] Origen, In Genesim homiliae 1, 13 (GCS 29, 15); cf. Philo, De opificio mundi 69 [23] (Cohn-Wendland 1, 18; tr. LCL, Philo 1, 55).

[5] Cf. Origen, Commentarium in Canticum canticorum, Prologus (GCS 33, 63–64); cf. also In Ieremiam homiliae 1, 10 (GCS 6, 8–9) for ποίησις and πλάσις: "What is made does not come into being in the womb; but what is molded from the dust of the earth, this is produced in the womb."

[6] Cf. Origen, Selecta in Genesim (PG 12, 93–96).

[7] Origen, In Genesim homiliae 13, 4 (GCS 29, 119).

[8] Origen, Selecta in Genesim (PG 12, 96).

[9] Cf. Bernard, op. cit., p. 27. It is in the superior part of the soul (λόγος, νοῦς, ἡγεμονικόν) that Origen locates the image; cf. Crouzel, op. cit., pp. 153–60.

[10] Athanasius, Contra gentes 34 (PG 25, 68). A passage of a sermon preserved in Syriac (PG 18, 585–604; E. A. W. Budge, Coptic Homilies in the Dialect of Upper

The Cappadocians are in substantial harmony. Basil says flatly that it is in the mind that we have the Creator's image.[11] Gregory of Nazianzus, it is true, indicates in one passage that the whole man, this composite of dust and breath, is "image of the Immortal."[12] Elsewhere, however, he declares more precisely that "the flesh is far inferior to that which is according to the image."[13] It is in the soul that we "bear the image of the sovereign God."[14] In the theology of Gregory of Nyssa the corporeal, sentient part of man does not share, save remotely, in the image of God.[15] Or, to phrase it more fully, it is the soul alone that is God's image in the proper sense of the word, even though this dignity finds a reflection in the body—not so much in its physical beauty as in the dignity of its carriage, its posture, its σχῆμα (a quality more psychical than physical), which destines him for dominion.[16] The same basic assertion confronts us in the homilies In verba: Faciamus hominem ad imaginem et similitudinem nostram: it is not in the form of the body that we image God.[17] Gn 1:26 has reference to the man within, to the soul, to reason.[18]

---

Egypt [London, 1910] pp. 407-24) and attributed to Alexander, the immediate predecessor of Athanasius in the See of Alexandria, apparently includes the body in the image and likeness: "God took dust from the earth and fashioned man in His image and in His likeness, and breathed into him the breath of life, that Adam might become a living soul"; De anima et corpore deque passione domini 2 (PG 18, 589). The external testimony to Alexander's authorship is uncertain and irresolute; we have it in Coptic under the name of Athanasius; cf. Budge, op. cit., pp. 115–32, 258–74. Bardenhewer provisionally regards it as probable that we have here a sermon of Alexander in Syriac and Coptic translations; cf. op. cit. 3 (1912) 35. Bernard, op. cit., p. 25, believes that the sermon savors rather of Irenaeus than of Alexandria and that this strengthens the suspicions against its authenticity.

[11] Cf. Basil, Epistolae 233, 1 (LCL, Basil 3, 364; PG 32, 864).

[12] Gregory of Nazianzus, Poemata dogmatica 8, 74–75 (PG 37, 452).

[13] Ibid. 10, 33 (PG 37, 467).

[14] Gregory of Nazianzus, Poemata moralia 10, 111–14 (PG 37, 688); cf. Orationes 38, 11 (PG 36, 321).

[15] Cf. Muckle, art. cit., pp. 55–84; cf. Gregory of Nyssa, De hominis opificio 16 (PG 44, 177–88).

[16] Cf. Leys, op. cit., pp. 50, 64–65; cf. Gregory of Nyssa, De hominis opificio 4 (PG 44, 136); ibid. 8 (PG 44, 144).

[17] Cf. In verba: Faciamus hominem 1 (PG 44, 261); the same idea, but different language, in De hominis structura 1, 6 (PG 30, 16). Cf. also In verba: Faciamus hominem 2 (PG 44, 280), and De hominis structura 2, 1 (PG 30, 40–41), where we have an echo of Origen's distinction between "make" (used of the soul, the image, the inner man) and "mold" (used of the body, the outer man).

[18] Cf. In verba: Faciamus hominem 1 (PG 44, 264); also De hominis structura 1, 7 (PG 30, 17).

If the Alexandrian tradition consistently refuses to concede the body any genuine resemblance to God, non-Alexandrian Greek literature is more complex. In the first two centuries it is not at all clear that the divine image is understood simply of man's spiritual faculties, whether on a natural or on a supernatural niveau. The Clementines locate God's image not in the soul but in the "form" of man. Distinctly anthropomorphic, they attribute to God a luminous corporeality. This form of God, invisible to the eye of flesh, man bears as something visible. The body is the real carrier of the divine image; the soul partakes thereof only through its link with the body, "invested with God's image to immortality."[19] However, this anthropomorphic exegesis of Genesis proper to the Clementines betrays their extra-ecclesiastical status; it paved the way for the fourth-century Audians.[20]

In more orthodox authors authentic anthropomorphism is not a peril; but the problem of interpretation remains.[21] For Clement of Rome, it is simply man who is stamped with God's image; nothing more is said.[22] The second-century Apologists are more disconcerting still. The author of the *De resurrectione*—possibly Justin—gathers from Genesis that "the man of flesh," that is to say, the whole empirical man, was fashioned to God's image. Just how the flesh images its Maker, he does not say.[23]

[19] Cf. *Clementina* hom. 10, 4 ff.; 16, 3 ff. (*GCS* 42, 155 ff., 230 ff.); cf. Struker, *op. cit.*, pp. 63-65. The *Oracula Sibyllina* see the whole man as God's image; they seem always to presuppose a certain inadequately defined participation of the human body in this prerogative; cf. Struker, *op. cit.*, p. 75.

[20] Cf. Struker, *op. cit.*, p. 133. He has shown (pp. 52-53) that in the developed Gnostic systems there can be no question of a genuine imaging of *God*.

[21] Seventy years ago Jeiler, "Ebenbild Gottes," *Kirchenlexikon* (Wetzer und Welte) 4 (2nd ed., 1886) 68, judged it unjust to accuse the pre-Nicene Fathers of a gross, Audian-type anthropomorphism. As he saw it, they placed the character of an image not so much in the similarity of nature with the prototype as in the sensibly perceptible representation of the same; they conceived the corporeal side of man as an expression of the animating spiritual form; they discerned in the body not merely a mirror of the soul but also, through its regal form, a visible representation of God's majesty.

[22] Cf. *Ad Corinthios* 33, 4-5 (Funk-Bihlmeyer 1, 53). Klebba, *op. cit.*, p. 23, believes that in this passage it is primarily the body which bears the impress of the divine; but Struker, *op. cit.*, p. 7 (note 4), justly accuses Klebba of stressing unduly Clement's use of πλάσσειν.

[23] Cf. *De resurrectione* 7 (Otto, *Corpus apologetarum* [3rd ed.] 3, 234). On the problem of authorship cf. B. Altaner, *Patrologie* (2nd ed.; Freiburg, 1950) p. 92; Bardenhewer, *op. cit.* 1 (2nd ed.; Freiburg, 1913) 246-47. For the interpretation of the passage cf. Struker, *op. cit.*, pp. 19-20. The *Cohortatio ad gentiles*, falsely ascribed to Justin, is clear enough. It asserts that the first human beings to make

Tatian sees no basis for comparison between the flesh and the fleshless God; neither is the soul godlike, because it is but the bond of the body; it is in the communication of the λόγος—πνεῦμα that we find God's image and likeness.[24] It would seem that, in Melito's mind, God possessed, even before creation, an outward human form, which He actually assumed thereafter for definite purposes, e.g., the Old Testament theophanies, and which He actually used as the archetype of the human body in the creation of man. If this interpretation of his thought is accurate, then the corporeality of God, of which Origen accuses Melito, would not be essential but transitory; so, too, the resemblance between God and man, on God's side. As far as man is concerned, however, the image of God is to be sought in the body.[25]

The author of the *Letter to Diognetus* has a vague, yet suggestive reference to the problem at issue: "For God loved men, and for their sake made the world and made all things on earth subject to them. He gave them their reason and their mind. Them only He allowed to look up to Him. Them He fashioned from His own image."[26] The immediate grammatical connection of the image with the one purely corporeal characteristic mentioned, man's gaze directed to heaven, his upright posture, might suggest anthropomorphic ideas, if the author's conception of God did not forestall any such approach. At best, as Struker proposes,

---

images of the gods in the likeness of men were inspired by a misunderstanding: they took Gn 1:26 to mean that "men were like God in external form, and they began to represent their gods accordingly"; *Cohortatio* 38 (Otto 3, 124). On the authorship cf. Altaner, *op. cit.*, p. 93. Bardenhewer, *op. cit.* 1, 233–36, sets the work in the second half of the third century, with A. Puech and A. Harnack.

[24] Cf. Tatian, *Oratio ad graecos* 12 and 15 (*TU* 4/1, 12 and 16). It is not clear whether Tatian composed this oration before or after his apostasy; cf. J. Quasten, *Patrology* 1 (Westminster, Md., 1950) 221.

[25] For the problem, as well as the reconstruction of Melito's thought, cf. Struker, *op. cit.*, pp. 40–41. The Syriac *Apology* of Ps.-Melito, chapter 6 (Otto 9, 427), discovers God's likeness in man's soul or mind. The work has not yet been satisfactorily dated; it is placed in Caracalla's reign by Altaner, *op. cit.*, p. 101, and Quasten, *op. cit.* 1, 247.

[26] *Epistola ad Diognetum* 10, 2 (Funk-Bihlmeyer 1, 147). The author and date of this letter are matters of conjecture; the suggestions of scholars range from Clement of Rome to its first editor, H. Stephanus, in 1592. H. Meecham leans to the middle of the second century for its composition; cf. *The Epistle to Diognetus* (Manchester, 1949) pp. 16–19. This date, or the latter half of the second century, is the prevailing view, though Wilamowitz-Moellendorff, Geffcken, and Zahn have assigned it to the third century. Cf. the closely reasoned thesis of P. Andriessen that this letter is the lost *Apology* of Quadratus; *Recherches de théologie ancienne et médiévale* 13 (1946) 5–39, 125–49, 237–60; 14 (1947) 121–56; *id.*, "The Authorship of the Epistula ad Diognetum," *Vigiliae christianae* 1 (1947) 129–36.

the writer "may actually have seen in the external appearance of man a mirror of divine perfection, yet have refrained from more accurate determination because sensible of the difficulties arising from the spiritual essence of God."[27]

The mind of Irenaeus is not easily grasped. For our present purpose, however, this much of his image theology seems clear: Adam was created after the model of the Word Incarnate. It follows that man's complete nature is to be understood as the image. The Word, becoming man, became what His image was. The divine image, then, comprises all the spiritual and bodily prerogatives of man that are not sheerly supernatural; in a word, the natural man, body and soul.[28]

Methodius is convinced that the soul was framed to "the image of His own Image" by "the unbegotten and unbodied Beauty";[29] and still he seems to see the whole man in God's image: "this human form" itself images the divine, is godlike.[30] This is especially true of Adam, since he was made immortal even in body.[31] Eusebius of Caesarea finds in St. Paul (Col 3:9-10) a proof that it is not the flesh that is the image of God.[32] Cyril of Jerusalem expressly locates the divine image in the soul.[33] Epiphanius reads, in one passage, like an epitome of caution. He will admit only the inescapable fact: man does image God. How he does it, God alone knows; and Epiphanius refuses to meddle.[34] And yet his

[27] Struker, op. cit., p. 15.

[28] Cf., e.g., Irenaeus, Adversus haereses 5, 16, 1 (Harvey 2, 367-68); Klebba, op. cit., pp. 23-25. From an analysis of Adversus haereses 5, 1-16, a synthesis has been fashioned by E. Peterson, "L'Immagine di Dio in S. Ireneo," Scuola cattolica 19 (1941) 3-11. Briefly: Adam was created on the model of the Word Incarnate. The latter is constituted of body, soul, and Holy Spirit; therefore the true man, perfect and living, formed to God's image and likeness, should consist of body, soul, and Holy Spirit. In other words, Adam before his sin possessed a body that imaged the body which the Word was to assume, and a Spirit corresponding to the Holy Spirit who generated and ruled the body of the Word. As the point of departure for the solution of difficulties in Irenaeus, Struker distinguishes between the image of God and the image of the Logos-Jesus Christ. For Irenaeus, he concludes, the image of God in the strict sense comprises man's reason and freedom; the image of the Logos embraces the whole corporeal-spiritual nature of man as such, with especial prominence given to the visible corporeality; cf. op. cit., pp. 97, 127.

[29] Methodius, Symposium 6, 1, 133-34 (GCS 27, 64); cf. De resurrectione 2, 24, 3 (GCS 27, 380).

[30] Cf. Methodius, De resurrectione 3, 15, 1 (GCS 27, 411); 3, 15, 2 (GCS 27, 411).

[31] Cf. ibid. 1, 35, 4 (GCS 27, 275); Gross, op. cit., p. 193.

[32] Cf. Eusebius, Contra Marcellum 1, 4 (GCS 14, 25).

[33] Cf. Cyril of Jerusalem, Catecheses 4, 18 (PG 33, 477).

[34] Cf. Epiphanius, Ancoratus 55 (GCS 25, 64-65).

conservatism does not prevent him, in another passage, from weighing the different opinions and rejecting them all: that the image is in the body, as the Audians claim; that Adam lost the image by sin; that the image is in the soul, or in virtue, or in baptism.[35] John Chrysostom and Severian of Gabala exclude the body from a share in the image.[36] Finally, Theodoret of Cyrus denies that the image is to be sought either in the soul's invisibility or in the human body; man is God's image because he sums up creation, dominates the earth, rules, and judges.[37] Nevertheless, he does discover an intimate imitation of the divine in the rational faculty of the human soul.[38]

The non-Alexandrian Greek tradition, therefore, like the Alexandrian, insists that man's resemblance to God is to be found in the soul. Unlike the Alexandrian, it seems—at least in its earlier representatives—in stumbling quest of a solution which will somehow include the body, the whole man, without running afoul of anthropomorphism. The Latin tradition is almost as inflexible as the Alexandrian. From Tertullian[39] through Hilary of Poitiers,[40] Zeno of Verona,[41] Philastrius of Brescia,[42] Ambrose of Milan,[43] and Jerome,[44] down to Augustine, who solidifies the

[35] Cf. Epiphanius, *Panarion*, haer. 70, 2–6 (*GCS* 37, 233–38).

[36] Cf. Chrysostom, *Homiliae in Genesim* 8, 3–4 (*PG* 53, 72–73); Severian, *In mundi creationem* 5, 3 (*PG* 56, 474).

[37] Cf. Theodoret, *Quaestiones in Genesim* 1, 20 (*PG* 80, 104); also *Interpretatio primae epistolae ad Corinthios*, 1 Cor 11:7 (*PG* 82, 312).

[38] Cf. Theodoret, *Quaestiones in Genesim* 1, 20 (*PG* 80, 104–8); Gross, *op. cit.*, p. 273.

[39] Cf. Tertullian, *Adversus Marcionem* 2, 5 (*CSEL*, 47, 340): the lines of man's body vary too much in the breadth and scope of humanity to mirror a God who "has but one form." The Latin *uniformem* seems to urge the anthropomorphic idea of unchangeable "shape"; but Tertullian's use of *corpus* with reference to God and spiritual beings in general is difficult to grasp; cf. A. d'Alès, *La théologie de Tertullien* (3rd ed.; Paris, 1905) pp. 61–65.

[40] Cf. Hilary, *In psalmum 118*, Iod 8 (*CSEL* 22, 443); *In psalmum 129*, 6 (*CSEL* 22, 651–52); *In psalmum 119*, 19 (*CSEL* 22, 556); *In psalmum 129*, 5 (*CSEL* 22, 651). Cf. also Ps.-Hilary, *Epistola seu libellus* 5 (*PL* 10, 737).

[41] Cf. Zeno, *Tractatus* 2, 19 and 20 (*PL* 11, 456 and 458).

[42] Cf. Philastrius, *Diversarum hereseon liber* 137, 2 and 5 (*CSEL* 38, 107–8). He speaks of the "heresy" which holds that man's body and not his soul is God's image; cf. *ibid.* 97, 1 (*CSEL* 38, 56).

[43] Cf. Ambrose, *Exameron* 6, 7, 40 and 43 (*CSEL* 32/1, 231 and 234); *ibid.* 6, 8, 44–45 (*CSEL* 32/1, 235); *Expositio psalmi 118*, 8, 23 (*CSEL*, 62, 164); *De institutione virginis* 3, 20 (*PL* 16, 324). For Ambrose, as for Hilary and Philastrius, Gn 1:26 refers to the soul, Gn 2:7 to the body; only the former is fashioned to God's image; cf. *Explanatio psalmi 43*, 4 (*CSEL* 64, 261); *Explanatio psalmi 118*, 10, 15 (*CSEL* 62, 212).

[44] Cf. Jerome, *Commentaria in Isaiam* 14 (*PL* 24, 508).

tradition,[45] the constant refrain of the West is that the image of God is to be found in man's soul and not in his body. There are exceptions, of course. In one passage, redolent of Irenaeus, Tertullian declares that the slime from which Adam's body was fashioned "was clothed even then in the image of Christ to come in the flesh."[46] It is an idea which Prudentius weds to dactylic hexameters:

> Christus forma Patris, nos Christi forma et imago;
> condimur in faciem domini bonitate paterna
> venturo in nostram faciem post saecula Christo.[47]

In Cyprian's warning to women not to mar God's handiwork (Gn 1:26) with rouge and the like, we may have a suggestion that woman somehow bears God's image in her native external appearance.[48] Lactantius gives the impression that he sees God's likeness in the whole man, soul and body.[49] Even Augustine suggests that our body is fashioned in such a way as to witness our superiority to the beast and consequently our likeness to God. This erect posture, unique in the animal world, means that our soul, our mind should be lifted to the spiritual things of eternity.[50] "The body of man, because better able to eye heaven, has in this respect a better right to be regarded as made to God's image and likeness than the bodies of all other animals."[51] Nevertheless, these exceptions, scattered as they are, do not invalidate the conclusion that on broad lines the Western Fathers agree in understanding the divine image, and in interpreting Gn 1:26–27, of human nature's distinctive feature, the rational soul in contrast to the body.[52]

When Cyril of Alexandria expressly defines man's inmost essence, he terms him "a rational, mortal animal, capable of understanding and

[45] Cf. Augustine, *Epistolae* 166, 12 (*CSEL* 44, 564): Gn 1:27 is to be understood of the rational soul. Cf. also *De Genesi ad litteram* 3, 20 (*CSEL* 28/1, 86): St. Paul's insistence on interior renewal shows sufficiently "where man has been created to God's image, that it is not in the features of the body but in some intelligible form of the mind illumined." Cf. likewise *De Genesi contra Manichaeos* 17 (*PL* 34, 186).

[46] Tertullian, *De carnis resurrectione* 6 (*CSEL* 47, 33); cf. *Adversus Praxean* 12 (*CSEL* 47, 245-46); *Adversus Marcionem* 5, 8 (*CSEL* 47, 597).

[47] Prudentius, *Liber apotheosis* 309–11 (*CSEL* 61, 94).

[48] Cf. Cyprian, *De habitu virginum* 15 (*CSEL* 3/1, 198).

[49] Cf. Lactantius, *Divinae institutiones* 2, 10 (*CSEL* 19, 147); also *Epitome divinarum institutionum* 22 [27] (*CSEL* 19, 694).

[50] Cf. Augustine, *De Genesi contra Manichaeos* 17 (*PL* 34, 187).

[51] Augustine, *De diversis quaestionibus 83*, q. 51, 3 (*PL* 40, 33).

[52] So, e.g., Slomkowski, *op. cit.*, p. 135.

knowledge";[53] or, more simply, "a rational, mortal animal."[54] As for his physical constitution, "man is by nature a composite being, not simple, a blend of two: a sensible body and an intellectual soul."[55] And it is precisely in the soul—this soul which comes from God,[56] which had no existence before its union with the body,[57] which will never cease to exist,[58] and which has no quality, no quantity, no form[59]—it is here, and

[53] *In Ioannem* 6 (Pusey 2, 128); *ibid.* 2, 5 (Pusey 1, 279); 10, 1 (Pusey 2, 522); *Thesaurus* 2 (*PG* 75, 28); *ibid.* 8 (*PG* 75, 109); 31 (*PG* 75, 444); *De sancta et consubstantiali trinitate* dial. 2 (*PG* 75, 728); dial. 7 (*PG* 75, 1081). The same definition, save for the omission of "mortal," is found: *In Ioannem* 1, 7 (Pusey 1, 80); 11, 7 (Pusey 2, 684).

[54] *Thesaurus* 31 (*PG* 75, 444); *Homiliae paschales* 12, 6 (*PG* 77, 689).

[55] *In Ioannem* 2, 1 (Pusey 1, 219); cf. *ibid.* 5, 5 (Pusey 2, 64); 6, 1 (Pusey 2, 200); *Adversus Nestorii blasphemias* 1, 4 (*ACO* 1, 1, 6, 24; *PG* 76, 37); *Epistolae* 17, 8 (*ACO* 1, 1, 1, 38; *PG* 77, 116); *ibid.* 39, 5 (*ACO* 1, 1, 4, 17; *PG* 77, 176–77). I see no persuasive evidence that Cyril holds for a trichotomy (πνεῦμα, ψυχή, and σῶμα or σάρξ) in man's essential physical structure. At times πνεῦμα seems but a synonym for ψυχή; cf. *In Ioannem* 3, 4 (Pusey 1, 439); *ibid.* 3, 6 (Pusey 1, 458); 12 (Pusey 3, 96); *In Matthaeum*, Mt 27:50 (*PG* 72, 465). At least once πνεῦμα is quite obviously identified with ψυχὴ νοερά; cf. *In Ioannem* 2, 1 (Pusey 1, 219). Again, πνεῦμα is used indifferently for νοῦς; cf. *In Ioannem* 1, 9 (Pusey 1, 117). On occasion Cyril points out that man's soul is πνεῦμα; cf. *De sancta et consubstantiali trinitate* dial. 7 (*PG* 75, 1108). He uses "body" (or "flesh") and "soul" without the addition of πνεῦμα, as though they satisfied man's essential constitution; cf. *In Canticum canticorum* (*PG* 69, 1284); *In Ioannem* 4, 7 (Pusey 1, 630); 7 (Pusey 2, 292). He notes that man's spirit is not something other than man himself; cf. *De recta fide, ad augustas* 19 (*ACO* 1, 1, 1, 15; *PG* 77, 21). And, at great pains to prove that Christ was man φυσικῶς and ἀληθῶς, with all things human save sin, Cyril accomplishes his purpose by showing that He assumed the whole of human nature because He had passions of the flesh and passions of the rational soul; cf. *In Ioannem* 8 (Pusey 2, 315–20). A body and a rational soul make Christ perfect man; cf. *Epistolae* 39, 5 (*ACO*, 1, 1, 4, 17; *PG* 77, 176–77; *De recta fide, ad augustas* 44 (*ACO* 1, 1, 5, 58–59; *PG* 76, 1413); *Apologeticus contra Theodoretum* 16 (*ACO* 1, 1, 6, 113; *PG* 76, 397). Cyril is consciously playing the philosopher when he observes that "we are compounded into one man made up of soul and body. Now the body is one thing, and the soul in the body is another, if you consider the essence of each; but they combine to form one living being, and after their union they admit no division whatsoever"; *In Ioannem* 12, 1 (Pusey 3, 155); cf. also the references in note 53 above. It is undeniable, however, that there are puzzling passages where the meaning of πνεῦμα fails to emerge clearly; cf. *In Ioannem* 2, 1 (Pusey 1, 187 and 220); *ibid.* 11, 9 (Pusey 2, 697); 11, 12 (Pusey 3, 2); *De sancta et consubstantiali trinitate* dial. 7 (*PG* 75, 1080); also *Adversus nolentes confiteri s. virginem esse deiparam* 9 (*ACO* 1, 1, 7, 23; *PG* 76, 265): body, soul, and mind (νοῦς) in Christ.

[56] Cf. *Epistolae* 1, 12 (*ACO* 1, 1, 1, 15; *PG* 77, 21).

[57] Cf. *ibid.* 81 (*PG* 77, 373).

[58] Cf. *De adoratione* 10 (*PG* 68, 697).

[59] Cf. *Thesaurus* 31 (*PG* 75, 452).

not in the body, that man's resemblance to his Maker is rooted. On this point Cyril's thought is clear, his expression unambiguous.

The simple fact emerges from several passages, in several ways; for Cyril plays the exegete and the apologete, the theologian and the philosopher. In his interpretation of Ps 32:9, "For He spoke and they were made, He commanded and they were created," Cyril explains that ἐγενήθη refers to "this body of ours fashioned from the earth," while ἐκτίσθη refers to "the soul created to God's image."[60] This resemblance to God in the soul is used to demonstrate man's superiority to the rest of animal creation:

> . . . Of all living creatures on earth, there simply is none the equal of man. . . . For we have been fashioned by [God], as by a potter, from the dust of the earth. But it is not sheerly in this that the dignity of human nature lies; there is something greater in us, a gracious gift of God's artistic skill. The fact is, we have been made to His image and likeness, and have been enriched with the impress of His glory, gleaming spiritually in our souls, even if we are, according to the flesh, earth and of earth. Man, then, is not a contemptible but an admirable creature on earth.[61]

Cyril denies categorically that the human body enjoys the same privilege. "Man upon earth, as far as his bodily nature is concerned, is dust and ashes; but he has been honoured by God, by having been made in His image and likeness—not in his bodily shape, that is, but rather because he is capable of being just and good, and fitted for all virtue."[62] It is in consequence of this prerogative that the soul is the more precious facet of the human composite. "The soul is more honorable than the substance of the body, seeing that it is God's image and inspiration (ἐμφύσημα). Still, the body is its instrument and its colleague in all that is best." That is why we must be concerned about both: the body in so far as this is imperative if it is not to obstruct the soul; the soul in every way, giving it always what it needs and deserves.[63]

The question, where does the image reside, is intimately allied with Cyril's polemic against anthropomorphism. It was reported to him that certain Egyptian monks were sowing confusion by drawing from Gn

---

[60] *In psalmos*, Ps 32:9 (*PG* 69, 876). Cyril's alternate exegesis, which refers the verbs in question to man's original existence and to his regeneration respectively, does not alter the information we derive from his first interpretation, namely, that he considers the soul alone God's image.

[61] *In Isaiam* 4, 2 (*PG* 70, 960).

[62] *In Lucam* hom. 96 (tr. R. Payne Smith, *A Commentary upon the Gospel according to S. Luke by S. Cyril* 2 [Oxford, 1859] 446).

[63] *In Matthaeum*, Mt 6:23 (*PG* 72, 384).

1:26 the conclusion that God has human form.[64] On this point he is intransigent. "Man is admittedly according to God's image, but the likeness is not corporeal; for God is incorporeal . . . . But if they think that God . . . was shaped after the nature of the human body, let them say whether He too has feet to walk, hands to work, eyes to see. . . ."[65] In fact, such a doctrine, predicating divine resemblance of the body's shape, has irreverent implications: God would be "conformed even to irrational animals."[66] Cyril's palmary argument against anthropomorphism is the fact that God is a spirit, not a body.[67] God is "incorporeal, immaterial, impalpable, beyond quantity and circumscription, beyond form and figure."[68] There, fundamentally, is the reason why those who claim that man's likeness to God lies in his body, in his visible form, "are mistaken."[69]

The anti-anthropomorphic argument in Cyril's hands is a blunt, indelicate instrument. Cyril bares a second weapon, more theological in its elaboration, against the theory that man's resemblance to God has something to do with the body. The force of this argument, as well as its accompanying peril for Cyril, will not be felt until we have exposed the specific content of his image concept. At any rate, Cyril argues that, if man were formed to his God in the nature and structure of his body, it would be impossible for anyone to lose the image; "for we have lost none of our essential components."[70] His point is that some men do reject, do lose the divine image; this they do by forsaking a life of justice, holiness, and virtue. In other words, Cyril's premise is that the image can be lost; if that is so, he concludes, then it is not in the body that our likeness to God lies.

In principle, therefore, Cyril excludes the body from God's image and likeness. In point of fact, however, two facets of Cyril's theology threaten

---

[64] An interesting page in the first series (composed 420–26) of the *Conferences* of John Cassian, a contemporary of Cyril, describes the anthropomorphic conception of God spread among the monks of Egypt on the basis of Gn 1:26–27; cf. *Collationes* 10, 3, 2–3 (*CSEL* 13, 288). It includes the patristic lecture of the deacon Photinus, "quidam diaconus summae scientiae vir," on the Oriental Church's interpretation of Gn 1:26. His answer: it is universally taught in the Orient that the words are not to be taken at their face value but spiritually, and that it is impossible to put human composition and human likeness in the incorporeal, simple nature of God. Cf. also *ibid.* 10, 5 (*CSEL* 13, 290–91).

[65] *Epistola ad Calosyrium* (Pusey, *In Ioannem* 3, 604).

[66] *Ibid.* (Pusey 3, 605).

[67] *Responsiones ad Tiberium* 10 (Pusey 3, 592–93).

[68] *Ibid.* 14 (Pusey 3, 599).

[69] *Ibid.* 10 (Pusey 3, 592–93).

[70] *Ibid.* (Pusey 3, 594).

his consistency in this matter. One of these developments cannot be adequately discussed at this point; it concerns man as mirror of the Immortal, and had best await our detailed treatment of the precise content of Cyril's image concept. The other problem is not quite as complex; it should be touched on here. There are many passages in Cyril's works where he insists that we have been made, or remade, in the image and likeness of Christ, the Word Incarnate, the Son of God in human flesh.[71] He tells us, for example, that, if we are scandalized at the ignorance of Christ as man, then the whole idea of the Incarnation will logically be destroyed—the mystery through which we have been saved. "For we were made like Him, when He was made like us."[72]

Is this Irenaeus redivivus? I do not think so. Cyril does not, of course, deny that the Son of God became like us in perfect humanity. He will not challenge the fact that all men without exception are conformed (συμμόρφους) to Christ by reason of the human nature common to them and to Him. But this is not the divine image of Scripture and theology, as Cyril sees it. The image texts of the New Testament (Rom 8:29; 2 Cor 3:17–18; Col 3:10; cf. Gal 4:19) do not refer to a graving of Christ in us after the flesh. Our transfiguration to Christ is a spiritual, a supernatural, a divine thing; we are images of divinity.[73] Cyril scouts as "highly ridiculous" the notion that reformation to our Lord involves some corporeal remodeling.[74] Our participation of the Son has reference to Him inasmuch as He is God. "For Christ is formed in us, not as created in created, but as Uncreated and God in created and produced nature, engraving us anew to His own image through the Spirit, and transferring the creature, that is, us, to the dignity that is above the creature."[75] Our specific imaging of God's Son comes down to this, that we have become sons of God.[76]

[71] Cf. *In Isaiam* 4, 5 (*PG* 70, 1121–24).

[72] *In Matthaeum*, Mt 24:36 (*PG* 72, 444–45); on Christ's likeness (ὁμοίωσιν) to us cf. *In Ioannem* 12, 1 (Pusey 3, 122–23).

[73] Cf. *Adversus Nestorii blasphemias* 3, 2 (*ACO* 1, 1, 6, 59–60; *PG* 76, 128–29).

[74] *De recta fide, ad Theodosium* 36 (*ACO* 1, 1, 1, 36; *PG* 76, 1188). Even here, however, one difficulty must await later discussion, i.e., Cyril's thesis that our definitive imaging of Christ will have place at the resurrection, when our bodies will be so transformed as to be like the glorified body of Christ; cf. *In 2 Cor.* 2, 1 (Pusey, *In Ioannem* 3, 338–39; *PG* 74, 929–32).

[75] *De sancta et consubstantiali trinitate* dial. 4 (*PG* 75, 904–5).

[76] Cf. *De dogmatum solutione* 4 (Pusey, *In Ioannem* 3, 557–58; *PG* 76, 1088–89). Note how Cyril uses image of *Christ* and impress of the *divine nature* indiscriminately; cf. *Homiliae paschales* 10, 1 (*PG* 77, 612). The Son Himself images the Father not in bodily structure, His human form, but in that He is everything the Father is, save for Fatherhood; cf. *Contra Iulianum* 10 (*PG* 76, 1013).

Modern exegesis, it must be confessed, is not in sympathy with Cyril's solution—at least where there is question of Gn 1:26–27. Today's exegete, in consequence of his effort to penetrate Hebrew thought patterns, Old Testament mentality, is more inclined to agree with the earlier non-Alexandrians that the whole empirical man was fashioned to God's image and likeness.[77] He sees that in Old Testament categories soul and body are so intimately one that the body is the soul in its outward form, its external expression.[78] And so he insists that, in the vision of the Priestly Tradition, man as such, fashioned of soul and body, is made in God's likeness—not simply one part of him. Or, in more nuanced terms:

> Man "in the image of God" means . . . that there is a correspondence between the total being of God and the total being of man. The thought cannot be confined to physical resemblance; indeed, it is improbable that the physical is in the center of attention. Instead, the emphasis must lie on the self-conscious, self-directing vitality which constitutes the sum of personal being. This, of course, does not exclude the corporeal because the Hebrews did not conceive of pure being in spiritual terms apart from material form. Yet it does mean that the "image" in man must primarily be concerned with the deeper aspects of personal being and not merely with the superficial.[79]

These nuances Cyril has not seen. One obvious reason is that his approach to a biblical text is not by way of the Hebrew mind; for one thing, he did not have the tools to unlock it. He reads the New Testament into the Old, theology into Scripture, the tradition of Alexandria into the Priestly Tradition, Christian anti-anthropomorphism into Semitic thinking about God. Nevertheless, another significant step in our quest has been realized. As Cyril and his Alexandrian ancestors see it, Scripture and theology agree in locating the image and likeness of God in man's soul, not in his body.

[77] Cf. E. F. Sutcliffe, in *A Catholic Commentary on Holy Scripture*, ed. B. Orchard *et al.* (London and New York, 1953) p. 183.

[78] On the Hebrew conception of soul and body cf. J. Pedersen, *Israel: Its Life and Culture* 1–2 (London and Copenhagen, 1926) 170–81.

[79] G. E. Wright, "The Faith of Israel," in *The Interpreter's Bible* 1 (New York and Nashville, c1952) 368. Cf. von Rad, *art. cit.*, pp. 388–89. Gunkel, *op. cit.*, p. 112, interprets Gn 1:26 primarily of man's body. G. Crespy, insisting that man in his totality, his integrity, his entirety, was made to God's image, considers impertinent the question, where in man is God's image? Man, he asserts, is not "after" God's image by his nature; man is "in" God's image by his destiny, his vocation as a creator-being (*homo faber*) to conduct creation, as well as his own efforts within creation, to the God who is sole Lord; cf. *Le problème d'une anthropologie théologique* (Montpellier, 1950) pp. 64–78.

# CHAPTER 3

# REASON

In his letter to Calosyrius, Bishop of Arsinoë, Cyril not merely marshalled objections against the disturbing thesis that man somehow images God with his body; he went on to take a more constructive stand:

Man's formation to God's image has other meanings—meanings on the surface and meanings deep within; for man alone, of all the living creatures on earth, is rational (λογικός), compassionate, with a capacity for all manner of virtue, and a divinely allotted dominion over all the creatures of earth, after the image and likeness of God. Therefore, it is inasmuch as he is a rational (λογικόν) animal, a lover of virtue, and earth's sovereign that man is said to have been made in God's image.[1]

When Cyril discerned in man's mind, in his reason, in his understanding, a facet of the divine image, he was inserting himself into a tradition that cut sharply across theological lines. The first two centuries are almost prophetic; for "wherever the doctrinal point of the divine image in man is considered in any detail at all, the natural, inamissible resemblance to God common to all men is found more or less clearly in the spiritual likeness between God and man revealing itself through reason and freedom."[2] The fact is luminous enough in Irenaeus: "man [is] a rational being, and on this ground he is like God, fashioned free in will and his own master. . . ."[3] But in the course of the next two centuries, from Irenaeus to Cyril, it is generally the element of intelligence rather than freedom that is underscored. Alexandrian thought, to which Cyril is so obviously heir, is permeated with this divine resemblance in human reason. We have but to page through Clement and Origen, with their

---

[1] *Epistola ad Calosyrium* (Pusey, *In Ioannem* 3, 605).

[2] Struker, *op. cit.*, p. 133.

[3] Irenaeus, *Adversus haereses* 4, 7 (Harvey 2, 154). It should be noted that, from Irenaeus' viewpoint, the rationality in question is not utterly inamissible; he goes on to state that, in setting himself up against God, man ceased to act rationally. Clement of Rome seems to see the principal element of the image in the gift of understanding; cf. *Ad Corinthios* 33, 4–5 (Funk-Bihlmeyer 1, 53). On the textual problem of κατὰ διάνοιαν, cf. Gross, *op. cit.*, p. 119, and Struker, *op. cit.*, p. 7 and note 2 *ibid.* Athenagoras may have seen in rationality the essence of man's resemblance to God; cf. *Legatio pro christianis* 12 (*TU* 4/2, 62). Cf. also *Oracula Sibyllina* 8, 402 (*GCS* 8, 168): "man is my image in possessing right reason."

anticipation in Philo, to be convinced of it. On this aspect of the image Philo waxes rhetorical:

. . . it is in respect of the Mind (νοῦν), the sovereign element of the soul, that the word "image" is used [in Gn 1:26]; for after the pattern of a single Mind, even the Mind of the Universe as an archetype, the mind in each of those who successively came into being was moulded. It is in a fashion a god to him who carries and enshrines it as an object of reverence; for the human mind evidently occupies a position in men precisely answering to that which the great Ruler occupies in all the world. It is invisible while itself seeing all things, and while comprehending the substances of others, it is as to its own substance unperceived; and while it opens by arts and sciences roads branching in many directions, all of them great highways, it comes through land and sea investigating what either element contains. Again, when on soaring wing it has contemplated the atmosphere and all its phases, it is borne yet higher to the ether and the circuit of heaven, and is whirled round with the dances of planets and fixed stars, in accordance with the laws of perfect music, following that love of wisdom which guides its steps. And so, carrying its gaze beyond the confines of all substance discernible by sense, it comes to a point at which it reaches out after the intelligible world, and on descrying in that world sights of surpassing loveliness, even the patterns and originals of the things of sense which it saw here, it is seized by a sober intoxication, like those filled with Corybantic frenzy, and is inspired, possessed by a longing far other than theirs and a nobler desire. Wafted by this to the topmost arch of things perceptible to mind, it seems to be on its way to the Great King Himself; but, amid its longing to see Him, pure and untempered rays of concentrated light stream forth like a torrent, so that by its gleams the eye of the understanding is dazzled.[4]

There is nothing in Cyril to match Philo's Platonic flight; but it is difficult to believe that in this matter Philo did not exercise a significant influence on the Christian theologians of Alexandria.[5] For Clement, the image of God of which there is question in Gn 1:26 is "the divine and

---

[4] Philo, De opificio mundi 69–71 [23] (Cohn-Wendland 1, 18–19; tr. LCL, Philo 1, 55–57). Cf. ibid. 139 [48] (Cohn-Wendland 1, 40): λογισμόν; also ibid. 146 [51] (Cohn-Wendland 1, 42): every man, in regard of his διάνοια, is kin to the divine Logos, because he has come into being as a copy (ἐκμαγεῖον) or fragment or ray of that nature. Cf. Quis rerum divinarum heres 231 [48] (Cohn-Wendland 3, 44): man was made "after the image": our νοῦς expresses God by being cast on the model (ἐκμαγεῖον) of the εἰκών. Cf. De fuga et inventione 68–72 [13–14] (Cohn-Wendland 3, 110–11).

[5] It is generally recognized that Philo exerted more influence than anyone else on Clement of Alexandria. For a study of their interpretation of Scripture, cf. C. Mondésert, Clément d'Alexandrie: Introduction à l'étude de sa pensée religieuse à partir de l'Ecriture (Paris, 1944) pp. 163–83.

royal Word, the impassible Man; and the image of the Image is the human mind (νοῦς)."[6] It is on mind and reason (νοῦν, λογισμόν) that the Lord impressed the seal of His likeness, because it is through judgments of the mind that man, like God, does good and exercises dominion.[7] The Image of God, Clement insists, is the Word of God; "an image of the Word is the true man, that is, the mind in man. It is on this account that he is said to have been made after God's image and after His likeness, because by his heart's understanding he is made like to the divine Word (λόγῳ) and therefore rational (λογικός)."[8] The passage is much akin, in its basic insight, to a paragraph in Philo:

> One of the two [forms of reason; λόγους] is the archetypal reason above us, the other the copy which we possess. Moses calls the first the "image (εἰκόνα) of God," the second the cast (ἐκμαγεῖον) of that image. For God, he says, made man not "the image of God" but "after the image". . . . And thus the mind (νοῦν) in each of us, which in the true and full sense is the "man," is an expression at third hand from the Maker, while between them is the Reason which serves as model for our reason, but itself is the effigies or presentiment (ἀπεικόνισμα) of God.[9]

We have heard Origen declare that it is in the rational (λογική) soul and not in the body that man is after God's image. He does not, however, restrict this rational soul to a cold, naked ability to think. It is the cognitive faculty, yes; but it comprises the power to make judgments, the disposition to do good, the ability to act justly, a purpose that is vigorous; "in a word, the faculty of achieving all that is noble and good."[10] It is a participation in the divine Logos:

> He who looks from heaven upon the irrational animals, even though their bodies may be large, will not see any origin for their impulses other than irrationality, so to speak. But when he looks at the rational beings, he will see reason (λόγον) which is common to men and to divine and heavenly beings, and probably also to the supreme God Himself. This explains why he is said to have

[6] Clement of Alexandria, *Stromata* 5, 14 (*GCS* 15, 388); cf. *ibid.* 6, 9 (*GCS* 15, 468).

[7] Cf. *ibid.* 2, 19 (*GCS* 15, 169). Note, however, *ibid.* 3, 5 (*GCS* 15, 215); this imaging seems to demand a pure mind free from all vice.

[8] Clement of Alexandria, *Protrepticus* 10 (*GCS* 12, 71).

[9] Philo, *Quis rerum divinarum heres* 230–31 [48] (Cohn-Wendland 3, 44; tr. *LCL*, Philo 4, 399).

[10] Origen, *Selecta in Genesim* (*PG* 12, 96). He goes on to reveal this image in action: loving justice and holiness, observing Christ's command to be merciful and to be perfect as the Father is.

been made in the image of God; for the image of the supreme God is His reason (λόγος).[11]

In a pregnant sentence Origen speaks of Christ as "the Word (λόγος) according to whom we are rational (λογικοί), He who is Himself identically the Image of God according to which man was made to God's image. ..."[12] To some extent at least, this divine resemblance is indestructible; this reasonableness is part and parcel of the human. Christians—so Origen reminds Celsus—have been told that the human soul was made in the image of God; they are convinced that this nature made in God's image "simply cannot efface entirely its distinguishing marks and assume others, I know not what, which are made after the image of some sort of irrational beings."[13]

The neo-Alexandrian development follows a similar pattern. Athanasius, who was a sympathetic reader of Origen, is inspired by his predecessors when he links κατ' εἰκόνα and λογικός, makes them not simply symmetrical but synonymous, and gives us in bold, unphilosophical strokes a doctrine of ontological participation.[14]

God ... seeing that the human race would be essentially impermanent, gave men a gift which other creatures lacked. He did not merely create them, as He had created all the irrational animals on earth; He made them after His own image, giving them a share in the power of His own Word, so that, possessing as it were some shadows of the Word (λόγου) and become rational (λογικοί), they might be in a position to abide in blessedness, living in paradise the true life which is actually the life of the saints.[15]

This is not the place to probe the thorny problem, whether Athanasius recognized a sheerly natural image in Adam or in man generally, a resemblance to God on the level of man's natural endowments.[16] This

[11] Origen, Contra Celsum 4, 85 (GCS 2, 356; tr. H. Chadwick, Origen: Contra Celsum [Cambridge, 1953] p. 251). Cf. Crouzel, op. cit., pp. 158-60, 168-75.
[12] Origen, Fragmenta in Ioannem 18 (GCS 10, 497).
[13] Origen, Contra Celsum 4, 83 (GCS 2, 354-55).
[14] Cf. Bernard, op. cit., pp. 32-42.
[15] Athanasius, De incarnatione Verbi 3 (PG 25, 101).
[16] Gross, op. cit., p. 204, believes that Athanasius recognized only a supernatural image, and that his philosophical views "did not allow him ... to recognize in the natural endowment of the soul an initial resemblance." Slomkowski, op. cit., p. 97, distinguishes: "When treating of creation, he expresses by 'image' all that which raised the first man above the condition of irrational beings, while, when he speaks of the state that followed the fall, he is led to specify his thought and then no longer sees 'the grace of the state of image' save in the gifts superadded to his nature, which man lost in consequence of his defection."

much at least may be said. In fashioning Adam to the image of God, in making him λογικός, the Creator graced man with a power which Athanasius finds genuinely gratuitous. This power was orientated to contemplation of the divine; this faculty made it possible for man to know the Logos, and in Him the Father whose Image He is. In Athanasius' eyes, men could not be properly λογικοί unless they knew the Logos, Reason, and through Him the Father. Without this gift, man impresses Athanasius as being on a level with the irrational (ἄλογος) among animals. The Aristotelian concept of sheer "rational animal" is not an Athanasian category.[17]

> When God . . . made humankind through His own Word, He saw clearly that owing to the limitation of their nature men could not of themselves know their Maker, could get no concept of God at all; for He is uncreated, while they have passed from non-being to being; He is incorporeal, while men have been molded with a body. . . . He did not leave them without knowledge of Him, lest their existence be profitless; for what profit can there be for creatures if they know not their Creator? Or how could they be rational (λογικοί) if they do not know the Father's Word (λόγον), in whom they have been made? They would be no different than the beasts (ἄλογον), had they no knowledge save of earthly things. And why should God have created them at all if He did not wish to be known by them? That is why . . . He made them share in His own Image, our Lord Jesus Christ, and made them after His own image and likeness, in order that by means of such a grace they might perceive the Image, I mean the Word of the Father, and through Him be able to come to a knowledge of the Father, and knowing their Maker they might live the life that is genuinely happy and blessed.[18]

Confronted with creation, Athanasius comprises the whole order of mind (νοῦς) within the concept of participation in the Word who divinizes. Confronted with the fact of sin, glimpsing the inadequacy of his tight little image-synthesis, he will fluctuate, hesitate, grope towards an answer complicated not merely by his philosophy but by the inner contradiction of the soul in sin.[19]

[17] Cf. Bernard, op. cit., pp. 61–62. This knowledge of God "through themselves" Athanasius expressly distinguishes from the knowledge of God "through the works of creation"; De incarnatione Verbi 12 (PG 25, 116–17).

[18] Athanasius, De incarnatione Verbi 11 (PG 25, 113–16); cf. Contra gentes 2 (PG 25, 5). It is striking that, even as early as Irenaeus, man's first "natural" knowledge of God is thought to be the result of some sort of divine revelation, probably by the Logos; cf. Adversus haereses 2, 4, 5 (Harvey 1, 263–64): "ratio mentibus infixa."

[19] Cf. Bernard, op. cit., pp. 69–70.

In the same Alexandrian tradition, Eusebius of Caesarea frequently reveals the rational soul imaging the Word of God.[20] Among the Cappadocians, Basil makes it sufficiently clear that the image and likeness of which Gn 1:26 speaks is, in part at any rate, a matter of mind and reason.[21] Specifically, the share in His own goods which God communicated to man in the beginning was "the power to know (νοεῖν) and understand (συνιέναι) their Creator and Maker."[22] Gregory of Nazianzus insists in bold language on the kinship between the divine and human νοῦς; God's image he places in the rational soul—if not exclusively, at least primarily.[23]

Gregory of Nyssa is far more subtle. Not, it is true, on the basic fact; that much is pellucid. If, he challenges Apollinaris, νοῦς (which Apollinaris designated πνεῦμα) was not linked to the body of Adam, in what are we to seek Adam's likeness (ὁμοιότης) to God? What was it streamed forth from the breath of God, if not νοῦς?[24] What is difficult to grasp, yet desirable, is the peculiar nuance which Gregory attaches to νοῦς καὶ λόγος. Νοῦς is reason—speculative, judicious, inquiring, in quest of synthesis. But it projects beyond the Greek concept of reason, mainly because Gregory envisions νοῦς in its openness to the whole realm of the supernatural.[25] He links the human λόγος, in so far as it is image, with God's Logos, principle of all truth in the order of reason as well as of faith. Life in harmony with νοῦς consists in contemplation of God; it is in this way that participation of God is achieved; it is in view of this participation that man was fashioned to God's image. Νοῦς is, in Gregory's pithy phrase, Θεία τε καὶ νοερὰ οὐσία, at once and indivisibly divine and rational.[26] Not that Gregory identifies the divine and the human in νοῦς;[27] but

[20] Cf. Eusebius, De ecclesiastica theologia 1, 20 (GCS 14, 81); ibid. 2, 14 (GCS 14, 118); Historia ecclesiastica 10, 4, 56 (GCS 9/2, 878); Demonstratio evangelica 4, 6, 6 (GCS 23, 159–60); cf. also Praeparatio evangelica 7, 10 (PG 21, 533–36).

[21] Cf. Basil, Regulae fusius tractatae 2, 3 (PG 31, 913).

[22] Basil, Homilia in psalmum 48, 8 (PG 29, 449). The "natural (φυσική) constitution" of which he speaks is, I believe, equivalent to "original" rather than "innate" or "essential"; cf. ibid. (PG 29, 432).

[23] Cf. Gregory of Nazianzus, Orationes 38, 11 (PG 36, 321): the "breath" which God infused is "the rational soul and the image of God." Cf. also Gross, op. cit., p. 245.

[24] Cf. Gregory of Nyssa, Adversus Apollinarem 12 (PG 45, 1145); cf. De hominis opificio 5 (PG 44, 137): λόγον καὶ διάνοιαν; and ibid. 16 (PG 44, 181): τὸ λογικόν τε καὶ διανοητικόν.

[25] For this insight I am indebted to Leys, op. cit., pp. 68–70.

[26] Gregory of Nyssa, De infantibus qui praemature abripiuntur (PG 46, 172, 173).

[27] Leys has shown that Gregory recognized a distinction equivalent to that

neither does he separate them. Νοῦς is divine not by its essence but by reason of its supernatural finality: it is destined to be the repository of faith. It is divine because either it contemplates God in fact or else, even in its prostitution to a creature, it is created for contemplation.

In Gregory, beyond any doubt, it is grace that makes man to God's image, even though this image comprises certain features (e.g., intelligence, freedom) which in our language we would designate as "from nature," but which, assumed into a supernatural finality (the intelligence is made for belief, freedom is given for the purpose of choosing God), no longer actually deserve to be called natural. It is indisputable, too, that Gregory is unaware of an historical state of pure nature; the world has been created in grace.[28]

It is a fusion rather than a confusion of perspectives. And Leys has pointed out that this outlook is not peculiar to Gregory; it is discoverable in all the Greek Fathers. We find it in Clement of Alexandria, in Origen, and especially in Athanasius, whose λογικός is best translated not "reasonable" but "participating in the Word," receiving from the Word reason and faith, gifts of nature and of grace.[29] It is a point worth making. We will fail to fathom the Alexandrian λογικός if we read it in an Aristotelian context. As "nature" is a perilous translation of the Alexandrian φύσις, so too is "rational" a deceptive version of λογικός. For the Alexandrians, man was a rational creature, a reasonable being, to the extent that his created νοῦς καὶ λόγος was attuned to, participated in, the uncreated Logos. In that lifelong process of assimilation the sheer faculty itself, the δύναμις,

---

which later Western theology would make between nature and grace; cf. *op. cit.*, pp. 97–106.

[28] Leys, *op. cit.*, p. 98. Gross, *op. cit.*, p. 233, declares more simply that, for Gregory, intelligence and free will constituted "a primordial resemblance of man to God, a resemblance that cannot be lost and is a sort of foundation for the ulterior likeness which God added to the former from sheer generosity." Muckle, *art. cit.*, pp. 62–63, points out that "it was in universal man that the image of God was first formed and this image consisted in the rational ruling principle in him. . . ." On the problem of double creation in Gregory, cf. J. Daniélou, *Platonisme et théologie mystique* (Paris, 1944) pp. 56–58; J. Laplace, *Grégoire de Nysse: La création de l'homme* (Paris and Lyons, 1943) pp. 48–52; H. Cherniss, *The Platonism of Gregory of Nyssa* (Berkeley, 1930) pp. 25–33.

[29] Cf. Leys, *op. cit.*, p. 70; Clement of Alexandria, *Protrepticus* 10 (*GCS* 12, 71); Origen, *Commentaria in Ioannem* 2, 2 (*GCS* 10, 54); *id., Fragmenta in Ioannem* 18 (*GCS* 10, 497); Athanasius, *De incarnatione Verbi* 3 (*PG* 25, 101). For Athanasius' λογικός, Leys has coined "Verbified."

is in God's image primarily in the sense that, as Origen has it, it is "the faculty of achieving all that is noble and good."[30]

Outside the Alexandrian school, the divine image is sought in human reason by Methodius and Cyril of Jerusalem,[31] who may be pigeonholed in the so-called traditionalist school; and, among the Antiochenes, by Theodoret of Cyrus and Isidore of Pelusium.[32] The same tendency is represented in Western thought by Tertullian, Lactantius, Gregory of Elvira, Hilary of Poitiers, Philastrius, and Ambrose.[33] In fact, it would

[30] Origen, *Selecta in Genesim* (*PG* 12, 96). This tendency of Gregory of Nyssa to envisage man's mind in terms of grace rather than of nature is so constant that it is perhaps the palmary reason why scholars have commonly refused to acknowledge him author of the two homilies *In verba: Faciamus hominem ad imaginem et similitudinem nostram.* The homilist states flatly that we have τό κατ' εἰκόνα by creation, in our original constitution; τό καθ' ὁμοίωσιν we achieve by exercising free choice. I am κατ' εἰκόνα in being λογικός; I become καθ' ὁμοίωσιν in becoming χριστιανός by embracing goodness; cf. *In verba: Faciamus* 1 (*PG* 44, 273). Apparently we are confronted with an unequivocal opposition between image, nature, reason on the one hand, and likeness, grace, living faith on the other—and presumably that is not authentic Gregory. However, Leys has shown, *op. cit.*, pp. 134–36, that in one instance Gregory does employ εἰκών of nature in abstraction from grace—man in his essential definition, "a rational, intellectual creature, capable of understanding and knowledge"; *Oratio catechetica magna* 33 (*PG* 45, 84). In other words, the concept, image = mind = nature, is not altogether alien to him. On the other hand, it can be persuasively argued that in the homilies under discussion ὁμοίωσις may still be the realization of εἰκών; Christianity and virtue realize a destiny germinally lodged in man's λογικόν. In short, the homilist's distinction is not necessarily nature versus grace. In any event, the author is in the Alexandrian tradition to this extent at least, that he situates the divine image in the human mind.

[31] Cf. Methodius, *Symposium* 6, 1 (*GCS* 27, 64); Cyril of Jerusalem, *Catecheses* 12, 5 (*PG* 33, 732). The latter's phrase, "rational image of God," is not as transparent as we should wish it to be.

[32] Cf. Theodoret, *Quaestiones in Genesim* 20 (*PG* 80, 104–8); Isidore, *Epistolae* 3, 95 (*PG* 78, 800). An adequate treatment of Theodoret's image concept may be found in E. Montmasson, "L'Homme créé à l'image de Dieu d'après Théodoret de Cyr et Procope de Gaza," *Echos d'orient* 14 (1911) 334–39; 15 (1912) 154–62. Note his summary of Theodoret, p. 337: "man, if we regard his soul, resembles God by the place he occupies among creatures; by his role of master, relatively free and independent; by his intelligence; by the unity of his spirit in the diversity of his mental faculties; by the power, in some sort creative, which he possesses; and by the holiness to which he ought naturally to tend."

[33] Cf. Tertullian, *Adversus Marcionem* 2, 9 (*CSEL* 47, 346): "qua rationalis, capax intellectus et scientiae"; Lactantius, *Divinae institutiones* 2, 10 (*CSEL* 19, 147): note Lactantius' quotation from *Oracula Sibyllina* 8, 402, translated above in note 3. For Gregory of Elvira cf. Slomkowski, *op. cit.*, p. 133. Cf. Hilary, *In psalmum 118*, Iod 7 (*CSEL* 22, 443); *id.*, *In psalmum 129*, 6 (*CSEL* 22, 651); Phi-

seem that the Latin Fathers of the fourth century agree, on the whole,
in recognizing the state of divine image in the natural nobility of human
nature.[34] Augustine rounds out the tradition. For him "the dignity of
image, taken in its proper sense, belongs only to man; in man it belongs
properly only to his soul; in the soul it belongs properly only to thought—
*mens*—which is the higher part of the soul and that most akin to God."[35]

Only in the light of this background can we penetrate the significance
of the sentence from Cyril of Alexandria which opened the present chapter: "it is inasmuch as he is a rational animal . . . that man is said to
have been made in God's image."[36] The unadorned fact is clear enough:
for Cyril, one facet of this many-sided image which is man is discoverable precisely in his rational nature. On this aspect of the divine resemblance Cyril expends precious little effort; in fact, he does not develop it
explicitly. We stumble upon it inserted inconspicuously in a passage like
the following:

> To marvel at the delights of the body and to put the premium on stuffing
> the belly is actually bestial and partakes of extreme irrationality. But devotion
> to the good, and serious effort to excel in virtue . . . I would regard as charac-
> teristic of the man who recognizes his own nature and is not unaware that he
> has been made a rational (λογικόν) animal according to the image of his Cre-
> ator.[37]

We have seen that, for Cyril, this rationality is a constituent part of
the human composite; man is defined as "a rational (λογικόν), mortal
animal, capable of understanding and knowledge";[38] or, more simply,
"a rational, mortal animal."[39] This essential definition is one and the

---

lastrius, *Diversarum hereseon liber* 97, 1–5 (*CSEL* 38, 56–57); Ambrose, *Expositio
psalmi 118*, 2, 13 (*CSEL* 62, 27).

[34] So Slomkowski, *op. cit.*, p. 134.

[35] E. Gilson, *Introduction à l'étude de saint Augustin* (Paris, 1929) p. 282. Cf.
Augustine, *De civitate Dei* 12, 24 (*CSEL* 40/1, 608); *De Genesi contra Manichaeos* 1,
17 (*PL* 34, 186–87); *De Genesi ad litteram* 3, 20 (*CSEL* 28/1, 86); *ibid.* 3, 22 (*CSEL*
28/1, 88–89); 6, 12 (*CSEL* 28/1, 187); *De Genesi ad litteram imperfectus liber* 16
(*CSEL* 28/1, 497); *Epistolae* 166, 12 (*CSEL* 44, 564).

[36] *Epistola ad Calosyrium* (Pusey, *In Ioannem* 3, 605).

[37] *In Ioannem* 3, 4 (Pusey 1, 439); cf. an analogous passage, *Homiliae paschales*
5, 2 (*PG* 77, 473–76). For another indication, not perfectly clear, cf. *In Lucam*,
Lk 16:10–12 (*PG* 72, 813–16). At times Cyril puts a verbal distinction (I do not
think it is more than a matter of distinct formal concepts) between the image
and reason: "man who is rational *and* made to the Creator's image"; cf. *Homiliae
paschales* 5, 2; 6, 3; 7, 1 (*PG* 77, 476, 504–5, 541); *Contra Iulianum* 2 (*PG* 76, 592).

[38] *In Ioannem* 6 (Pusey 2, 128).

[39] *Thesaurus* 34 (*PG* 75, 596).

same for all men,[40] obviously because human nature is itself one.[41] Intelligence (σύνεσις) is a gift man receives concurrently with existence;[42] for "the God of all . . . created man upon the earth with a mind capable of wisdom and possessed of powers of understanding."[43] Nor is rationality, like riches, a mere accretion from without, an appendage of man;[44] rather is there in the human mind a natural aptitude for understanding and knowledge.[45] Rationality is a prerogative of his nature, and so man cannot cease to be a rational animal.[46]

At first glance Cyril's thesis is quite simple. Man images God with his mind, his reason, his intelligence, his understanding. This faculty is native to man; without it man would not be man. Here, then, if anywhere, we seem to confront a natural resemblance, a likeness to God on the level of unmodified human nature, a divine image with no overtones of grace. In point of fact, however, this aspect of Cyril's image is complex. In harmony with the Alexandrian insight, Cyril insists that understanding, like being and life,[47] is possessed only in virtue of a human participation in the divine; the light of reason is a sharing in Him who is Light by nature, the Word of God. In this connection the indispensable pages are the three chapters in Cyril's *Commentary on John* where he interprets that section of the Johannine Prologue which presents the Word of God as the true Light, as the Light of men.[48] Regrettably, Cyril's exposition is elusive, primarily in consequence of a fluctuating or at least an ambiguous terminology. Still, an attempt to capture the content of those pages is imperative.

Everything which a created nature has, Cyril informs us, it has from God. Since man is a rational (λογικόν) animal, he necessarily partakes of wisdom (σοφία) from God. The giver of that wisdom is the Word, who enlightens the rational animal and lavishes intelligence (σύνεσις) on those who are capable of intelligence. As Wisdom and Intelligence, He mingles

[40] Cf. *De sancta et consubstantiali trinitate* dial. 3 (*PG* 75, 852); *In Ioannem* 2, 1 (Pusey 1, 176); *ibid.* 4, 1 (Pusey 1, 494); 7 (Pusey 2, 261).

[41] Cf. *In psalmos*, Ps 103:25 (*PG* 69, 1264); *In Matthaeum*, Mt 12:33 (*PG* 72, 409); *De sancta et consubstantiali trinitate* dial. 4 (*PG* 75, 905–8).

[42] Cf. *In Ioannem* 1, 9 (Pusey 1, 113).

[43] *In Lucam* hom. 130 (Smith, Eng. tr. 2, 603).

[44] *In Lucam* hom. 109 (*PG* 72, 816).

[45] Cf. *In Ioannem* 4, 5 (Pusey 1, 600–601).

[46] Cf. *ibid.* 2, 6 (Pusey 1, 325). Cyril locates the rational faculty (λογικόν) in the heart and inward parts (σπλάγχνα), or, more specifically, the breast (στέρνον).

[47] Cf. *In Lucam* hom. 122 (Smith, Eng. tr. 2, 566–67); *In Ioannem* 4, 3 (Pusey 1, 544); *ibid.* 1, 6 (Pusey 1, 74–79). Cyril's doctrine of the Word as Life is based on his punctuation of Jn 1:3–4: "Whatever was made, in it was Life."

[48] Cf. *In Ioannem* 1, 7–9 (Pusey 1, 80–113).

Himself with creatures, that the rational may be rational and those capable of understanding may have understanding (φρόνησις).[49] The light (φῶς) which man has, he has in consequence of God's love for man; the faculty of understanding is provided him simultaneously with existence.

The Word alone is properly Light, alone able to enlighten, alone not in need of light; it is proof that He is not a creature. The Word is Light by nature (κατὰ φύσιν, φύσει), creatures by grace (κατὰ χάριν); He is participated, they participate; He gives, they receive. He is Light by His very essence (οὐσιωδῶς); they have light as a contingent dignity, an adventitious grace, an acquired gift, a participation by way of imitation (κατὰ μίμησιν), a sharing in God's nature.

What someone has by his very nature (φύσει), properties of a nature, these things are a fixed and fast possession; they are rooted in that nature. What is a matter of free choice, however, what depends on will, does not have the same kind of stability, the same immovability. An example of the former is rationality (τὸ ἄνθρωπος εἶναι λογικός); it is not acquired by choice; it derives from nature (παρὰ τῆς φύσεως). An example of the latter is virtue or vice; to be good or bad, to be just or unjust, is a question of deliberate choice; and the choice is in man's power. Now, if man were light by his very nature, he could never love darkness rather than the light (cf. Jn 3:19); virtue would flow not from choice but from essence. In point of fact, however, we were in darkness and we have been called into the light (cf. 1 Pt 2:9). It follows, then, that the Son alone is properly Light, that creatures have light by participation. According to Ps 4:7, the Son "is stamped on us, making us conformed to Himself and engraving on those who believe in Him the illumination that is through His own Spirit, like a divine image (εἰκόνα), that they too may be gods and sons of God like Him."[50]

Cyril adds a similar approach to the same conclusion. Essential properties, he notes, are not lost by negligence; neglect can result in the loss of those possessions alone which have been acquired by the will, by free choice, or which can be added or taken away without corruption of the substance. He takes three examples: man is rational by nature (λογικὸς κατὰ φύσιν), a shipwright by choice, an invalid by accident. It is impossible for him to become irrational (ἄλογος), but he can lose his shipbuilding skill by negligence, and he may recover from his illness by medical atten-

---

[49] Here we confront an initial ambiguity. When Cyril attributes wisdom, intelligence, understanding to the self-communication of the Word to creatures, is he speaking merely of the faculty itself, or does he intend its proper exercise, or does he embrace both?

[50] *In Ioannem* 1, 8 (Pusey 1, 103).

tion. The point is, essential properties of a thing remain rooted in it. If, then, a creature can be true light by his nature, how can he possibly lose the light (as Scripture says he does) by refusing to believe? Or how can he become a son of light by believing? Cyril's conclusion: the light in us is a result of deliberate choice; it is a question of will, not of essence. It is love that wins for creatures the light which they do not have.[51]

The above digest of *In Ioannem* 1, 7–8, presented in Cyril's own phraseology, may reveal how difficult it is to determine the exact sense in which man the λογικός participates in God the Logos, the precise way in which human reason is a reflection of divine Mind. Several ambiguities are basic. First, Cyril fails to discriminate the expression, κατὰ φύσιν, as it applies to God and to man. Second, he oscillates rapidly and bewilderingly between the natural order and the supernatural. Third, he employs σοφία, σύνεσις, and φρόνησις in such haphazard fashion that one cannot determine whether they are simply synonymous with τὸ λογικόν or connote something Christian. We know from other passages that man images God inasmuch as he is rational; we gather from *In Ioannem* 1, 7–8, that in some sense man's rationality is a participation in the Light that is the Logos; but the precise meaning of this participation, and the level on which the rational resemblance operates, these escape us.

Fortunately, the chapter which immediately follows in the *Commentary on John* provides a small measure of clarification; more importantly, it may serve as a springboard for a radical solution.[52] Cyril is interpreting Jn 1:9b: the true Light "enlightens every man who comes into the world."[53] He remarks that everything that exists owes to God not only its existence but its nature as well; anything and everything which belongs to a creature's essence is a gift from the munificence of the Creator; its root is His "grace." So, too, there is no light in rational creatures save by participation. The focal problem is: how does the Light enlighten every human being called into existence? Cyril knows that rational creatures enlighten one another by transferring ideas from mind to mind; this sort of thing, he suggests, is rather instruction or revelation. Not so the Word of God:

The Word of God "enlightens every man who comes into the world" not by way of instruction, as angels do and men; but rather as God, in creative fashion (δημιουργικῶς), He stores in each of those who are called into existence a seed of wisdom (σοφίας) or of the knowledge of God, and implants the root of intel-

[51] Cf. *ibid.* 1, 7–8 (Pusey 1, 80–107).
[52] Cf. *ibid.* 1, 9 (Pusey 1, 108–13).
[53] Cyril states explicitly that "coming into the world" is to be understood not of the Word but of man; cf. *In Ioannem* 1, 9 (Pusey 1, 112).

ligence (συνέσεως), and thus renders the animal rational (λογικόν), making it partaker of His own nature, and instilling in the mind as it were some luminous vapors of the inexpressible Splendor, in the manner and proportion known to Him (for on subjects like this we should not, I think, say too much). It is, therefore, evident that our forefather Adam did not acquire wisdom (τὸ εἶναι σοφός) in time, as we do, but from the very first moments of his creation he appears perfect in understanding (συνέσει)—as long as he preserved pure and unsullied in himself the enlightenment given to his nature by God, and did not prostitute the dignity of that nature. The Son enlightens, therefore, in creative fashion, inasmuch as He is Himself the true Light, while the creature is illumined by participation in the Light, and consequently is called and becomes light, mount-ing to the supernatural (τὰ ὑπὲρ φύσιν) through the grace (χάριν) of God who glorifies him and crowns him with various honors. . . .[54]

Part of the picture is clear. Each human being receives rationality as a gift from a generous God; with the body it is constitutive of his essence, but it is still a gift; it stems from χάρις. Specifically, the gift of rationality is communicated by the Logos. What does He communicate? Not ideas, but something apparently physical—a "seed," a "root," "vapors." What-ever it is, through it man participates in the nature of the Logos; it involves, inchoatively at least, supernatural life, life above the human.

Part of the picture is obscure. Cyril all but confesses that he does not know just what the Word imparts. Seed or root or vapors, the language is metaphorical, embarrassingly vague, and Cyril acknowledges as much. Consequently, he cannot specify the meaning which participation as-sumes in this context, or the sense in which this gift can be denominated supernatural.

It may be argued, of course, that the "light" in question (*In Ioannem* 1, 9) is not supernatural (ὑπὲρ φύσιν), is not a grace (χάρις), in the sense in which contemporary theology understands these terms; that it is "above nature" in the sense, so dear to Cyril, that everything which man pos-sesses is a "grace," a favor, a gift of God. Such a thesis would find support from passages where Cyril presents a divine illumination whose effects are strictly on the level of the human. He insists that all souls are illu-mined by God with a certain divine law.[55] This is "the natural (φυσικός) law, the law of creation, according to which we know our duty and we recognize our Maker from conscience and from creatures."[56] For "the

---

[54] *Ibid.* (Pusey 1, 111). Cf. *ibid.* 5, 2 (Pusey 1, 711–12): Anyone who does not have the divine light in himself walks necessarily in darkness. It is the Son who instils intellectual light in all men; He sows in each human being the σύνεσις that is proper to man.

[55] Cf. *In Matthaeum*, Mt 25:5 ff. (*PG* 72, 448).

[56] *In psalmos*, Ps 18:8 (*PG* 69, 832). Cyril insists that the Creator can be known

God of the universe framed man in the beginning and engraved on him a natural law that leads him like a child to a knowledge of evil and of good."[57] It is this natural law that calls men to offer sacrifice to God, "instilling without instruction the knowledge of the Creator."[58] It is "the law in us of the innate knowledge of God" that inspires men to thank-offerings.[59] For, though idol-worshipers miss the mark and fail to discern who is the Maker of the universe, yet "an innate and necessary law spurs them, and a spontaneous knowledge rouses them, to conceive of One incomparably superior to mortal men, that is, God."[60]

I would suggest, however, that a more adequate solution is to be sought in Cyril's Alexandrian background and outlook. Like his predecessors, he is not disposed to contemplate man in a state of pure nature, in isolation from his concrete destiny. Rationality, and therefore

---

from the beauty, order, and magnificence of His creatures; cf. *ibid.*, Ps 18:2-3 (*PG* 69, 828-29); *ibid.*, Ps 95:5 (*PG* 69, 1245); *In Isaiam* 1, 3 (*PG* 70, 149-52); *ibid.* 3, 3; 3, 5; 4, 1; 4, 5; 3, 4 (*PG* 70, 752, 816, 817-20, 873, 1116-17, 773); *In Oseam* 7 (Pusey 1, 263-64); *In Ioannem* 6, 1 (Pusey 2, 166). Conscience is generally introduced by Cyril as something that judges and pricks, saddens and burdens the sinner; cf. *In psalmos*, Ps 37:7 (*PG* 69, 960); *In Isaiam* 4, 3 (*PG* 70, 1033); *In Ioannem* 9 (Pusey 2, 350).

[57] *In Isaiam* 2, 5 (*PG* 70, 540). In the same passage Cyril changes the metaphor: this law "steers us naturally to a knowledge of good and evil." He claims that it is the natural law to which reference is made by the "enlightenment" in Jn 1:9; by the promise of a "law in their hearts" in Jer 31:33; and by the expression, "man was created for good works."

[58] *In Ioannem* 6 (Pusey 2, 98).

[59] *Glaphyra in Genesim* 1 (*PG* 69, 36). Cf. *In Ioannem* 2, 5 (Pusey 1, 277-78, 283): adoration of God is a duty most befitting men; it divides the servant and slave from the king and master; it is the gateway to divine worship (λατρεία) in deeds.

[60] *Glaphyra in Genesim* 1 (*PG* 69, 36). Comprised within the natural law whereby "we know our duty" would seem to be those individual "laws of nature" mentioned by Cyril, e.g., the love of mother or father for child (*In Isaiam* 4, 4 [*PG* 70, 1065]; *In Oseam* 1 [Pusey 1, 34]); of son for father (*In Michaeam* 3 [Pusey 1, 728]); of brother for brother (*Glaphyra in Genesim* 5 [*PG* 69, 257]; *In Malachiam* 1 [Pusey 2, 550]); and, in general, the law of affection within a family, inscribed by God on human nature, "even without our will" (*In Michaeam* 3 [Pusey 1, 719]; *In Lucam* hom. 42 [*CSCO* 70, 113; Lat. tr. 140, 76; Smith, Eng. tr. 1, 171]; *In Lucam* hom. 105 [*PG* 72, 793; cf. Smith, Eng. tr. 2, 491, note g, for interpolations]); so, also, the prohibition of incest (*In Isaiam* 2, 3 [*PG* 70, 440]; cf. *In Amos* 1 [Pusey 1, 405]). But there are "natural laws" of a different order, e.g., savagery in beasts (*In Isaiam* 3, 3 [*PG* 70, 748]); the serpent is hostile to man "by the law of its nature" (*In Isaiam* 5, 6 [*PG* 70, 1428]); cf. "the laws of human nature" with respect to the conception of Christ and of Isaac (*In Isaiam* 5, 1; 4, 5 [*PG* 70, 1180, 1105]); "something like a natural law" makes the Son of God exactly like the Father (*In Ioannem* 2, 6 [Pusey 1, 324]); in dying, man yields to "the laws of [his] nature" (*ibid.* 6 [Pusey 2, 118]).

the divine image under this formality, is for him fundamentally a natural thing; it is "from nature." But potentially and in its divinely decreed finality it is supernatural: through the proper use of reason man achieves his actual destiny; in this sense he "mounts to the supernatural through the grace of God who glorifies him and crowns him with various honors." The general idea comes off clearly enough in a passage where Cyril declares that the human mind is the most productive, the most fruitful possession of our nature; for the mind has in itself the seeds of all virtue; like the earth, it supplies unceasingly from its inner self our desires for everything that is noblest and best; that is the way God has made it.[61] Specifically, what Cyril sees in the mind of every man born into the world is reason in quest of faith. This attitude emerges strikingly from his *Commentary on Isaiah*, when he interprets the Septuagint version of Is 53:10–11: βούλεται πλάσαι τῇ συνέσει:

> They who are in sins, and worship the creature rather than the Creator, have their heart in some way ugly and their understanding (διάνοιαν) exceedingly unsightly. . . . But when they welcome [faith] in Christ, they are transformed spiritually to His divine and excellent beauty. . . . God the Father wishes, therefore, to mold to Him [i.e., Christ] those who believe, to mold them by understanding (συνέσει), that is, by His own Wisdom, divine I mean, and to make them conformed to Him through sanctification in the Spirit; "for," it says, "those whom He foreknew and predestined to be conformed to the image of His Son, those He called" (Rom 8:29–30).[62]

In Cyril's eyes, it is faith that fashions man's mind, his intelligence, to divine Wisdom, to God the Word; it is in belief that the natural image of God implanted by the Word at man's formation finds its supernatural fulfilment.[63] In the wake of Clement and Origen, of Athanasius and Gregory of Nyssa, Cyril's interest in the human mind, in human reason, in human understanding, centers in its supernatural finality: it is created to be Christian. The key to the problem that has puzzled us may well be Cyril's trenchant sentence: "Faith is the beginning of understanding."[64]

[61] Cf. *Homiliae paschales* 6, 8 (*PG* 77, 517).

[62] *In Isaiam* 5, 1 (*PG* 70, 1188–89). I have presumed to add the word "faith" in brackets, because it is obvious that πίστιν or a related expression has accidentally been omitted from the printed text. Cf. also *In Ioannem* 1, 8 (Pusey 1, 103).

[63] Cf. *De adoratione* 11 (*PG* 68, 740): implanted in the rational faculty by nature is correct, just, righteous judgment (δικαιοκρισία); *In Ioannem* 11, 2 (Pusey 2, 645): perfect knowledge is correct knowledge of the Trinity; *ibid.* 11, 7 (Pusey 2, 682); *ibid.* 11, 12 (Pusey 3, 13): knowledge of the Father through θεωρία, and knowledge of the mystery of Christ, this is what brings to man the Father's perfect love.

[64] *Contra Iulianum* 7 (*PG* 76, 877).

CHAPTER 4

# FREEDOM

Closely allied with rationality in any humanistic outlook on life is the human attribute we call free will. Man's power under God to control his own soul's destiny was consistently an object of predilection to Christian Greek optimism. To the Alexandrians especially, determinism in any shape or form was repugnant. The war waged by Clement and Origen against Gnostic pessimism is convincing evidence of that.[1] But to the early Greek authors free will was not merely a matter of apologetical, polemical concern; it crops up rather frequently within the Eastern theology of the divine image.

During the second century the concept of human freedom as a facet of God's image in man emerges most clearly in Irenaeus. For him, the formal element of the primitive, natural, inamissible, genuinely divine image is not simply rationality but equally the freedom of the will which flows from it. He states it bluntly in *Adversus haereses*: "Man is free in will from the beginning, and free in will is God, to whose likeness he was made...."[2] He repeats it plainly in *Demonstratio apostolicae praedicationis*: "So he was free and his own master, having been made by God in order to be master of everything on earth."[3]

The tradition of Christian Alexandria is preluded by Philo, who makes human freedom an attribute of the mind and in that power of self-determination discovers the soul's most remarkable likeness to God:

... It is mind (διάνοια) alone which the Father who begat it judged worthy of freedom (ἐλευθερίας), and loosening the fetters of necessity, suffered it to range as it listed, and of that free-will (ἑκούσιον) which is His most peculiar possession and most worthy of His majesty gave it such portion as it was capable of receiving. For the other living creatures in whose souls the mind (νοῦς), the element set apart for liberty (ἐλευθερίαν), has no place, have been committed

[1] Cf. A. de la Barre, "Ecole chrétienne d'Alexandrie," *DTC* 1, 817; C. Bigg, *The Christian Platonists of Alexandria* (Oxford, 1913) pp. 108–11.
[2] Irenaeus, *Adversus haereses* 4, 60, 2 (Harvey 2, 289); cf. *ibid.* 4, 7 (Harvey 2, 154): God wanted faith and obedience to be man's own in a genuine sense. Cf. also Struker, *op. cit.*, pp. 97, 99–101, 117, 127.
[3] Irenaeus, *Demonstratio apostolicae praedicationis* 11 (*PO* 12, 667–68; tr. J. P. Smith, *ACW* 16, 54). Struker, *op. cit.*, p. 21, believes that Justin too may well have counted moral freedom in the content of the divine resemblance.

40

under yoke and bridle to the service of men, as slaves to a master. But man, possessed of a spontaneous and self-determined will (γνώμης), whose activities for the most part rest on deliberate choice, is with reason blamed for what he does wrong with intent, praised when he acts rightly of his own will (ἑκών). In the others, the plants and animals, no praise is due if they bear well, nor blame if they fare ill: for their movements and changes in either direction come to them from no deliberate choice or volition of their own. But the soul (ψυχή) of man alone has received from God the faculty of voluntary movement (τὴν ἑκούσιον κίνησιν), and in this way especially is made like (ὁμοιωθεῖσα) to Him. . . .[4]

For Philo, then, it is the rational soul, the mind, which has been made to God's image; but within the soul, within the mind, it is the faculty of self-determination, voluntary movement, free will, that reveals man's closest likeness to his Creator.[5]

Clement, Origen, and Athanasius do not follow perceptibly in the footsteps of Philo. Each, it is true, is enamored of human freedom; but none of them ties it explicitly to the divine image. Thus, free will is a human possession of which Clement is quite aware;[6] for him, it is the independent, natural movement of the mind or soul;[7] it plays a significant role in his theology of perfection.[8] And yet, I cannot find that he deals with it consciously as an aspect of the divine image in man. Nevertheless, a resemblance to God through freedom may well be implicit in this, that for Clement it is the mind which has been molded to the divine, and free will is simply the spontaneous, uncompelled movement of the mind.[9]

Similarly, Origen emphasizes the fact of human freedom; free will is indissolubly woven into the fabric of Christian doctrine:

This also is laid down in the Church's teaching, that every rational soul is possessed of free will and choice. . . . There follows from this the conviction that we are not subject to necessity, so as to be compelled by every means,

[4] Philo, *Quod Deus sit immutabilis* 47–48 [10] (Cohn-Wendland 2, 64–65; tr. *LCL*, Philo 3, 33–35).

[5] Wolfson has devoted a penetrating chapter to the problem of free will in Philo; cf. *op. cit.* 1, 424–62. He points out, e.g., that a voluntary act does not mean for Philo, as it does for Plato and Aristotle, simply an action performed with knowledge; knowledge is but a condition for the exercise of freedom. Again, he shows that Philo leaves the choice of evil wholly to the power of man, but leaves room for God's help in man's effort to pursue the good.

[6] Cf. Clement of Alexandria, *Stromata* 5, 13 (*GCS* 15, 381): τὸ αὐτεξούσιον; cf. *ibid.* 7, 3 (*GCS* 17, 11): τὸ αὐθαίρετον.

[7] Cf. Clement of Alexandria, *Fragmenta* 4 (*GCS* 17, 220).

[8] Cf. Clement of Alexandria, *Quis dives salvetur* 10 (*GCS* 17, 165).

[9] Cf. Clement of Alexandria, *Stromata* 2, 19; 5, 14 (*GCS* 15, 169, 388); *Protrepticus* 10 (*GCS* 12, 71); *Fragmenta* 4 (*GCS* 17, 220).

even against our will, to do either good or evil. For if we are possessed of free will, some spiritual powers may very likely be able to urge us on to sin and others to assist us to salvation; we are not, however, compelled by necessity to act either rightly or wrongly. . . .[10]

Origen can prove the existence of freedom from the common experience of men.[11] He knows how to distinguish the free, inner-directed movement of man from the actions of inanimate objects, plants, and irrational animals.[12] He understands how indispensable free will is for meritorious activity;"for, if you take from virtue the element of freedom (τὸ ἑκούσιον), you take away its essence as well."[13] And yet, despite his insistence on its reality, its nature, and its significance for Christian living, Origen does not, to my knowledge, ever link freedom formally to the image of God in man. Again, it would be incautious to conclude that he is not sensible of such a connection or even identification. I would suggest rather that his concept of reason, of the rational faculty in man, which is de facto God's image, is so broad that, as with Clement, it embraces the will as well.[14]

In like vein, Athanasius is aware that the human soul was fashioned free (αὐτεξούσιος),[15] that God gave Adam mastery over his own will (θέλησιν αὐτεξούσιον),[16] but he does not professedly incorporate this aspect of human living into his vision of the divine image in man.[17] Here too, however, as

[10] Origen, De principiis 1, praefatio 5 (GCS 22, 12–13; tr. G. W. Butterworth, Origen on First Principles [London, 1936] p. 4); this passage we have only in Rufinus' translation.

[11] Cf. Origen, De oratione 6, 2 (GCS 3, 312).

[12] Cf. Origen, De principiis 3, 1, 2 ff. (GCS 22, 196 ff.); cf. a similar passage in De oratione 6, 1 (GCS 3, 311–12).

[13] Origen, Contra Celsum 4, 3 (GCS 2, 276).

[14] Cf. Origen, Selecta in Genesim (PG 12, 96); also De principiis 3, 1, 4 (GCS 22, 199; tr. Butterworth, op. cit., p. 162): ". . . [evil] sensations and incitements are there, but his reason (λόγος) . . . repels the incitements and gradually weakens the desire." The connection we are seeking is almost made in Contra Celsum 8, 72 (GCS 3, 288–89; tr. Chadwick, op. cit., p. 507): "But we believe that at some time the Logos will have overcome the whole rational nature, and will have re-modelled every soul to his own perfection, when each individual simply by the exercise of his freedom will choose what the Logos wills and will be in that state which he has chosen."

[15] Cf. Athanasius, Contra gentes 4 (PG 25, 9).

[16] Cf. Athanasius, Contra Apollinarium 1, 15 (PG 26, 1120).

[17] The closest we come to such incorporation is a reference to the ἐλευθερία brought by Christ, which frees the whole man, body and soul, and renews him in the image of Christ; cf. Contra Apollinarium 1, 14 (PG 26, 1117–20).

with Clement and Origen, the concept which Athanasius has of νοῦς, where the image of God is lodged, seems broad enough to include the will. This becomes transparent if we can trust a fragment allegedly from Athanasius' *Sermo maior de fide*: "Willing (θέλησις) is nothing else than the mind (νοῦς) moved with reference to some object, or the free (αὐτεξούσιος) movement of the rational soul."[18]

In light of the above, it is almost startling to find Basil of Caesarea, Gregory of Nyssa, and Didymus of Alexandria utterly unambiguous. Basil asks how it is that man's soul, which was created for union with God in love, was susceptible of sin. His answer: "Because its movements were free (διὰ τὴν αὐτεξούσιον ὁρμήν)—which is particularly appropriate for a rational nature. For it was set free of all compulsion and received from the Creator a life of free choice, because it was made to God's image."[19]

In a number of places Gregory of Nyssa reveals that the image of God within man is constituted by free will. The fact itself is simply put: "Freedom (τὸ αὐτεξούσιον) is a godlike thing."[20] In what sense does human freedom image the divine? Man "was image and likeness of the power which rules all things that are; and for this reason even in freedom of choice he resembled Him who exercises universal authority. He was not enslaved by any external compulsion, but directed himself by his own mind and will to whatever he wanted, and chose autocratically what pleased him."[21] Why was this prerogative conceded to man? In order that goodness and virtue might not be an involuntary achievement but the fruit of deliberate decision.[22] Man had to be free if he was to image God; and he had to be free if he was to merit God.[23]

Didymus of Alexandria is brief but clear. He tells us that in baptism we recover the image and likeness of God which we received originally from God's inbreathing (Gn 2:7) and lost subsequently through sin.

[18] Athanasius, *Fragmentum ex Sermone maiore de fide* (*PG* 26, 1292).

[19] Basil, *Quod Deus non est auctor malorum* 6 (*PG* 31, 344); cf. *Homilia in psalmum 48*, 8 (*PG* 29, 449).

[20] Gregory of Nyssa, *De mortuis* (*PG* 46, 524). According to Muckle, *op. cit.*, p. 76, Gregory "teaches that when God created man after His own image and likeness, He endowed him with the perfections which correspond to all the attributes of the divine nature according to the capacity of a finite creature to receive them. . . . Among these are immortality, mind, free-will and the virtues." Cf. J. Gaïth, *La conception de la liberté chez Grégoire de Nysse* (Paris, 1953), especially pp. 40–66.

[21] Gregory of Nyssa, *De virginitate* 12 (ed. J. P. Cavarnos, *Gregorii Nysseni opera* 8/1, 298).

[22] Cf. Gregory of Nyssa, *In Canticum canticorum* hom. 2 (*PG* 44, 796).

[23] Cf. Gregory of Nyssa, *Oratio catechetica magna* 5 (*PG* 45, 24).

Now we are once more what we were of old in Adam, "sinless and free (αὐτεξούσιοι); for these are what the image and likeness signifies. . . ."[24]

Of the more conspicuous Alexandrians, therefore, some unequivocally find a facet of divinity in human freedom; others can be persuasively interpreted in the same sense. Outside Alexandria it is difficult to discover even this rather moderate enthusiasm. Methodius, one of the better pre-Nicene theologians, wrote a treatise on free will (περὶ τοῦ αὐτεξουσίου), in an effort to prove that responsibility for evil stems from the free will of man.[25] Naturally, he makes much of this prerogative; in fact, he does not hesitate to call it "the greatest gift God gave to man";[26] but he does not expressly link it to the divine image within him.[27] Cyril of Jerusalem, on the other hand, tells his candidates for baptism:

Know yourself; know who you are. Your condition is this: you are a dual human being, compounded of soul and body; and . . . the same God is fashioner of the soul and of the body. Know, too, that you have a soul which is its own master (αὐτεξούσιον), God's fairest achievement, after its Maker's image; immortal, because of the God who gives it immortality; an incorruptible rational animal because of Him who gave freely of these, who has power to do what He wants.[28]

Early Latin theology reveals an analogous lack of fervor. There are exceptions, admittedly. Tertullian confesses that he can find no better image in man, no closer resemblance to God, than in his freedom.[29] Jerome discerns the possibility of sin in man's free will, "according to which man was made to God's image and likeness."[30] But the references are rare. In regard of the image, human freedom scarcely strikes the

[24] Didymus, De trinitate 2, 12 (PG 39, 680).

[25] Cf. GCS 27, 145-206. The title of the Slavonic version, On God, Matter, and Free Will, is a more faithful reflection of its contents.

[26] Methodius, De autexousio 16 (GCS 27, 186; PO 22, 795).

[27] The statements of Gross, op. cit., p. 193, to the effect that, for Methodius, man is initially an image of the Logos "by his reasonable and free soul," and that in Adam the state of image was constituted "by his intelligent and free nature," are ambiguous. I can find no passage where Methodius expressly locates the image in man's freedom, or even in all the powers of man's soul. The references given by Gross do not touch this precise point; cf. Methodius, Symposium 6, 1 (GCS 27, 64); ibid. 1, 4-5 (GCS 27, 12-13); De resurrectione 2, 24 (GCS 27, 380); De autexousio 16 (GCS 27, 186; PO 22, 795).

[28] Cyril of Jerusalem, Catecheses 4, 18 (PG 33, 477); cf. X. Le Bachelet, "Cyrille (Saint), évêque de Jérusalem," DTC 3, 2554.

[29] Cf. Tertullian, Adversus Marcionem 2, 5; 2, 6; 2, 9 (CSEL 47, 340, 341, 346).

[30] Jerome, Epistolae 21, 40 (CSEL 54, 139-40).

responsive chord in tradition that intelligence invokes—perhaps because free will is so intimately linked with reason as to bask often unnoticed in the reflected light of the latter.

Cyril of Alexandria is noticeably in the line of Basil, Gregory of Nyssa, and Didymus; but he pays far more attention than any of his predecessors to the will precisely in the context of divine resemblance. In a single passage of his commentary on Genesis he has condensed the three facts on human freedom which especially attract him. First, man was gifted with freedom of choice from the very first moment of humanity's creation. Second, the existence of freedom, its reality in man, can be proved from its existence, its reality, in God. Third, freedom is an indispensable condition for meritorious action, imperative if human activity is to be commendable or censurable.

For man, from the beginning of his creation, had been entrusted with the reins of his own volitions ($\theta\epsilon\lambda\eta\mu\acute{a}\tau\omega\nu$), with unrestricted movement towards his every desire; for the Deity is free ($\grave{\epsilon}\lambda\epsilon\acute{\upsilon}\theta\epsilon\rho\upsilon$) and man had been formed after Him. It was in this way, I think, and in no other that he could win admiration, if it was clear that he practiced virtue of his own accord, and that the purity of his actions was the fruit of judgment, not the result, as it were, of natural necessity which simply would not permit him to be borne beyond the good, even though he might wish to do otherwise. Man, therefore, had been equipped from the start with unrestricted, unimpeded movement of purpose ($\delta\iota\alpha\nu\sigma\acute{\iota}\alpha s$) in all his actions.[31]

And what he has said in dealing with the Book of Genesis, Cyril reaffirms more succinctly in his *Commentary on John*: Adam was "self-determining ($\alpha\grave{\upsilon}\tau\sigma\pi\rho\sigma\alpha\acute{\iota}\rho\epsilon\tau\sigma s$) and entrusted with the reins of his own volitions ($\theta\epsilon\lambda\eta\mu\acute{a}\tau\omega\nu$); for this too is a part of the image, seeing that God exercises lordship over His personal volitions."[32] To this extent, at least, Adam was master of his soul, of his fate. Freedom of will meant that man's thoughts, his desires, and his volitions were not inexorably predetermined by fate from without or by his nature from within, but were in a very true sense subject to his choice. Nor was this gift peculiar to Adam; every man has the power to do what he wants without compulsion, because human nature itself has been fashioned free by its Creator.[33] And in this inner freedom, as in his reason, man was molded on a divine model, a God whose will is uncompelled, unconstrained.

[31] *Glaphyra in Genesim* 1 (*PG* 69, 24).

[32] *In Ioannem* 9, 1 (Pusey 2, 485); cf. *Contra Iulianum* 8 (*PG* 76, 925): $\alpha\grave{\upsilon}\tau\sigma\kappa\rho\alpha\tau\grave{\eta}s$ $\kappa\alpha\grave{\iota}$ $\grave{\epsilon}\lambda\epsilon\acute{\upsilon}\theta\epsilon\rho\sigma s$.

[33] Cf. *De adoratione* 6 (*PG* 68, 457); *In Ioannem* 1, 7 (Pusey 1, 93).

Cyril, however, is not concerned with a psychological fact, the sheer power of man to will one thing rather than another. His concern is Christian; he is preoccupied, above all, with virtuous living; and so freedom of the will regularly means in the concrete the power to choose the good and refuse the evil, or vice versa. For man, despite a natural aptitude for goodness and justice, is actually good or evil, just or unjust, because he wills to be such.[34] Fate, fortune, and birth do not govern the actions of men. His argument is the experience of humanity: "If I should choose to be good, there is nothing to hinder me from it; and if I should elect to be evil, nothing would keep me from sinking down to it."[35] This unrestricted momentum in whatever direction the human will pleases is man's special prerogative. Without it, Cyril reminds us, there would be no reason to praise virtue or censure vice; there would be no point to a divine law or divine castigation.[36] It is here that Cyril finds the key to the paradox of Adam's sin:

... man was made in the beginning with an intelligence that was superior to sin and passions. However, he was not at all incapable of turning aside in any direction he pleased; for the excellent Artificer of the universe thought it right to attach to him the reins of his own volitions, and to leave it to self-directed movements to achieve whatever he wanted. The reason is, virtue had to be a matter of deliberate choice, not the fruit of compulsion, nor so firmly fixed by nature's laws that man could not stumble; for this is proper to the supreme essence and excellence.[37]

In a trenchant, almost untranslatable phrase, "virtue is not a totalitarian (ἀδέσποτον) thing."[38]

If we are to do justice to Cyril's assertion that freedom "is a part of the image," two extremes must be avoided. On the one hand, it would

[34] Cf. In Ioannem 1, 8 (Pusey 1, 101); In Matthaeum, Mt 7:11 and 12:35 (PG 72, 385-88, 409). This is not Pelagianism, the thesis that man can lift himself to heaven by his bootstraps. Cyril, as we shall see, recognizes the need of grace if oneness with God is to be achieved. In the present context the problem is reduced by Cyril to one point: is virtue (or vice) forced or free?

[35] In Isaiam 1, 1 (PG 70, 48); cf. De adoratione 6 (PG 68, 456 ff.); also In Ioannem 5, 1 (Pusey 1, 663-72), where Cyril argues at length against the "Greek error" that human affairs are the pawns of times, hours, days, and years; goodness and wickedness are the result of our own deliberate choice. Cf. also Homiliae paschales 6, 4 (PG 77, 509-12).

[36] Cf. In Romanos, Rom 7:15 (Pusey, In Ioannem 3, 202-6).

[37] De adoratione 1 (PG 68, 145); cf. Contra Iulianum 8 (PG 76, 937-40).

[38] Contra Iulianum 5 (PG 76, 744).

be a mistake to press to excess the resemblance attested by Cyril between God's freedom and man's. Actually, he simply states a fact and draws a conclusion. The fact is scriptural: man was made from the beginning to God's image and likeness. The conclusion is his own: since God's will is self-determining, so too is man's. Both are genuinely free. But Cyril recognizes that we are dealing with analogy, that similarity between God and man involves dissimilarity, that the chasm of infinite perfection yawns between God and all that is not God. This point he makes clear when discussing another aspect of the image, conformity to God in the tenor of our lives:

... if our ideas are sound, we shall not believe that those who have God's image (τὸν θεῖον ἐξεικονισμόν) gleaming in their souls by the quality of their way of life bear a likeness (ἐμφέρειαν) to Him which is substantial and unchangeable and extends commensurately to everything that is properly His, on the ground that, since we have been created to His image and likeness, God is like us without any distinction whatsoever. This is not so; far from it. There is an infinite distance between us. We are not simple in nature; but God is utterly simple, without any composition, all-perfect, in need of nothing. . . . We are of earth, as far as the flesh is concerned, corruptible, as quick as grass to wither, like lilies in a field; not so God. Besides, the soul of man is easily led astray and experiences all sorts of changes, from virtue to vice, and from vice back to virtue again; but God is, I might say, firmly and irrevocably fixed in the prerogatives that are His; change is not His to experience; in fact, His immovability, unlike our steadfastness, is a matter of essence, not an invention of will. It is obvious, then, that in creatures there is no natural likeness (φυσικὴ ἐμφέρεια) to God; rather does the likeness reveal itself somehow in deed and in the quality of one's way of life.[39]

This is not yet the place to discuss Cyril's rejection of a natural likeness between God and man, and his insistence on an exclusively dynamic resemblance. The point at present is this: it is precisely the significant role of analogy in his works that preserves Cyril from suspicion of having debased the freedom of God, and keeps us from misconstruing his doctrine of divine resemblance into some manner of univocal concept, applicable without distinction to God and to man.[40]

On the other hand, it will not do to minimize Cyril's conception of the image in man's will. I said above that Cyril's concern is not man's basic

[39] *De sancta et consubstantiali trinitate* dial. 1 (*PG* 75, 673–76).

[40] The role of analogy in Cyril's theology has been recognized by H. du Manoir, "Le problème de Dieu chez Cyrille d'Alexandrie," *Recherches de science religieuse* 27 (1937) 404, 556. On the concept of freedom in God, cf. L. Billot, *De Deo uno et trino* (7th ed.; Rome, 1935) pp. 252–60.

power to will some one thing in preference to another; freedom in the concrete means for him the power to choose between good and evil. Still another refinement is imperative if Cyril's image concept is to gain in clarity. The facet of freedom which makes man an image of God is not merely the perilous power to elect either good or evil. What copies the divine perhaps more accurately is man's ability to freely elect the good. One suspects as much in a passage from Cyril's exegesis of Isaiah: men were "free (ἐλευθέρους) upon the earth, and well made to God's image, and 'created for good works,' as blessed Paul says" (Eph 2: 10).[41] The same idea is expressed in Cyril's apologetic against Julian the Apostate, when he links human freedom so intimately with the life of virtue which was Adam's God-given destiny:

. . . once heaven and earth and, in short, everything in them had been brought into being, the body of man was fashioned of earth. Animated by the ineffable power of the Creator of all things, it was on the instant a rational animal and most godlike (λογικὸν καὶ θεοειδέστατον); for it had been made to the image of its Creator. Now, no one would doubt that, since he is the artistic product of a good God, man was brought to existence not for shameful works but for all that is praiseworthy. The fact remains, he was made self-directing and free (αὐτοκρατὴς καὶ ἐλεύθερος), capable of moving by the momentum of his own volitions in whatever direction he might choose, be it towards good or towards evil.[42]

Finally, man's creation "for good works" leads logically to a fascinating feature of Cyril's image theology: the fact that it is not only in conscious, deliberate activity that the will images God. In Cyril's view, man is gifted with a natural, inborn appetite for the good; in this sense man can be denominated "naturally good" and an image of God. This native endowment, with its link to the image, emerges from Cyril's interpretation of Gn 2:7:

. . . the Creator of the universe fashioned man, that is, his body, from the earth. Animating it with a living and intellectual soul in the manner known to Him, He instilled in it a natural appetite (ἔφεσιν) for, and knowledge of, everything that is good. This, I think, is the meaning of the blessed evangelist John's words, "He was the true Light which enlightens every man who comes into the world" (Jn 1:9); for the [human] animal is born with a natural aptitude

[41] In Isaiam 1, 5 (PG 70, 249).
[42] Contra Iulianum 8 (PG 76, 925). My translation, "the fact remains," is an attempt to grasp the meaning behind the connective γε μήν; PG has "quippe" in its Latin version. It might well be adversative, "nevertheless"; if so, it would mean that, although God made man for good works, He did not want virtue to be compelled but free.

(ἐπιτηδειότητα) for the good. This we will learn from the all-wise Paul when he writes: "His workmanship we are, created for good works . . ." (Eph 2:10). Man, you see, governs himself by his own deliberate choice (προαιρετικῶς), and he has been entrusted with the reins of his own purpose (διανοίας), so that he can move quickly in whatever direction he pleases, to good or to its opposite. Now, his nature has instilled in it the appetite (ἔφεσιν) and the desire (προθυμίαν) for every kind of good, and the will (τὸ θέλειν) to cultivate goodness and justice; for this, we say, is the way man was made to [God's] image and likeness, inasmuch as the [human] animal is naturally (πέφυκεν εἶναι) good and just. But, since he had to be not merely rational and fit for well-doing and justice, but also sharer of the Holy Spirit, in order that he might have the distinctive marks (χαρακτῆρας) of the divine nature more limpid in him, He breathed into him the breath of life. This is the Spirit given to the rational creature through the Son and transforming it to the supreme, that is, the divine, form.[43]

In short, man's will is not merely endowed with a potency, an unrestricted ability to choose between good and evil; it is divinely oriented towards the good by man's very make-up. It is part of his nature; it is a tendency that was implanted in Adam independently of his participation of the Holy Spirit. It does not destroy his freedom; he can still elect evil. And it is a facet of God's image within man; for in some genuine sense man can be called "naturally good and just." This apparently is what Cyril means when he writes: "It is not in being rich that we are rational and capable of all good activity; rather our very nature was made in such a way that it is fit for, capable of, such things—and it is this that is [really] our own; for, as blessed Paul writes, 'we have been created for good works . . .' " (Eph 2:10).[44] Or when he states: "Man was made to the image [of the Logos] in the beginning, and his nature was fit to assume all good and to achieve virtue; for He created us 'for good works'. . . . In the man who was first formed there was every aptitude (ἐπιτηδειότης), carrying with it the power (δύναμιν) to embrace virtue, but not the actuality (ἐνέργεια) as well. . . ."[45]

This natural aptitude for goodness Cyril proves from history and from Scripture, when he has occasion to deny any difference between image and likeness:

[43] *De dogmatum solutione* 2 (Pusey, *In Ioannem* 3, 552-53).
[44] *In Lucam* hom. 109 (*PG* 72, 816).
[45] *Responsiones ad Tiberium* 8 (Pusey, *In Ioannem* 3, 590). The passage is somewhat obscure, because it deals primarily with the supernatural order, and yet seems to regard the aptitude for virtue as native to man. We are faced once again with Cyril's understandable indifference to sheerly natural powers in isolation from their concrete finality.

The likeness to God we obtained in our primal constitution, and we are images of God; for, as I said, man's nature is capable of goodness and justice and holiness, and has the appetite (ἔφεσιν) for these things implanted in it from God. And this can be seen from the following argument: when man's mind (διανοίᾳ) turned aside, it turned not from evil to good but from good to evil. . . . That an appetite (ἔφεσις), a desire (προθυμία), and a knowledge of all that is good was sown in man's soul from his primal constitution, the eminently wise Paul points out clearly in these words: "When the Gentiles who have no law do by nature what the Law prescribes, these having no law are a law unto themselves; they show the work of the Law written in their hearts; their conscience bears witness to them" (Rom 2:14–15). Now, if the knowledge of the Law or of the mind of the lawgiver is present naturally even in the Gentiles who are outside the Law, it will be clear to everyone that man's nature was made just and good in the beginning, and was brought to this by God, bearing His form and the image of His goodness; for the first period of man's life was holy. . . .[46]

The passage, in isolation, is not unambiguous. One might argue from text and context (e.g., this facet of the image was disfigured by sin) that this appetite for goodness, this "holiness," was a supernatural thing, and that Cyril calls it "natural" only in the sense that it was original, a constitutive part of man's primitive state; it is not inbred in every man. On the other hand, the presence of this γνῶσις, and presumably of the ἔφεσις as well, in the Gentiles after Adam's sin, justifies the interpretation that, sin or no sin, there is in the human will an innate appetite for the good.[47] It is this natural appetite for goodness that Cyril seems to have in mind when he lists among the aspects of the image the fact that man "alone, beyond all the living beings on earth, is rational . . . with an aptitude (ἐπιτηδειότητα) for all virtue. . . ."[48]

A summary is in order. As Cyril sees it, man images God with his will. In the first place, man, like God, is not compelled by fate or by his nature to elect this rather than that as an object of volition; more specifically, he can choose between good and evil; best of all, he can freely refuse the evil, prefer the good. Secondly, man, though not predestined to good or evil, is predisposed to good. If actual virtue is achieved by deliberate choice, proclivity to virtue is rooted in created nature. In that sense man is "naturally good"; naturally good, he resembles his God.

[46] De dogmatum solutione 3 (Pusey, In Ioannem 3, 555–56).

[47] This problem will return for more detailed discussion when we consider the impact of sin on the divine image and likeness in man.

[48] Epistola ad Calosyrium (Pusey, In Ioannem 3, 605).

# CHAPTER 5

## DOMINION

At the outset of his *Glaphyra in Genesim* Cyril of Alexandria pens a spirited account of creation.[1] It is one of the rare lyrical passages in a generally lusterless exegete.[2] Digested in Cyrillic language, it runs like this:

In the beginning, before all else, God fashioned heaven and earth in His incomparable way through the Son, His own all-producing Power.[3] Then, always working through the Word, He gathered the waters into one place, decked the earth with herbs and trees, set the sun to rule the day and the moon to rule the night, sprinkled the whole of heaven with stars, and, being Life by nature, formed the fish and the birds, the wild beasts and herds. Then, pleased with His artistry, God turned to the reason for all His creation: man. The point is, "the earth had to be filled with those who would know how to give glory, and from the beauty of creatures . . . gaze upon the glory of their Creator."[4] And so He had to

[1] Cf. *Glaphyra in Genesim* 1 (*PG* 69, 17-20).

[2] Anyone who has read Cyril extensively will echo the mild judgment of Altaner, *op. cit.*, p. 244: "Cyril's writings, which are very important for Church history and the history of dogma, do not rank very high as literary productions." Especially in exegesis, his style is as prolix as his output is prolific. Cf. M. Jugie, "Cirillo d'Alessandria, santo," *Enciclopedia cattolica* 3, 1721: Cyril is clear, precise, and incisive in polemics; otherwise he is wordy and redundant.

[3] The Father is ἐξ οὗ, the Son, δι' οὗ, of creation; cf. *In Ioannem* 1, 9 (Pusey 1, 128). It is a constant refrain in Cyril that the Son is the "hand" or the "right hand" of the Father, because through Him the Father brought all things into being and executes all His operations; cf. *In Ioannem* 7 (Pusey 2, 253); *Glaphyra in Genesim* 3 (*PG* 69, 128); *In Isaiam* 2, 1 (*PG* 70, 329). Cyril justifies the expression by appealing to experience (we do all things through our own hand: *In psalmos*, Ps 88:11 [*PG* 69, 1212]), to typology (the hand is the type of practical activity: *In Isaiam* 3, 1 [*PG* 70, 568]), and to Scripture (*Glaphyra in Exodum* 2 [*PG* 69, 473]). Cyril extends the metaphor to include the Spirit as "the finger of God" (Lk 11:20), because whatever is done by the Father through the Son, is done by the Son ἐν πνεύματι (*In Lucam* hom. 81 [*PG* 72, 704; cf. Smith, Eng. tr. 2, 371]). A theological explanation of creation by the Father through the Son is found in *In Ioannem* 1, 5 (Pusey 1, 65-73). Cyril often insists that all God's operations *ad extra* are common to Father, Son, and Spirit; cf., e.g., *Adversus Nestorii blasphemias* 4, 1 (*ACO* 1, 1, 6, 77; *PG* 76, 172).

[4] *Glaphyra in Genesim* 1 (*PG* 69, 20). Cf. *In Matthaeum*, Mt 24:29 (*PG* 72, 441); also *In Ioannem* 1, 9 (Pusey 1, 124); *In Isaiam* 3, 5; 4, 3 (*PG* 70, 816, 977); *In Lucam* hom. 96 (Smith, Eng. tr. 2, 446); *In epistolam 1 ad Corinthios* 6 (Pusey, *In Ioannem* 3, 316).

fashion a rational animal. Every other creature He extemporized with a word,[5] but the formation of this creature God had conceived of old. It was not fitting for the copy ($\mu\ell\mu\eta\mu\alpha$) of the supreme glory, a creature most like God ($\theta\epsilon o\epsilon\iota\delta\epsilon\sigma\tau\alpha\tau o\nu$), to be formed like other creatures; consequently, God dignified this creation with deliberate forethought and personal activity. "He molded an image ($\check{\alpha}\gamma\alpha\lambda\mu\alpha$), made it a rational animal, and that it might rise above its own natural essence He straightway engraved on it the incorruptible, life-giving Spirit."[6] Then God bestowed on man paradise and pleasure, and empire ($\kappa\rho\acute{\alpha}\tau o\varsigma$) over everything on earth, the fish of the sea and the fowl of the air, the wild beasts and the venomous among animals. These He persuaded by the laws of their nature to fear man as was fit. "And so man was the impress ($\dot{\epsilon}\kappa\mu\alpha\gamma\epsilon\hat{\iota}o\nu$) of the supreme glory, and the image ($\epsilon\dot{\iota}\kappa\dot{\omega}\nu$) upon earth of divine power ($\dot{\epsilon}\xi o\upsilon\sigma\acute{\iota}\alpha\varsigma$)."[7]

Several pertinent ideas emerge from this passage. First, Adam was given empire, power, authority over all irrational life on earth. Second, these creatures were made subservient to Adam, and fear of man was implanted in their nature. Third, in virtue of this dominion the lord of earth resembled God, who exercises supreme lordship over the universe.

[5] The temptation is to translate $\dot{\alpha}\pi o\sigma\chi\epsilon\delta\iota\acute{\alpha}\zeta\omega\nu$ $\dot{\rho}\acute{\eta}\mu\alpha\tau\iota$ "extemporized with His own Word," but the Greek in context lends itself ill to such a turn. The contrast is not between creation through the Word and creation by personal activity; rather is it between extempore speech and deliberate action. Irrational creation God fashioned by a simple fiat; man is the product of divine reflection and labor. The latter interpretation, moreover, is more in keeping with the biblical account of creation which Cyril is expounding, and is borne out by a strikingly parallel passage, *In Isaiam* 1, 2 (*PG* 70, 81), where Cyril exemplifies the extempore word by quoting Gn 1:6, "Let there be a firmament made." Cf. *De sancta et consubstantiali trinitate* dial. 3 (*PG* 75, 804), where Cyril uses $\dot{\alpha}\pi o\sigma\chi\epsilon\delta\iota\acute{\alpha}\zeta\epsilon\iota\nu$ of man's creation, but without the explanatory "word." The idea of $\sigma\chi\epsilon\delta\iota\acute{\alpha}\zeta\epsilon\iota\nu$ is that of doing something off-hand or on the spur of the moment (cf. Liddell-Scott, *s.v.*), and is used by Cyril of Jonas setting up his booth outside Ninive (Jon 4:5; Cyril, *In Ionam* [Pusey 1, 595]).

[6] *Glaphyra in Genesim* 1 (*PG* 69, 20). $\Pi\nu\epsilon\hat{\upsilon}\mu\alpha$ here I understand of the Holy Spirit, for the following reasons. (a) This $\pi\nu\epsilon\hat{\upsilon}\mu\alpha$ raises man above his natural essence—which, as we have shown earlier, man's own $\pi\nu\epsilon\hat{\upsilon}\mu\alpha$ does not do. (b) The $\pi\nu\epsilon\hat{\upsilon}\mu\alpha$ engraved on man is Cyril's interpretation of "the breath of life" breathed by God into the face of Adam (Gn 2:7); cf. the present context and the parallel passage, *In Isaiam* 1, 2 (*PG* 70, 81). But, for Cyril, the "breath" in Gn 2:7 is the Holy Spirit given by God to Adam; cf. *In Matthaeum*, Mt 24:51 (*PG* 72, 445); *In Ioannem* 1, 9; 5, 2 (Pusey 1, 139, 691); and elsewhere, where the Holy Spirit is likewise presented as "life-giving" and the principle of human incorruption.

[7] *Glaphyra in Genesim* 1 (*PG* 69, 20).

This aspect of the divine image within man is, Cyril confesses, a secondary resemblance, but it is none the less authentic. Having declared that the primary, most proper fashion in which man can be formed after God's pattern is through virtue and sanctification, he adds: "It is not improbable to say that the likeness (ὁμοίωσιν) to God is in man in regard of sovereignty (κατὰ τὸ ἀρχικόν) as well; for dominion (τὸ ἄρχειν) was given him over all things that are on earth. And this is the second aspect of the likeness (ὁμοιώσεως) to Him."[8] In the light of Cyril's categorical affirmations elsewhere, "not improbable" (οὐκ ἀπίθανον) must be regarded as litotes; his own mind is unwavering. At any rate, there are no reservations in the letter he wrote to Calosyrius. The image of God, he thunders, is not in the body:

Man's formation to God's image has other meanings—meanings on the surface and meanings deep within; for man alone, of all the living creatures on earth, is rational, compassionate, with a capacity for all manner of virtue, and a divinely allotted dominion (τὸ ἄρχειν) over all the creatures of earth, after the image and likeness of God. Therefore, it is inasmuch as he is a rational animal, a lover of virtue, and earth's sovereign (ἀρχικόν) that man is said to have been made in God's image.[9]

It is, I suggest, in the context of the passages just quoted that a number of texts should be interpreted wherein God's image and man's dominion are closely linked in thought and expression, without being formally identified. For example, Cyril tells us that Adam "was made to the Creator's image and was appointed to rule (ἄρχειν) over the things of earth. . . ."[10] Again, Adam "was made to the image and to the likeness of God, and like some ruler (ἄρχων) he was set over (κεχειροτόνηται) the things of earth."[11] In man's primal constitution "we had been made by God to His image and likeness, and had been richly honored, obtaining dominion (ἄρχειν) over the things of earth."[12] Cyril asks why Julian the Apostate "pokes fun at the fact that the thinking, rational being, the most godlike (θεοειδέστατον) of all earth's animals, I mean man, was honored with dominion (ἀρχῇ) over all things. Why, the very nature of things agrees with Moses' words!"[13] On another occasion he insists that

8 *Responsiones ad Tiberium* 10 (Pusey, *In Ioannem* 3, 593-94).
9 *Epistola ad Calosyrium* (Pusey, *In Ioannem* 3, 605).
10 *De adoratione* 2 (PG 68, 244).
11 *In Isaiam* 1, 2 (PG 70, 81).
12 *In Hebraeos*, Heb 2:7-8 (Pusey, *In Ioannem* 3, 382; cf. 383).
13 *Contra Iulianum* 2 (PG 76, 592).

Christ's death was intended to benefit all men, not simply, as Caiphas said, the Jewish nation:

> For all of us are called God's race and children, inasmuch as He is Father of all in that He begot us by way of creation and brought into existence the things that were not. Still more because we have the honor of having been made from the beginning after His image, and of having obtained dominion (ἄρχειν) over the creatures of earth. . . .[14]

In each of these texts dominion follows hard upon image; in none of them is dominion expressly identified with image. In view of Cyril's indisputable doctrine elsewhere formulated, it is legitimate to conclude that even in these less obvious passages the Bishop of Alexandria implies that an aspect of man's resemblance to God is his sovereignty over irrational creation.

Is it possible to discover whether Cyril visualized man's dominion on earth as a natural prerogative? To clarify the issue (and clarification is needed, given Cyril's ambiguous use of φύσει and κατὰ φύσιν), is man lord of creation simply because he is a man? Because he is rational and it is irrational? In a world of finny, four-legged, and winged creatures, is dominion inseparable from human nature? Or is dominion something superadded—decorative and advantageous, yes, but indifferent as far as his essence and his destiny are concerned?

The solution will not come from Cyril's distinction between God's kingship and man's. For him, God alone is King by His very nature;[15] divinity and natural kingship go together;[16] God's dominion, unlike man's, is a matter of essence.[17] With man, kingship is an adventitious

---

[14] *In Ioannem* 7, fragmenta (Pusey 2, 295). On the idea that the whole race was given this privilege, cf. *Homiliae paschales* 5, 4 (*PG* 77, 484): "It was human nature that was divinely appointed to rule over (ἄρχειν) all things." In somewhat obscure language Cyril says that only the divine nature has universal lordship; all rational creatures are on the level of servants; their dignity is their ability to maintain their assigned ἀρχή; cf. *Homiliae paschales* 12, 2 (*PG* 77, 676). But the context has reference to the faithless angels (Jude 6) who did not keep their own ἀρχή, i.e., "did not preserve their original state" (Confraternity translation), "did not hold to their own domain" (Westminster), their "dignity" or "first state" (Zorell), their "due order" (Knox).

[15] Cf. *In Isaiam* 3, 4 (*PG* 70, 769); *Thesaurus* 31 (*PG* 75, 444). In such passages the human kingship in question is concretely man's empire over men within a political community; but, I believe, the principles enunciated can be transferred to man's dominion over irrational creation.

[16] Cf. *In Ioannem* 12, 1 (Pusey 3, 151); *Thesaurus* 32 (*PG* 75, 485).

[17] Cf. *In Amos* 4 (Pusey 1, 533).

thing.[18] Here again, however, essence and nature are perilous terms. Cyril himself admits that everything which God has, He has by His nature (φυσικῶς); everything which we have, we have adventitiously (εἰσποιητόν); everything we have is a gift (χάρις). Even rule over others we borrow from God, simply because we borrow everything from God.[19] In this terminology "natural" is contrasted with "given," not with "supernatural" or "preternatural." Our one valid and pertinent conclusion from such texts is that, for Cyril, man's sovereignty is, like rationality and free will, freely bestowed by God. He does not imply that dominion over irrational beings is not a necessary consequence of human nature as concretely constituted, rational and free.

The solution will not emerge from Cyril's exegesis of Gn 1:26. Almost invariably his reference to the original grant of sovereignty is curt and unenlightening.[20] The *Glaphyra in Genesim* passage digested above is somewhat more developed but still perplexing. It is not clear from the text or the context whether dominion is an aspect of the human animal's elevation "above its own natural essence" or simply a consequence of the radical difference between man and beast. On the one hand, Adam appears to be already constituted in his essential structure; in fact, he has been gifted with the Spirit; dominion is a prerogative God "gave in addition" (προσνενέμηκε), much like paradise itself. On the other hand, fear of man has been instilled into the nature of irrational creation.[21]

One paragraph suggestive of a solution confronts us in a fragment on the Epistle to the Hebrews. Cyril finds David astonished at the excess

[18] Cf. *In Ioannem* 3, 1 (Pusey 1, 374).

[19] Cf. *ibid.* 11, 4 (Pusey 2, 665–66).

[20] Cf. the texts mentioned above: *Responsiones ad Tiberium* 10 (Pusey, *In Ioannem* 3, 593–94); *Epistola ad Calosyrium* (Pusey, *In Ioannem* 3, 605); *De adoratione* 2 (*PG* 68, 244); *In Isaiam* 1, 2 (*PG* 70, 81); *In Hebraeos*, Heb 2:7–8 (Pusey, *In Ioannem* 3, 382); *Contra Iulianum* 2 (*PG* 76, 592); *In Ioannem* 7, fragmenta (Pusey 2, 295).

[21] Cf. *Glaphyra in Genesim* 1 (*PG* 69, 20). Note, however, the order of events in *In Isaiam* 1, 2 (*PG* 70, 81): Adam "was made to the image and to the likeness of God, and like some ruler he was set over the things of earth. And *besides this* he was honored with the Spirit of life; for He breathed into his face the breath of life" (italics added). Here the dominion is described as if given prior to the gift of the Spirit, whereas in the *Glaphyra* text the order is the reverse: first Spirit, then dominion. I am afraid that the order of events, as portrayed by Cyril, is unreliable and unserviceable. In another passage he interprets Gn 2:7 apparently of both natural and supernatural life: "at one and the same time the Spirit infused life in the creature and in divine fashion stamped on him His own features"; *In Ioannem* 2, 1 (Pusey 1, 182).

of God's graciousness to men: "What is man that you should be mindful of him?" (Ps 8:5). He proceeds to answer the question:

[What is man? He is] this animal so little, so paltry, earthsprung. [God] made him somewhat less than the angels; for we are admittedly inferior to the holy angels in nature and glory. And so the God of the universe deigned to "crown [us] with honor and glory" (Ps 8:6) and made us illustrious; for He appointed [man] to rule (εἰς ἀρχήν) over the earth and "set him over the works of His hands" (Ps 8:7).[22]

By his sheer nature, therefore, in so far as he was a human being and nothing more, Adam apparently did not have sovereignty over the earth. Man's nature is of itself unprepossessing; God dignified it with dominion.

A perhaps more impressive indication stems from the impact of sin on the image in Cyril's theology; and this we must anticipate here, if only fragmentarily. It is Cyril's stated principle that we have lost nothing which is ours by our essence (οὐσιωδῶς).[23] Nevertheless, he reminds us in the fragment on Hebrews quoted above, we have fallen from God's free gift (χάριτος) in Adam; "for in him as the first man God said to man's nature, 'Increase and multiply, and exercise complete dominion (κατακυριεύσατε) over [the earth].' 'But,' [Paul] says, 'now we do not see as yet all things subject to him' (Heb 2:8)." Therefore, Cyril argues, there must be another time when God's words will be verified; that is why Paul says that God has subjected the world to come not to angels but to men. It is through Christ that we have regained the blessings which our nature had in the beginning; it is through Him that we possess them securely. "Just as Adam's transgression dishonored us dreadfully, so we have been glorified through Christ's obedience for us. . . ."[24] The passage is not crystalline; but it would seem that human nature had dominion in Adam, lost it in Adam, recovered it in Christ, and will actually exercise it in the world to come.[25] One gathers that the preroga-

[22] *In Hebraeos,* Heb 2:7 (Pusey, *In Ioannem* 3, 382–83).

[23] Cf. *Responsiones ad Tiberium* 10 (Pusey, *In Ioannem* 3, 594). It should be pointed out that Cyril goes on immediately to speak of the loss of holiness and justice, without reference to this "second aspect of the likeness." Note, however, *De adoratione* 2 (*PG* 68, 245): Christ brought us back through holiness to the kingly honor (βασιλίδα) we formerly had.

[24] *In Hebraeos,* Heb 2:7–9 (Pusey, *In Ioannem* 3, 383–84).

[25] On the other hand, cf. Cyril's Easter message: On Easter it is not simply irrational nature, the world of field and flower, that blossoms again; what has come to life as well is man, the nature that has command over (ἡγεμονεύουσα) everything on earth; cf. *Homiliae paschales* 9, 2 (*PG* 77, 581).—It is of some pertinence that, when listing various kinds of image, Cyril says that one kind consists in

tive of sovereignty is neither constitutive of, nor consequent upon, man's nature.

To sum up: two of Cyril's positions are clear. One is the biblical fact: in the person of Adam, human nature was endowed by God with sovereignty over irrational creation. The other is a personal exegesis: this dominion is one aspect of the divine image in man. Cyril does not specify the nature of this imperial power; he does not reveal how it was exercised. It is not a constituent part of man's nature; in all probability it does not flow necessarily from his essence. This facet of the divine image was affected by Adam's sin; but, because we are so ill-informed on the nature of Adam's dominion, it is difficult to determine whether it was totally lost or merely diminished. And though we have recovered our primeval domination through Christ our Lord, its actualization seems reserved for the life to follow.

The striking feature in the history of this facet of the divine image is its attraction for the exegetes of Antioch. This is not to say that Alexandria disdained it or that the interpretation in question was unknown to the West.[26] Gregory of Nyssa, for example, frequently finds God's image in the kingship which man exercises over the rest of creation. In honoring man with His image, the Creator subjected irrational nature to him.[27] This destiny is written for all to read in the qualities of man's soul (virtue, immortality, justice) and in the carriage of his body.[28] In the very first moment of humanity's creation human

---

"dignity and honor and glory and supremacy (ὑπεροχῇ); for example, if someone should succeed to another's government (ἀρχήν) and should perform with authority (ἐξουσίας) everything that would be fit and proper for his predecessor"; *In Ioannem* 2, 8 (Pusey 1, 339–40). It is under this head, if anywhere in Cyril's catalog, that dominion falls.

[26] I have not found a convincing ἀρχή-image in Origen or Athanasius. There may be a reference to the ἀρχέτωσαν of Genesis in Clement's *Stromata* 2, 19 (*GCS* 15, 166): "This is the man 'according to the image and likeness': the gnostic, who imitates God as far as he can, who neglects nothing that makes for the likeness to the extent that it is possible . . . ruling over (βασιλεύων) his passions. . . ." At the end of the same chapter (*GCS* 15, 169), however, Clement insists that the image is a matter of mind and reason, "on which the Lord duly impresses the likeness in respect of well-doing and the likeness in respect of dominion (τὸ ἄρχειν); for principalities are made to prosper not by qualities of body but by judgments of mind. . . ." He does not elaborate. Cf. also *ibid.* 7, 3 (*GCS* 17, 12): the gnostic, image of the Image, "rules over (ἄρχων) himself and what is his."

[27] Cf. Gregory of Nyssa, *Contra Eunomium* 1 (*PG* 45, 308–9). The edition of W. Jaeger (2 vols.; Berlin, 1921), which restores the proper order of the books, has not been available to me.

[28] Cf. Gregory of Nyssa, *De hominis opificio* 4 (*PG* 44, 136).

nature was fashioned royal, as image of the nature which exercises universal lordship.[29] In harmony with Genesis, Gregory has man wield dominion over all inferior creatures; but he does so, as Leys has pointed out, in a perspective that is no longer Semitic but Greek, that is, by the natural advantage which his intelligence obtains for him, the while his physical endowments are comparatively slender.[30] The author of *In verba: Faciamus hominem ad imaginem et similitudinem nostram* has phrased it pithily: "Where you have the ability to dominate (τοῦ ἄρχειν), there you have the image of God."[31] And he applies this dominion not simply to man's power to dominate irrational creation by his reason (διὰ τοῦ λογισμοῦ), but also and primarily to those who exercise sovereignty over their passions.[32] In a letter to Bishop John of Jerusalem dated 394, Epiphanius, Bishop of Salamis, reports that some of Origen's disciples discover the resemblance in "man's universal dominion after the image of God." With his accustomed anti-Origenist invective Epiphanius appraises this, and other efforts to localize the divine image, as "drunken belches."[33]

The fascinating unknown whom we call Ambrosiaster,[34] writing apparently in Rome about 375, knows of some who hold that the Genesis image consists in man's sovereignty over irrational creation, on the strength of the close connection between the image concept and the domination idea in Gn 1:26-28. He finds this thesis groundless on two counts. First, if it were true, God would have addressed His "Let us make" not to the Son but to the heavenly dominations mentioned by St. Paul (Col 1:16; Eph 1:21). Second, if it were true, woman too would

[29] Cf. *ibid.*

[30] Cf. Gregory of Nyssa, *Adversus eos qui castigationes aegre ferunt* (*PG* 46, 308-9); Leys, *op. cit.*, p. 71. Leys remarks that another expression of this kingship is free will considered primarily as independence of all external constraint, then as the faculty of self-domination; and he reminds us again that, for Gregory, there is no tight partition between the various aspects of the image; here, e.g., the kingship image leads, in connection with the intelligence image, to the virtue image; cf. *op. cit.*, pp. 71-72.

[31] *In verba: Faciamus* 1 (*PG* 44, 265).

[32] Cf. *ibid.* (*PG* 44, 261-68); notice here (*PG* 44, 264), as in the certainly authentic works of Gregory, the concept of man's physical feebleness counterbalanced, or rather outweighed, by his reason.

[33] Epiphanius, in the epistolary corpus of Jerome, *Epistolae* 51, 7 (*CSEL* 54, 409); we have the letter in Jerome's translation.

[34] The conclusion of C. Martini is that the author flourished at Rome during the pontificate of Damasus (366-84), though he apparently had some connection with the Milanese Church and with Spain; cf. *Ambrosiaster: De auctore, operibus, theologia* (Rome, 1944) p. 160.

be God's image—an absurd suggestion, seeing that woman is subject to her husband's dominion and has no authority.[35] "It is in this that man is God's image: just as in heaven there is one God from whom all spiritual beings subsist, so on earth there was to be one man from whom all the rest would have their descent in the flesh."[36] There is a subtle addition to Ambrosiaster's thesis when he writes: "This, then, is the image of God in man, that one was made as it were the lord (*dominus*) from whom all the rest would derive their origin; he would have God's sovereignty (*imperium*) as if His vicegerent (*vicarius*), seeing that every king has God's image."[37] It would seem that Ambrosiaster is interpreting merely Gn 1:26–27; he applies the image to the first man, not to all men; he locates it in Adam's role as physical head of the human race; he refuses it to woman, even apparently to Eve. In the last-quoted text he appears to include sovereignty in the image; not sovereignty over irrational creation, but simply over wife. In the circumstances, wife can only be Eve.

In Augustine's understanding of Genesis, the reason why God immediately added, "Let him have dominion" over irrational animals, was to have us grasp the truth that man was made to God's image precisely under the formality which raises him above the brute beast; and that is mind, reason, intelligence.[38] Nevertheless, as we have seen, an identification of image and dominion is not unfamiliar to the West, as it was not strange to Alexandria.

The extant evidence, however, points to a decided predilection for this interpretation among the Antiochenes. The exegesis in question finds its springboard in the juxtaposition of the two ideas, image and dominion, within the same biblical verse, Gn 1:26. Diodore of Tarsus, with whom the School of Antioch opened its golden age, presents the pith of the interpretation: "How, then, is man God's image? By way

---

[35] Cf. Ambrosiaster, *Quaestiones veteris et novi testamenti 127*, 45, 3 (*CSEL* 50, 82–83).

[36] *Ibid.* 45, 2 (*CSEL* 50, 82). Cf. *ibid.* 21 (*CSEL* 50, 47–48): "That man was made to the image of God means this: One made one, so that, just as all things are from one God, so too the whole human race might be from one man. The likeness, however, is this: as the Son is from the Father, so too is the woman from the man, to preserve the pattern of a single origin. . . ." Cf. the similar doctrine and expression in the same author's commentary, *In epistolam b. Pauli ad Corinthios primam* (*PL* 17 [ed. 1866] 253), which forms a part of *Commentaria in 13 epistolas b. Pauli* (*PL* 17, 47–536). He is a representative of literal, historical exegesis, averse to the allegorical altogether; cf. Altaner, *op. cit.*, p. 341.

[37] Ambrosiaster, *Quaestiones veteris et novi testamenti 127*, 106, 17 (*CSEL* 50, 243).

[38] Cf. Augustine, *De Genesi ad litteram* 3, 20 (*CSEL* 28/1, 86).

of dominion (τὸ ἀρχικόν), in virtue of authority (τὸ ἐξουσιαστικόν)." For proof he is content to quote Gn 1:26. His development—at least as we have it in this catena fragment—is similarly brief: "Just as God rules over the whole universe, so too man rules over (βασιλεύει) the things of earth."[39] Chrysostom, the most remarkable of Diodore's disciples,[40] is seemingly inspired by his master when he writes: "What is this 'to our image and likeness'? An image of sovereignty (ἀρχῆς) is signified. As no one is superior to God in heaven, so let no one be superior to man upon earth." A threefold honor, Chrysostom adds, is here involved. God made man to His image; man's sovereignty is not a recompense for effort expended, but a gift of love; and it is a natural (φυσικήν) dominion, like the empire of the lion among beasts or the eagle among birds, not an elective thing, like the rule of their Emperor.[41]

Severian of Gabala, whose aversion to all but the simplest allegory ranks him with the Antiochenes,[42] is brief and clear. We are God's image if we are holy, or if we are just, or if we are merciful; for Paul ascribes the image to the virtues (cf. Col 3:9–10). But Severian adds: "In what does the image consist? Again, in authority (ἐξουσίᾳ)." And he quotes Gn 1:26.[43] Inasmuch as Ephraem used Antiochene principles of hermeneutics,[44] it may be significant that the glory of the School of Edessa saw one aspect of the image in man's dominion over creation: "Moses explained wherein we were God's image when he said, 'That they may rule over the fishes of the sea and the birds and the herds and the whole earth.' It was, therefore, by the power which Adam received over the earth and over all things which are in it, that he was the likeness of that

[39] Diodore, *Fragmenta in Genesin*, Gn 1:26 (*PG* 33, 1564–65).

[40] Cf. Chrysostom's panegyric on Diodore, *Laus Diodori episcopi* (*PG* 52, 761–66), in which he compares Diodore to John the Baptist in spirit (φρόνημα) and in tenor of life.

[41] Cf. Chrysostom, *Homiliae de statuis* 7, 2 (*PG* 49, 93). Cf. also *Homiliae in Genesim* 8, 3 (*PG* 53, 72): God "says 'image,' therefore, by way of dominion (ἀρχῆς), not in any other way; . . . nothing on earth is greater than [man], but all things are subject to his authority (ἐξουσίαν)." Cf. *ibid*. 9, 2 (*PG* 53, 78). This is indubitably the interpretation of his predilection. The fact that human reason, though basically the cause of man's domination in Chrysostom's thinking, is never presented as the element which makes us like God, prompts Gross to ask if we have here "a manifestation of the anti-intellectualism of the Antiochenes"; *op. cit.*, p. 256, note 3.

[42] Cf. G. Bardy, "Sévérien de Gabala," *DTC* 14, 2003, 2006.

[43] Severian, *De mundi creatione* 5, 4 (*PG* 56, 475).

[44] Cf. F. Cayré, *Patrologie et histoire de la théologie* 1 (Paris, 1953) 443: his exegetical method is historical and literal in his commentaries, allegorical and mystical in his hymns and discourses. Cf. Altaner, *op. cit.*, p. 300.

God in whose power were the things which are above and the things which are below."[45]

Isidore of Pelusium, whom Cyril called his "father," and who wedded such sharp criticism with genuine admiration for the Bishop of Alexandria,[46] denies that the image has anything to do with God's essence or man's: "Man is an image of dominion (ἀρχῆς) and kingship (βασιλείας), not of essence." The word ἀρχέτωσαν, "let them have dominion," following hard upon "let us make man to our own image and likeness," convinces him that the characteristic note of the image is to be discovered in sovereignty (ἐν τῷ ἀρχικῷ).[47] It is a sovereignty which was equally Eve's, but in consequence of sin woman's dominion was "diminished and mutilated," and she was made subject to her husband.[48] The words of the Psalmist, "Thou hast crowned him with glory and honor, and hast set him over all the works of thy hands" (Ps 8:6–7), reveal the image of God in man's lordship over the things of earth; for (the words are an echo of Diodore) "just as God rules over all things, so too man rules over (βασιλεύει) the things on earth."[49]

Precisely what Isidore understands by this God-given dominion becomes more luminous from a difficulty which he records: If man was given dominion over everything on earth, why is he afraid of wild animals? Isidore refuses to pronounce on the merits of a reply which some propose, namely, that dominion over undomesticated beasts is not a part of the original biblical text, but was added later. He prefers to meet the objection head on. While the image was radiant in man, all things were subject to him; that is why Adam gave the animals names. But when he disobeyed God, his dominion was "mutilated." He was not deprived of it entirely—God did not want His gift to go unused; but a certain mutilation did take place. And it was by fear of wild beasts that man was to be recalled to his senses. Isidore finds his proof in Noah,

[45] Ephraem, *Commentarius in Genesim* 1, 29 (*CSCO* 152, 23; Latin tr., *CSCO* 153, 17). The *Commentaries on Genesis and Exodus* were written between 364 and 370; cf. R. M. Tonneau, in *CSCO* 152, Praefatio, p. II.

[46] Cf. du Manoir, *Dogme et spiritualité*, pp. 22–24. From certain letters of Isidore to Cyril, du Manoir considers it probable that Cyril spent some time as a monk in the Pelusium monastery where Isidore was superior for about forty years, or in a neighboring monastery. Cf. also du Manoir, "Cyrille d'Alexandrie (saint)," *Dictionnaire de spiritualité* 2, 2672–73. Isidore stood flatly against Alexandrian allegorism; cf. Cayré, *op. cit.* 1, 571.

[47] Isidore of Pelusium, *Epistolae* 3, 95 (*PG* 78, 801).

[48] Cf. *ibid.*; he is led to this conclusion by 1 Cor 11:7 and Gn 3:16.

[49] *Ibid.* Isidore believes that the likeness either is synonymous with image, or else means that the sovereignty received at creation should flower in deliberately elected virtue; cf. *ibid.* (*PG* 78, 801–4).

who purified the mutilated image by taking justice to his heart, so that "all the wild beasts came to him, acknowledging their primeval bondage and all but accusing him who sinned in the beginning and lost part of his domination." He finds his proof in Daniel, whom the lions feared; in the three young men, of whom the fire was afraid; in Paul, whom the viper did not hurt. From the fact that these individuals recovered Adam's dominion Isidore concludes that he received it in its entirety and lost it in part. The good Abbot betrays a latent insecurity when he ends, perhaps belligerently, probably in humility: "If anyone has something better to say, let him speak and be heard!"[50]

Theodoret of Cyrus, among several aspects of the image, such as rationality, cites with obvious approval the opinion that man is God's image by reason of his authority over irrational creation. "Some have said that man was made to God's image with respect to dominion (κατὰ τὸ ἀρχικόν); and they have made use of a very clear proof, the fact that the Creator added, 'And let them have dominion. . . .' For, just as He holds absolute sway (δεσποτείαν) over the whole universe, so He has given to man authority (ἐξουσίαν) over the irrational animals."[51] And in a poetic passage that is almost certainly Theodoret's we read that the human mind (νοῦς) was made to the Creator's image; for it is "imitator of the Creator, king of visible creation, or image of the King. It collects tribute from earth, from sea, from air, from sun and moon and stars, from sky and clouds, from sheep and oxen and the other beasts; better, it culls all their fruits. For its sake, you see, the things that are visible were made; for of these God stands not in need."[52]

Strangely enough, however, another disciple of Diodore, the warmly debated Theodore of Mopsuestia,[53] sounds a dissonant note in this

---

[50] It is not clear whether woman's mutilated image was likewise repaired; and, if so, in what sense. She remains subject to her husband; and this subjection, in Isidore's view, is a diminishing of her dominion.

[51] Theodoret, *Quaestiones in Genesim* 20 (*PG* 80, 105).

[52] *De incarnatione domini* 17 (*PG* 75, 1445). This work (*PG* 75, 1420–77) has been mistakenly placed among the writings of Cyril of Alexandria. It is almost certainly to be attributed to Theodoret of Cyrus, after the research of A. Ehrhard, "Die Cyrill v. Alexandrien zugeschriebene Schrift Περὶ τῆς τοῦ Κυρίου ἐνανθρωπήσεως ein Werk Theodorets von Cyrus," *Tübinger theologische Quartalschrift* 70 (1888) 179–243, 406–50; cf. du Manoir, *Dogme et spiritualité*, p. 59.

[53] On modern efforts to reverse the traditional opinion of Theodore's Christology, cf. J. L. McKenzie, "A New Study of Theodore of Mopsuestia," *Theological Studies* 10 (1949) 394–408; and F. A. Sullivan, "Some Reactions to Devreesse's New Study of Theodore of Mopsuestia," *ibid.* 12 (1951) 179–207; and especially the latter's full-length study, *The Christology of Theodore of Mopsuestia* (Rome, 1956).

singular harmony; he takes exception to such an interpretation. If we may trust the passage preserved in Theodoret of Cyrus, Theodore rejects as ridiculous the opinion that man is God's image by intelligence or power of domination (κατὰ τὸ ἀρχικόν). His argument is that man shares these advantages with other beings, e.g., the angels, whereas no other creature but man is said to have been made God's image.[54] "What is certain is that, for Theodore, man is the image of God because he is like the center of the universe to which all other beings are related, so that, while being part of the world, he holds there, so to say, the place of God."[55]

In general, however, the Antiochenes do detect at least a facet of the divine image in man's sovereignty. They do so on the basis of Gn 1:26, the contiguity of divine image and human dominion in the one verse; but this does not lead them, save in an Isidore, to allege for Adam a preferential status, an ἀρχή more perfect than our own. Apart once more from an Isidore, this sovereignty is not linked to sanctity; man is lord of earth because he is man; he is rational, the rest of earth is irrational. The content of this human resemblance to God is consistently kept quite abstract: man holds a position with reference to earth's creatures analogous to the position which God occupies in regard to all creatures; God is Lord of the universe, man is lord of earth. Irrational creation's rebellion against man rarely strikes the Antiochenes as an argument against man's sovereignty, any more than man's rebellion against God occurs to them as evidence against God's kingship. Finally, engrossed in the literal sense of Scripture, Antiochene exegesis cannot be persuaded to pass from dominion over birds and beasts to empire over passions and irrational impulses.

With much of this Antiochene outlook Cyril of Alexandria is in agreement. Perhaps his most significant divergence is the tendency to find man's domination of irrational creation affected by the sin of Adam. It would be an engaging discovery if we could trace this aspect of Cyril's image theology to the influence of his father in Christ, Isidore of Pelusium.

From the standpoint of sound exegesis, it is worth noting that Cyril's effort to identify the image with man's earthly suzerainty can claim considerable support in contemporary biblical criticism. True, scholars like Wright and Clamer see this lordship as rather a consequence of man's resemblance to God;[56] the Priestly Tradition does not formally

[54] Cf. Theodore, *apud* Theodoret, *Quaestiones in Genesim* 20 (*PG* 80, 109-13).
[55] Gross, *op. cit.*, p. 264.
[56] Cf. Wright, *art. cit.*, p. 368; Clamer, *op. cit.*, p. 113. In similar vein, von Rad, *art. cit.*, p. 390.

64       CYRIL OF ALEXANDRIA: IMAGE OF GOD IN MAN

identify *ṣelem* and *dᵉmût*. Others are less cautious. Sutcliffe, for example, finds in the immediate context of God's determination to mold man divinely a suggestion that "the likeness is to be found primarily in man's lordship of created things, which bear a relation of subordination to him analogous to that which he bears to his Creator."[57] A recent article by D. T. Asselin on the concept of dominion in Gn 1–3 is categorical on the point.[58] Asselin claims that the second part of Gn 1:26 is an explanation of the first part:

> Man is God's image not because of what he is, but because of what he is given: a share in the divine sovereignty over creation. He is lord of the world, yet Yahweh's vassal. In the light of the Israelite's synthetic mode of conceiving the constitution of man and of his experimental knowledge of God in dynamic, historical categories, no other explanation appears plausible. The absence of any influence of Greek philosophy prevents him from conceiving the relation of resemblance between God and man on either a purely natural (physical or spiritual) or a purely supernatural level. It is thought of as based upon a conferred dynamism.[59]

Cyril would agree that man is God's image in virtue of what he is given. As we shall shortly see, however, Cyril will go further; he will insist, almost paradoxically, that man's primary resemblance to God is in virtue of a gift which allows him to image the divine in virtue of what he is.

[57] Sutcliffe, *op. cit.*, p. 183. In this connection cf. the observations of K. L. Schmidt, "Homo imago Dei im Alten und Neuen Testament," *Eranos-Jahrbuch* 15 (1947) 149–95, but especially 182 ff.

[58] Cf. D. T. Asselin, "The Notion of Dominion in Genesis 1–3," *Catholic Biblical Quarterly* 16 (1954) 277–94.

[59] *Ibid.*, pp. 293–94.

# CHAPTER 6

# SANCTIFICATION

To this point we have examined those facets of the divine image which Cyril, explicitly or by implication, considers secondary: (a) rationality, with its supernatural finality; (b) freedom, together with the will's natural orientation to goodness; and (c) sovereignty over irrational creation. With this as background, we can focus on man's prime resemblance to his God.

The problem at issue in the tenth of Cyril's *Responsiones ad Tiberium* is precisely this: how are we to understand the concept, "man to the image of God"? There are individuals who are anxious to know.[1] The Bishop's response is categorical and it is a two-edged sword. Negatively, he characterizes as mistaken the view that it is the body which images God; for, "since God is a spirit, He is surely shapeless, beyond all form and figure and circumscription."[2] Positively, he proceeds to answer the question:

We have been formed (μεμορφώμεθα) to [God] in the primary and most proper way in which it can be understood: according to virtue and sanctification (ἁγιασμόν); for the Deity is holy (ἅγιον), and the fount, beginning, and origin of all virtue. Now, that we should so understand man's creation to God's image, the all-wise Paul will tell us in his words to the Galatians: "Little children, with whom I am in labor again, until Christ be formed in you" (Gal 4:19). For He is formed in us through the sanctification (ἁγιασμοῦ) which comes through the Spirit, through the calling which consists in faith in Him. Now, in those who sin against this faith the distinctive features (χαρακτῆοες) do not shine forth clearly; that is why they need another spiritual travail and suprasensuous (νοητῆς) regeneration, in order that they may be formed once more to Christ, inasmuch as the Holy Spirit makes the divine image gleam in them through sanctification (ἁγιασμοῦ).[3]

In a word, God is holy, and man images God if he is himself holy. In fact, this is divine resemblance at its loftiest level. Time and again Cyril identifies the image of God with the holiness of man. This resemblance to God which is holiness was one aspect of the divine image in Adam;

---

[1] Cf. *Responsiones ad Tiberium* 10 (Pusey, *In Ioannem* 3, 592).

[2] *Ibid.* (Pusey, *In Ioannem* 3, 593).

[3] *Ibid.*

for "in the beginning man's nature was enriched with participation in the divine Spirit, and with the resemblance (ἐξεικονισμόν) to God that comes through sanctification (ἁγιασμοῦ); for in this way too he was made to the Creator's image."[4] And holiness has been a significant aspect of the divine image ever since the Son of God was enfleshed. Cyril admits to Nestorius that all men without exception are conformed (σύμμορφοι) to Christ in a genuine sense: He is perfect man and they are perfect men. But there is more; conformity to Christ is not simply a matter of sheer humanity. Some men bear "the image of the heavenly" (1 Cor 15:49), and that image is "utter absence of slavery to passion, ignorance of sin, superiority to death and corruption, holiness (ἁγιασμός), justice.... These, I think, are possessions that befit the divine, undefiled nature; for it is superior to sin and corruption; it is holiness (ἁγιασμός) and justice."[5] And so, to Nestorius' objection, "Surely you do not mean to say that God the Word had brethren who were like the divinity (θεότητι),"[6] Cyril presents man's primary conformity to God's very nature:

[Christ] has, therefore, brethren like (ἐοικότας) Himself, who bear the image of His divine nature by way of sanctification (κατά γε τὸν τοῦ ἡγιάσθαι τρόπον); for that is the way Christ is formed in us, inasmuch as the Holy Spirit as it were transforms us from what is human to what is His.... On those who have been made partakers of His divine nature through participation in the Holy Spirit, there is somehow stamped the suprasensuous likeness (ἐμφέρεια) to Christ, and the beauty of the inexpressible divinity gleams in the souls of the saints. How, then, can you attribute to us, without blushing, sheer likeness (ἐμφέρειαν) of the flesh, and that alone, with utter disregard for the divine, suprasensuous formation? More accurately, you have done away with it altogether.[7]

[4] De sancta et consubstantiali trinitate dial. 6 (PG 75, 1008); cf. In Ionam (Pusey 1, 565), where the dynamic element of holiness is accentuated.

[5] Adversus Nestorii blasphemias 3, 2 (ACO 1, 1, 6, 59-60; PG 76, 128-29). Cf. De adoratione 17 (PG 68, 1076) for a comparison between the "holy time of man's life" in Adam and the "holy and far better" period inaugurated with Christ.

[6] Adversus Nestorii blasphemias 3, 2 (ACO 1, 1, 6, 58; PG 76, 124).

[7] Ibid. (ACO 1, 1, 6, 60; PG 76, 129); cf. De sancta et consubstantiali trinitate dial. 7 (PG 75, 1088): "the image which is in sanctification." Cyril stresses the conformity to Christ which sanctification effects. Cf., e.g., De adoratione 16 (PG 68, 1013, 1020): the ἅγιοι are conformed always to Christ, who has an incomparable, unsurpassable ἁγιότης; they are in His μορφή; Glaphyra in Genesim 5 (PG 69, 260): we who have faith in Christ are conformed to Him, because we have been regenerated through the Spirit to incorruption and sanctification; Glaphyra in Exodum 2 (PG 69, 436): those saved in Christ have a conformity to Him through sanctification in the Spirit; In Isaiam 4, 1 (PG 70, 892): by conformity to Christ

In this connection an initial desideratum is to unearth Cyril's concept of sanctification, his understanding of holiness: what is ἁγιασμός? Not the detailed process, with its total configuration, but the underlying definition.[8] The material for such a study is discouragingly opulent and scattered through the Cyrillic corpus. Fortunately, two passages are quite synthetic in approach. The first is a paragraph in the *Commentary on John*.[9] The Johannine phrase, "whom the Father has sanctified (ἡγίασε)" (Jn 10:36), leads Cyril to remark that Scripture takes ἁγιάζεσθαι in many senses; he lists five. First, something is sanctified if it is dedicated (ἀνατιθέμενον), if it is consecrated to God, like the first-

---

believers have the beauty of the divine nature gleaming in their souls; through sanctification we have returned to our nature's original beauty, the image of God; *ibid.* 5, 1 (*PG* 70, 1189): the Father wants to make believers conformed to Christ through sanctification in the Spirit; *In Lucam* hom. 67 (*PG* 72, 673; *CSCO* 70, 264; Lat. tr. 140, 181): the Son took flesh to make us conformed to Himself; through sanctification and justice He engraved on us the beauty of His own divinity; *In Lucam*, Lk 15:8 ff. (*PG* 72, 800): we have been formed to Christ through sanctification and justice; *In Ioannem* 7, fragmenta (Pusey 2, 252): to preserve the kinship with Christ inaugurated by the Incarnation, we must preserve "the conformed image of holiness (ἁγιότητος)"—which seems to mean that we must continue to be like Christ in holiness of life; *In epistolam 2 ad Corinthios* 1 (Pusey, *In Ioannem* 3, 326): formed to Christ, we image God; *Contra Iulianum* 9 (*PG* 76, 948): we have been formed to the Son, the Spirit impressing on us through sanctification a singular beauty like God's; *Adversus Nestorii blasphemias* 3, 2 (*ACO* 1, 1, 6, 60; *PG* 76, 129): Christ is formed in us by way of sanctification through participation in the Spirit; *Responsiones ad Tiberium* 10 (Pusey, *In Ioannem* 3, 593): Christ is formed in us through the sanctification which comes through the Spirit; *Homiliae paschales* 13, 3 (*PG* 77, 700): Christ became man to make us conformed to Himself.

[8] A particularized account of Cyril's understanding of sanctification is available in the first part of J. Mahé's informative study, "La sanctification d'après saint Cyrille d'Alexandrie," *Revue d'histoire ecclésiastique* 10 (1909) 30–40, 469–92. Cf. also some detailed analyses and exhaustive documentation in du Manoir, *Dogme et spiritualité*, pp. 163–84, 243–56, 393–439.—On broad outlines, ἁγιασμός is the act or process whereby holiness is effected (to this corresponds the verb ἁγιάζειν), and so I have generally translated it "sanctification"; ἁγιότης or ἁγιωσύνη is the resultant state of sanctity (to this corresponds the adjective ἅγιος), which I regularly translate "sanctity" or "holiness." Nevertheless, the concrete meaning or nuance is frequently to be determined by the context; sometimes the exact shade of thought (act, process, state) cannot be determined. Cyril himself is rarely concerned to make such distinctions, perhaps because the act of sanctifying involves sanctity, while the state of holiness implies a ceaseless self-communication of God.

[9] Cf. *In Ioannem* 7, fragmenta (Pusey 2, 259–60). Because the passage is not consistently clear, an interpretative digest seems preferable to a literal translation. Cyril's examples, for one thing, could at times be more accurately assigned.

born in Israel (Ex 13:2). Second, someone is sanctified if he is chosen (προχειρισθέν) by God to carry out His will, like Cyrus and the Medes elected to war against the Babylonians (Is 13:3), or like the Son of God chosen by the Father to reform human life. Third, that is sanctified which has come to partake (ἐν μεθέξει) of the Holy Spirit. Fourth, persons and things are called holy if they are set apart (ἀφοριζόμενα) for sacrifice to God; e.g., the Christ of the passion. Fifth, that is sanctified which has the Word of God united (ἐνωθέντα) to it; so the flesh of Christ in the Incarnation.

The second synthetic effort to define sanctification occurs in the sixth of the *Dialogues on the Trinity*.[10] Cyril is concerned to explain in what sense it can be said that the Incarnate Word was sanctified. Once again he observes that Scripture reveals many disparate meanings of ἁγιάζεσθαι; he lists four. First, some are said to be sanctified in this sense: God sees in advance that, "leading an admirable life in harmony with His law, they will be fit for participation in the Holy Spirit."[11] These are the "predestined" of Paul (Rom 8:29–30). This was the lot of Jeremiah: "Before I formed you in the belly, I knew you; and before you came forth out of the womb, I sanctified you" (Jer 1:5). This concept of sanctification differs from each of the five meanings given in the passage from the *Commentary on John*; here sanctification is not participation in the Spirit but precisely God's foreknowledge thereof. Second, others are sanctified (in the usage of Scripture), even though they do not know God. Their sanctification is not a relationship to, a kinship with, the Spirit; it means that they have been designated to accomplish some facet of God's will. This notion of sanctification is identical with the second meaning in the *Commentary on John*—even to the example of Cyrus and the Medes. Third, that is holy which has been dedicated to God by way of sacrifice, like the "sanctified flesh" of which God spoke to Haggai (Hg 2:13). This concept seems a combination of the first (dedication) and fourth (set apart for sacrifice) meanings in the *Commentary on John*. Finally, "we call those persons holy who have been genuinely sanctified through the Spirit and have been made sharers in the divine nature." This concept corresponds to the third meaning given in the preceding paragraph. In brief, the *Dialogue* supplies but one biblical use of sanctification which is not to be

---

[10] Cf. *De sancta et consubstantiali trinitate* dial. 6 (*PG* 75, 1004–1005).

[11] Cyril does not explain how these individuals will lead an "admirable life" prior to participation in the Spirit. We may achieve a clearer understanding of his mind in this matter when we discuss the effect of sin on the image in man.

found in the *Commentary*: God's foreknowledge of man's share in the divine.[12]

These varied definitions crop up with fair frequency to fill out and illustrate Cyril's total conception. Man's sanctification is consecration to God;[13] it is selection to do God's will;[14] it is sacrifice of self.[15] But Cyril's definitions cannot be used indiscriminately; not every consecration, not every segregation, not every sacrifice is participation in the Spirit. Cyril takes occasion to mention that the sanctification of the Chaldaeans (Zeph 1:7) is not to be understood in the sense that they have been made ἅγιοι. In their case it is not a question of having laid wickedness aside; it is not participation in the Holy Spirit; it is simply that they have been appointed by God to burn Judaea.[16] When Christ tells the Father that He "sanctifies" Himself for the disciples (Jn 17:19), He is not speaking of a sanctification which consists in purification of soul or spirit, nor does He mean participation in the Spirit. He means, "I dedicate and offer myself as a spotless victim ... ; for that was sanctified, or called holy according to the Law, which was offered on God's altar."[17]

[12] The passage in the *Commentary on John* may represent Cyril's more mature thought; it is indisputably a later production than *De sancta et consubstantiali trinitate*, as we learn from two formal references to the latter work in the *Commentary*; cf. *In Ioannem* 1, 9 (Pusey 1, 128, 137–38). Jouassard, *art. cit.*, p. 170, dates *John* from 425 on; he places *De trinitate* between 423 and 425.

[13] Cf. *De adoratione* 10 (*PG* 68, 688); *ibid.* 16 (*PG* 68, 1013–16); *Homiliae paschales* 10, 2 (*PG* 77, 620); *Adversus Nestorii blasphemias* 2, 4 (*ACO* 1, 1, 6, 41; *PG* 76, 81); *In Isaiam* 1, 6 (*PG* 70, 292).

[14] Cf. *Adversus Nestorii blasphemias* 2, 4 (*ACO* 1, 1, 6, 41; *PG* 76, 81); *In Sophoniam* 1 (Pusey 2, 178).

[15] Cf. *Contra Iulianum* 2 (*PG* 76, 593): by passionless contemplation of God; *In Ioannem* 4, 7 (Pusey 1, 640): by not living to ourselves. The concept of sanctification as sacrifice (often used in connection with dedication) is notably applied to Christ; cf. *In Ioannem* 5, 1 (Pusey 1, 662–63).

[16] Cf. *In Sophoniam* 1 (Pusey 2, 178).

[17] *In Ioannem* 4, 2 (Pusey 1, 519). Cyril notes that the altar (Lv 8:11) was sanctified through the Spirit, not as the human soul participates in the Spirit, but from contact with the sacrifice; "for even a place is holy if Christ is there"; *De adoratione* 11 (*PG* 68, 764). On the sanctity of places cf. *ibid.* 12 (*PG* 68, 829); *In Ioannem* 4, 5 (Pusey 1, 599–600). For the sanctification of things cf. *In Isaiam* 5, 2 (*PG* 70, 1224); *In Ioelem* 1 (Pusey 1, 307); *ibid.* 2 (Pusey 1, 354); *In Zachariam* 6 (Pusey 2, 542). Things are holy in the sense that they make people holy (e.g., fear of God) or are separated from profane use and reserved for God's glory (e.g., sacred vessels); they are sanctified (e.g., wars, fasts) in the sense that they are dedicated to God. Christ's body is holy because it belongs properly to the Word; cf. *Contra Iulianum* 8 (*PG* 76, 941–42).

In any event, the concept of human holiness which Cyril accentuates, the sanctification which is man's preeminent imaging of God, is participation in the divine nature. We encounter a splendid illustration of this emphasis in the *Dialogues on the Trinity*. Cyril is making the point that, when the Holy Spirit communicates Himself to a creature, He makes the nature of that creature holy. In constituting man superior to sin, He "transforms him to the Creator's image through sanctification; for the Maker of all things is holy; that is why He says, 'Be holy, because I am holy' (Lv 19:2). . . . For we too, we ourselves, have been created to God's image and likeness. Now, that which produces the divine resemblance (ἐξεικονισμόν) in us is surely sanctification (ἁγιασμός), that is, participation (μέθεξις) of the Son in the Spirit."[18] In summary, participation is sanctification, and sanctification produces resemblance: holy men image the holy God.

This aspect of the image is more than the natural capacity for goodness and virtue which concerned us in a previous chapter. Man "was indeed animated by God's inexpressible power, and was made in His likeness in so far as he was naturally good and just and capable of all virtue; but he was sanctified when made partaker of the Holy Spirit. . . ."[19] Sanctification, participation in God's own Son through His Spirit, is not innate in human nature.

In this work of sanctification twin graces are given us. On the one hand, there is a sanctifying grace which is a created quality. This aspect of sanctification is evident in a lovely paragraph occasioned by Is 44:21: "I have formed (ἔπλασα) thee, thou art my servant, O Israel, forget me not." Cyril catalogs the various formations possible for man. First, there is a simple, uncomplicated formation which was uniquely Adam's; he was fashioned from the dust of the earth. Second, ever since Adam, man has been formed in the womb of a mother; that formation is proper to us; it is the way we come into existence. Third, there is a formation by which we become children of God; by knowledge of God's laws we are elevated to a spiritual (πνευματικόν) beauty effected in the soul through the adornment provided by the virtues. Fourth (and this Cyril seems to distinguish from the preceding), men

[18] *De sancta et consubstantiali trinitate* dial. 6 (*PG* 75, 1013). That holiness is participation of the Son in this passage, rather than immediately of the Spirit, is not significant, in view of Cyril's constant oscillation between Spirit and Son. The justification of this fluctuation stems from the fact that, for Cyril, our participation in God, as well as our resemblance to God, has reference to the three Persons; we share in the divine nature.

[19] *De dogmatum solutione* 2 (Pusey, *In Ioannem* 3, 553–54).

are fashioned in Christ, through participation (μετοχῆς) of the Holy Spirit, to His form (εἶδος). The amazing Paul writes to the Galatians: "Little children, with whom I am in labor again, until Christ be formed in you" (Gal 4:19). Now, Christ is formed (μορφοῦται) in us inasmuch as the Holy Spirit implants in us some divine form (μόρφωσιν) through sanctification (ἁγιασμοῦ) and justice. It is in this way, you see, it is in this way that the impress of the substance of God the Father is conspicuous in our souls—since the Holy Spirit reforms us, as I said, to Him through sanctification.[20]

The sanctified soul, therefore, is graced with a created quality, a μόρφωσις, whose function is to form Christ in us.[21] On the other hand, Cyril will not tolerate the thought that this grace is something separated from the essence of the Spirit. He gives Himself—what theologians call the Uncreated Grace. Those who deny the divinity of the Spirit, Cyril argues, will have to conclude that it is not the Spirit Himself who is stamped on us in sanctification, but grace through Him. This is not true. Christ "is formed through the Spirit, who renovates us to God through Himself (δι' ἑαυτοῦ)." Since, then, we are formed to Christ and He is stamped on us, molded in us, through the Spirit who is like Him by nature, it follows that the Spirit is God, "seeing that He forms to God, not as if through a ministerial grace, but as a participation in the divine nature He gives Himself to those who are worthy."[22] Even more strikingly:

[20] In Isaiam 4, 2 (PG 70, 936). The "impress" (χαρακτήρ) here is apparently the Son of God, from the context and in view of Cyril's obvious use of Heb 1:3.

[21] Mahé, art. cit., pp. 480–85, has shown that Cyril presents a grace which is a sanctifying quality (ποιότης), a divine form (μόρφωσις) impressed on our souls by the Spirit, a seal, a force, an ornament, a garment, the nourishment and sap of the soul, the pledge and earnest of eternal life—all features which fit perfectly what we call sanctifying grace. The texts which seem to reject such a created grace actually endeavor to show the totality of the supernatural reality: this is something genuinely divine, not a purely created quality separable from, and independent of, the Spirit. Mahé's conclusion is that Cyril admits a sanctifying grace, but it is not a kind of instrumental quality, separated from the Spirit, with the help of which He would transform our souls; it is the infusion and action of the Spirit in the just soul.

[22] De sancta et consubstantiali trinitate dial. 7 (PG 75, 1089; cf. 1088); cf. Thesaurus 34 (PG 75, 597): the sanctifying Spirit does not need to sanctify "by some means"; sanctification is a work which He accomplishes personally (αὐτουργόν) within us. Cf. Adversus Nestorii blasphemias 2, 2 (ACO 1, 1, 6, 37; PG 76, 72): the Word "anoints with His own Spirit those who are fit to partake of His holiness (ἁγιότητος)."

Surely the Holy Spirit does not paint the divine essence in us like a scene-painter, with Himself something other than it. It is not in this way that He brings us to God's likeness. Rather, being Himself God and proceeding from God, He is Himself impressed invisibly in the hearts of those who receive Him, like a seal in wax. Through communion and likeness to Himself He paints our nature completely to the archetypal beauty and makes man once again to God's image. How, then, will He be a creature, He through whom our nature is re-shaped to God, inasmuch as it is made partaker of God?[23]

This sanctification involves union with God. In fact, such union, such oneness, is impossible unless the Holy Spirit allows us to share in His own proper holiness. In the *Commentary on John*, for example, Cyril is stressing the fact that it was not exclusively for the disciples' sake that our Lord prayed His Father to send the Spirit. As all men bore the image of Adam when he fell, so all the justified express the image of Christ:

We say that the very ugly image of the earthy man is visible in certain pattern forms like the filth that is sin, the feebleness that is death and corruption, the impurity involved in fleshly lust and in a mind earth-bound. In like fashion, we think, the image of the heavenly man, Christ, is conspicuous in cleanness and purity, in total incorruption and life and sanctification (ἁγιασμῷ). But it would have been impossible for us to be restored to our original beauty, once we had fallen from it through the transgression in the first man, had we not achieved that inexpressible communion (κοινωνίας) and union (ἑνώσεως) with God; for that is the way in which man's nature was adorned in the beginning. But union with God is impossible of achievement for anyone save through participation (μετουσίας) in the Holy Spirit, instilling in us His own proper sanctification (ἁγιασμόν) and refashioning to His own life the nature that fell subject to corruption, and thus restoring to God and to God's semblance (μόρφωσιν) what had been deprived of this glory. For the perfect image of the Father is the Son, and the natural likeness of the Son is His Spirit. The Spirit, therefore, refashioning as it were to Himself the souls of men, engraves on them God's semblance (μόρφωσιν) and seals the representation (εἰκονισμόν) of the supreme essence.[24]

An aspect of the divine image is holiness; man's holiness is a share in the holiness which is a property of the Holy Spirit; by participation in the Spirit's holiness, oneness with God is realized. In point of fact, holiness *is* union with God. In a pregnant sentence, "Each of those who

[23] *Thesaurus* 34 (*PG* 75, 609–12).
[24] *In Ioannem* 11, 11 (Pusey 2, 730–31).

believe in Christ is made a temple of the Spirit, receiving within himself, so to say, the whole fount of sanctification."[25]

It is this "fount of sanctification," the Holy Spirit, who fashions us to God's image through holiness.[26] The role of the Spirit, Cyril makes clear, is indispensable. When our Lord asked the "holy Father" to keep the disciples "holy through thy truth" (Jn 17:17), He was referring to Himself, to the Word, "in whom and through whom the sanctifying (ἀγιάζον) Spirit proceeds. What was the Savior's purpose in speaking like this? He was calling sanctification (ἀγιασμόν) upon us from the Father, the sanctification that is in and through the Spirit. He wanted to rekindle in us what was in us at the time of our original formation, the beginning of God's creation."[27] Man's primeval fashioning included sanctification through the Spirit; else man could not have been molded to God's image. Man's refashioning is a like process, effected by participation (μετουσίας) in the Spirit, who is given to redeemed humanity by the Incarnate Word.[28] In point of fact, through sanctification we are formed to the Spirit as well as to the Son; and since the accurate likeness (ἐμφέρεια) of the Father is the Son, and the natural likeness (ὁμοίωσις) of the Son is the Spirit, in being formed to the Spirit "we are molded to the very life of God."[29] In Cyril's eyes, the sanctifying role of the Spirit is essential. There is no convincing evidence that Cyril considered it exclusive, that he attributed to the Spirit a personal function in sanctification which belongs only to the Spirit, to the exclusion of Father and Son.[30]

[25] *Homiliae paschales* 4, 5 (*PG* 77, 464–65). This union with God, this participation, involves an indwelling of God; cf., e.g., *Glaphyra in Genesim* 1 (*PG* 69, 29), and *passim* in Cyril.

[26] Cf. *In Isaiam* 1, 5 (*PG* 70, 236): the Son, Image and Likeness of the Father, sends into us the Holy Spirit, who seals us, refashions us to the original image through holiness. Cf. also *Scholia de incarnatione Unigeniti* 1 (*PG* 75, 1372).

[27] *In Ioannem* 11, 10 (Pusey 2, 719).

[28] Cf. *ibid.* (Pusey 2, 719–23).

[29] *De sancta et consubstantiali trinitate* dial. 7 (*PG* 75, 1089). It is difficult to turn εἰδοποιούμεθα with a single English word or phrase; the noun εἰδοποιία is the specific nature of a thing, and so Cyril may be indicating not simply an imaging of the *Father* through Son and Spirit, but specifically a resemblance to the divine nature as common to all three. Cf. *ibid.*: "We are refashioned so as to image the Holy Spirit, that is, so as to image God."

[30] On this point controversy has been acute since Petau concluded that for the Greek Fathers, Cyril in particular, the Holy Spirit is united to us substantially (οὐσιωδῶς), is in some fashion the formal cause of our adoption, and that therefore

This image of God which is holiness is resemblance and not equality. There is a striking difference between God's holiness and man's. Cyril observes that in His high-priestly prayer our Lord

does a splendid service in calling the Father "holy" (Jn 17:11): He all but reminds Him that, since He is holy, He takes delight in those who are holy. Now, everything is holy which is free of this world's defilement. And this is in Christ by His very nature, just as it is in the Father; but in the holy disciples it is something adventitious, introduced from the outside, by means of the sanctification (ἁγιασμοῦ) that comes by way of grace, and by means of splendid, virtuous living; for this is the manner in which one is fashioned to the divine, supramundane image.[31]

---

sanctification, though common to the one divine nature, belongs to the Holy Spirit by a special, personal title; cf. D. Petavius, *Dogmata theologica* 3 (Paris, 1865) 453–95. Mahé, *art. cit.*, p. 480, is convinced that, for Cyril, the work of sanctification is not so proper to the Spirit that it belongs to Him alone, to the exclusion of the other two Persons. He believes that it may be called proper to the Spirit in a certain sense, by a special title which is not true of Father and Son—for three reasons based on the Greek conception of the Trinity: (a) He is the *bond* of union which links our souls to Father and Son; (b) He is the *Image* of the Son; in impressing Himself on our souls, He refashions them to the image of the Son and consequently to the image of the Father; (c) He is the *sanctifying power* of the divinity; holiness is as essential to the Spirit as paternity is to the Father and filiation to the Son. P. Galtier found totally alien to the Greek Fathers, including Cyril, the conception attributed to them of an intervention of the Spirit in our souls which would belong to Him by a personal title and remain exclusively proper to Him; cf. *L'Habitation en nous des trois personnes: Le fait, Le mode* (Paris, 1928) p. 94. Du Manoir has found Galtier thoroughly convincing on Cyril; cf. *Dogme et spiritualité*, pp. 236–51. Cf., however, J. Sagüés, "El Espíritu Santo en la santificación del hombre según la doctrina de San Cirilo de Alejandría," *Estudios eclesiásticos* 21 (1947) 35–83: Although Cyril teaches that God's external activity proceeds from the one divine nature, and consequently is due equally to the three Persons as efficient cause, still he somehow conceives of distinct functions of the distinct Persons in man's sanctification. It is a "proper and personal function" of the Spirit to unite God and the soul; He brings us the restoring influence of the Father by deifying us in conforming us to the Son through divine filiation. Sanctification must be "from" the Father "through" the Son "in" the Spirit.

[31] *In Ioannem* 11, 9 (Pusey 2, 716). Cf. *De sancta et consubstantiali trinitate* dial. 6 (*PG* 75, 1016): because adventitious, our holiness can be lost; cf. also *ibid.*, dial. 7 (*PG* 75, 1089). Cf. *In epistolam 1 ad Corinthios* 1 (Pusey, *In Ioannem* 3, 326–27): Unlike Christ, who is image and likeness of the Father by nature, by essence, we are called to likeness (ὁμοιότητα) by participation in holiness (κατὰ μέθεξιν ἁγιασμοῦ); the Father, as it were, inscribes Himself on the nature of the Son, impresses Himself substantially. Cf. *De sancta et consubstantiali trinitate* dial. 6 (*PG* 75, 1009): "sanctification (ἁγιασμός) is proper to divinity"; the Spirit is holy

This last quotation introduces us to a concept of holiness not formally included in what has thus far been discussed. "Everything is holy which is free of this world's defilement"—a status which is achieved through "sanctification by way of grace" and through "virtuous living." That is why Cyril can, on another occasion, oppose holiness (ἀγιασμός) and moral uncleanness (ἀκαθαρσία), and insist that the two cannot coexist in the same individual.[32] It is in the same vein that he defines sanctification as "a rubbing away, a getting rid, of wickedness and sin."[33]

In other words, Cyril's theology of sanctification, his image which is holiness, embraces a dynamic aspect as well as an ontological. If one is to be holy, he remarks in connection with Jn 15:4, it is not enough to be received among the branches on the vine; what is needed above and beyond that is a genuine following of Christ "through perfect, unfailing love." This is the best way in which we can be welded to divinity; this is holiness.[34] God wants man's nature to become like (ἀφομοιοῦσθαι) Him through every kind of virtue; He wants us to be spiritually sealed to Him by holy living, and so to engrave His beauty on our souls.[35] "It is when we keep ourselves believing and holy (ἁγίους) that Christ is obviously formed in us, and His own features flash intelligibly in our minds."[36] Christ, the Renewer, "refashions us once more to His own image, so that the distinctive marks of His divine nature are conspicuous in us through sanctification and justice and the good life according to virtue. ... The beauty of this most excellent image shines forth in those of us

by nature, and it is He who sanctifies (ἀγιαστικόν) whatever in created nature is holy. For a summary of the difficult problem of our Lord's holiness as conceived by Cyril, cf. Mahé, art. cit., pp. 34–35. As God, Christ is holy by nature; as man, He is holy by participation; He receives the Spirit in His human nature, even though it is He Himself who effects the sanctification of His human nature by His own Spirit. It is His own Spirit He receives; He receives the Spirit as man; He gives the Spirit to Himself as God. Moreover, it is not for Himself that Christ receives the Spirit, but for us, to communicate Him to each of us.

[32] Cf. In Romanos, Rom 8:9–10 (Pusey, In Ioannem 3, 214); also De adoratione 2 (PG 68, 248).

[33] De sancta et consubstantiali trinitate dial. 6 (PG 75, 1016).

[34] Cf. In Ioannem 10, 2 (Pusey 2, 558); ibid. 5, 5 (Pusey 2, 81).

[35] Cf. Contra Iulianum 2 (PG 76, 593).

[36] De dogmatum solutione 3 (Pusey, In Ioannem 3, 557). Cf. the moving exhortation in Homiliae paschales 27, 3 (PG 77, 936) to express in our souls the innate goodness of God, to practice justice, self-control, mildness, humility, forbearance, absence of anger, because the beauty of virtue involves variety of virtues. Cf. also In Lucam hom. 79 (CSCO 70, 324; Lat. tr. 140, 224).

who are in Christ, as long as we have played the part of good men
through works themselves."[37] The desirable thing is to try to resemble
(ἀφομοιοῦσθαι) the all-holy God by good deeds and virtue.[38] In this connection Cyril links human holiness with the concept of dedication or
consecration. "Our life must be holy; for such was Christ's life. And if
we do choose to lead holy lives, we shall be enriched with His admirable
image; conformed to Him ... we shall really be a holy, acceptable of-
fering (ἀνάθεμα) to God the Father."[39] The basic fact seems to be this:
the divine essence is "the whole form (εἶδος) and beauty of virtue."[40]

In the concrete, Cyril finds it difficult to dissociate ἁγιασμός and ἀρετή,
the ontological and the dynamic, in his theology of the image. A fine
illustration of his tendency to blend the two is to be found in the tenth
of his Easter Homilies—not surprising in a letter destined for his flock.[41]
Sin, Cyril tells his Christians, has first been put to death in Christ;
now it is to be put to death in us. How? By making Christ at home in
our souls through participation in the Spirit, who conforms us to Christ
through sanctification and impresses the divine resemblance on us
through His own self, in order that the Father, seeing the features of
His Son conspicuous in us, may love us as His children. Briefly, the
impress of the divine essence is seen in our souls only if we are made
partakers of God's nature. But it is in deeds and in the power to act
virtuously that we discover within ourselves that "remodeling in sanctification" which leads to everything that is pleasing to God, casts all
weakness from our will, and creates an unyielding frame of mind—like
God, who yields to nothing and is inexpressibly vigorous in bringing
His will to successful issue.

[37] Responsiones ad Tiberium 8 (Pusey, In Ioannem 3, 590). When our Lord said
that the purpose of His Incarnation was to give life, to restore sanctification,
"more than abundantly" (cf. Jn 10:10), He meant that He would make men
"holy in act," "remarkable for good actions." This holiness κατ' ἐνέργειαν Cyril
contrasts curiously with Adam's δύναμις for all virtue without the ἐνέργεια.

[38] Cf. Contra Iulianum 4 (PG 76, 680); also In Ioannem 5, 5 (Pusey 2, 72, 81–82).
In subjection to sin we bear the image (εἰκών) of Adam; in victory over sin we bear
the form (μόρφωσις) of Christ; cf. In Ioannem 11, 2 (Pusey 2, 657).

[39] Glaphyra in Exodum 2 (PG 69, 437). Cf. In Lucam, Lk 6:36 (PG 72, 597): the
virtue of mercy "fashions us to God and produces in our souls as it were some
features of the supreme nature."

[40] Contra Iulianum 2 (PG 76, 592).

[41] This letter is to be dated 422; cf. the table in PG 77, 395–96. It must be remembered that the table is drawn up on the justifiable assumption that there is no
lacuna in the Easter Homilies, despite the fact that we have no homily numbered
3; therefore, what is traditionally known as Hom. 10 is correctly listed as 9 in
the table.

Therefore . . . it is the Spirit who makes us conformed to Christ, and it is through activated virtue that God's features gleam in us. . . . If, then, we hold it sweet and dear to bear the image so glorious of the Savior, and to be refashioned to that divine, celestial beauty, let us renounce this most unsightly stamp of sin; let us shun the spirit that is soft and an easy prey to the stubborn assaults of the devil. Let us play the man, after the manner of Christ, that we may be found partakers of His life. . . .[42]

Again, a brief synthesis is advisable. In this aspect of Cyril's image theology we seem to confront two distinct but complementary facets, one ontological, the other dynamic. The ontological is a share in God's own nature effected by participation in the Spirit, and is generally termed ἁγιασμός. The dynamic is a life lived in harmony with the exigencies of that participation, and is often termed ἀρετή. Each aspect—the ontological participation and the dynamic activity—is a reflection of the divine. We resemble God if we share His nature; we resemble God if we imitate His actions. Here, I suggest, is the key to the fuller interpretation of the sentence which we found fundamental earlier in this chapter: "We have been formed to God in the primary and most proper way in which it can be understood: according to virtue and sanctification (κατ' ἀρετὴν καὶ ἁγιασμόν); for the Deity is holy, and the fount, beginning, and origin of all virtue."[43]

It is intriguing to discover that an image of God formally denominated holiness does not play the same recognizable role among Cyril's predecessors, particularly those whose theological tradition is kin to his. It is not that sanctification is a matter of indifference to them; it is rather a difference in emphasis, and at times in sheer terminology. Irenaeus, for example, is unmistakably aware of a loftier, supernatural resemblance to God which is achieved when the soul receives the Spirit;[44] he knows that the Word Incarnate restored the "likeness," refashioning man so

[42] *Homiliae paschales* 10, 2–4 (*PG* 77, 617–25).

[43] *Responsiones ad Tiberium* 10 (Pusey, *In Ioannem* 3, 593); cf. *De recta fide, ad Theodosium* 20 (*ACO* 1, 1, 1, 55; *PG* 76, 1164): the image of Christ is "steadfastness in holiness (ἁγιασμόν)"; *Contra Iulianum* 6 (*PG* 76, 816): the temper of genuine holiness (ἁγνεία) includes care for all virtue, taking pains to excel in all that is best; cf. also *Homiliae paschales* 20, 3; 24, 1; 27, 2 (*PG* 77, 845, 885, 932). Cyril declares that we cannot come close to God by way of sanctification unless we have first removed all stain of sin and fleshly desires; cf. *ibid.* 26, 1 (*PG* 77, 916). In *Responsiones ad Tiberium* 14 (Pusey, *In Ioannem* 3, 599–600) Cyril states that angels as well as men—all rational creatures—are in God's image, "formed to God through sanctification (ἁγιασμοῦ) and justice and all virtue."

[44] Cf. Irenaeus, *Adversus haereses* 5, 6, 1 (Harvey 2, 334); *Demonstratio apostolicae praedicationis* 5 (*PO* 12, 663).

as to make him like the Father.[45] His accent, however, is not specifically on the sanctification involved; he stresses rather the "spirituality," incorruption, and immortality which Christ and the Spirit introduce.[46]

In this respect Clement of Alexandria represents an advance. His just and holy (ὅσιος) gnostic is an image (εἰκών) of God;[47] he is "divine and already holy (ἅγιος), God-bearing and God-borne."[48] It is the soul of a just man that is preeminently God's image (ἄγαλμα),[49] truly a holy (ἅγιον) altar.[50] Moreover, the gnostic is actually made sacred (καθιέρωται) in virtue of God's excess of holiness (ἁγιότης).[51] There is a sanctification (ἁγιασμός) of soul and body which is effected by reception of the Holy Spirit.[52] Nevertheless, in harmony with Clement's theology of progressive assimilation, in line with the destiny of the human image to realize in himself the divine likeness, he accentuates virtuous activity. The divine and holy ἄγαλμα is discoverable in the just soul when it is purified, when it performs blessed deeds,[53] when the Eternal Word is enshrined therein through obedience to the commandments.[54] The gnostic, who is after God's image and likeness, who imitates God as far as is humanly possible, lives righteously, rules over his passions, does good by word and deed.[55] If it is on reason, in the mind, that God stamps His likeness, He does it in so far as man does good.[56] To recapitulate the pedagogy of the Word:

As I see it, He Himself fashioned man from dust, regenerated him by water, made him grow by the Spirit, and educated him by word, guiding him to adoptive sonship and salvation by holy precepts, with this in view, that, refashioning the earthborn man into a holy (ἅγιον) and heavenly man by His coming, He might fulfil to perfection those words of God, "Let us make man to our image and to our likeness."[57]

[45] Cf. Irenaeus, Adversus haereses 5, 16, 1 (Harvey 2, 368); Demonstratio apostolicae praedicationis 97 (PO 12, 729).
[46] Cf. Irenaeus, Adversus haereses 4, 43, 2; 5, 1, 1; 5, 8, 1 (Harvey 2, 296, 314, 339).
[47] Cf. Clement of Alexandria, Stromata 6, 12 (GCS 15, 480).
[48] Ibid. 7, 13 (GCS 17, 58); cf. ibid. 7, 3 (GCS 17, 10).
[49] Cf. ibid. 7, 3 (GCS 17, 12).
[50] Cf. ibid. 7, 6 (GCS 17, 24).
[51] Cf. ibid. 7, 5 (GCS 17, 21).
[52] Cf. ibid. 4, 26 (GCS 15, 320).
[53] Cf. ibid. 7, 5 (GCS 17, 21-22).
[54] Cf. ibid. 7, 3 (GCS 17, 12).
[55] Cf. ibid. 2, 19 (GCS 15, 166).
[56] Cf. ibid. (GCS 15, 169); also ibid. 6, 12 (GCS 15, 484).
[57] Clement of Alexandria, Paedagogus 1, 12 (GCS 12, 148); cf. ibid. 1, 7 (GCS 12, 123): Jesus is our holy (ἅγιος) Teacher and God.

It would appear that Clement's distinction between image and likeness induces him to stress the dynamic in a Christian's imaging of the divine, while Cyril's refusal to discriminate makes him more conscious of the sublime dignity resident in the ontological. Whatever the reason, Cyril reveals a greater interest than Clement in the fact of participation and in the concept of sanctification.

In this matter Origen's approach is somewhat similar to Clement's. True, we do read that "the grace of the Holy Spirit is at hand, that those beings who are not holy by their essence may be made holy by participating in this grace."[58] But Origen's emphasis is on the dynamic, on the progressive acquisition of perfection:

> The fact that [Moses] said, "He made him to God's image," and said nothing about the likeness (Gn 1:27), points to nothing else but this: man did indeed receive the dignity of image in his first creation, but the perfection which is likeness was reserved for him at the consummation. The purpose was that he should acquire the latter for himself by his own sedulous efforts to imitate God. The possibility of perfection was given him in the beginning through the dignity of image; he was expected to achieve perfect likeness for himself at the end by the fulfilment of works.[59]

It is this basic principle, I believe, which underlies concrete applications such as this: "The Lord is just and holy (ὅσιος), merciful and compassionate. Therefore, he who loves justice and holiness (ὁσιότητα), and is careful to carry out what the Savior commanded, 'Be merciful, as your Father is merciful,' and 'Be perfect, as your heavenly Father is perfect,' becomes an image of God in every way."[60]

If the category of participation plays a conspicuous role in the totality of Athanasius' theology, it is rarely more in evidence than in his image doctrine.[61] The Word does not participate; creatures participate in Him.[62] To participate in the Word is to be κατ' εἰκόνα; they are equivalent expressions.[63] And κατ' εἰκόνα, as Bernard has pointed out, is

[58] Origen, De principiis 1, 3, 8 (GCS 22, 61); cf. the whole context on sanctification.

[59] Ibid. 3, 6, 1 (GCS 22, 280). For the process in detail, cf. the splendid treatment of Origen's ideal of perfection by W. Völker, Das Vollkommenheitsideal des Origenes (Tübingen, 1931); also H. Rahner, "Das Menschenbild des Origenes," Eranos-Jahrbuch 15 (1947) 197–248; Merki, op. cit., pp. 60–64. For Origen's conception of human participation in the divine, and its application to the divine image in man, cf. Crouzel, op. cit., pp. 160–79.

[60] Origen, Selecta in Genesim (PG 12, 96).

[61] Cf. Bernard, op. cit., pp. 32–38.

[62] Cf. Athanasius, Contra gentes 41 (PG 25, 84); ibid. 46 (PG 25, 93).

[63] Cf. Athanasius, De incarnatione Verbi 3 (PG 25, 101); ibid. 11 (PG 25, 116).

not mere resemblance, the reproduction of a form; it is ontological participation.[64] It is, in Athanasius' terse phrase, τὸ κατὰ θεὸν ζῆν; God communicates His own divine life.[65]

But the perspective in which Athanasius views participation, the configuration of his thought on the image, is not identical with Cyril's. There is similarity. Athanasius claims that participation in the Word confers on man a stability, ἀφθαρσία, ἀθανασία, which he does not possess of himself; and in virtue of this incorruptibility he is a being like God. This aspect of the image, as we shall see, finds a strong echo in Cyril. But Athanasius' approach to ἀφθαρσία, and to the divine image as a whole, is strikingly different from Cyril's. For Athanasius, to be κατ' εἰκόνα is to be κατὰ Λόγον; to be κατὰ Λόγον is to be λογικός; and to be λογικός is to be not simply rational in an Aristotelian-Scholastic sense, but contemplator of the divine.[66] Such was man in his primeval creation; such was every man's vocation; this was the destiny of our race:

God ... through His own Word, our Savior Jesus Christ, made the human race to His own image. Through the likeness it had to [the Word], He made it contemplate and know genuine realities. He gave it thought and knowledge of His own eternity. ... With no obstacle to impede his knowledge of the divine, he contemplates unceasingly through his purity the Father's Image, God the Word, to whose image he has been made. ... He is raised above the sensible, above every corporeal representation; he is linked by the power of his mind to the divine and suprasensible realities in heaven. For, when the mind of men keeps from communion with bodies, when it has no contact with the concupiscence which corporeal reality induces from without, but lives entirely alone and above, as it was made in the beginning, then, transcending the sensible and all things human, it is raised high above this world and, seeing the Word, it sees in Him as well the Father of the Word; it takes delight in the contemplation of Him; it is made new with its yearning for Him. ... The purity of the soul qualifies it to reflect God in itself as in a mirror. ...[67]

[64] Cf. Bernard, op. cit., p. 38.
[65] Cf. Athanasius, De incarnatione Verbi 5 (PG 25, 104).
[66] For the imprecisions of Athanasius' language and the fluctuations in his thought (including λογικός and the knowledge of God), cf. Bernard, op. cit., pp. 64-70.
[67] Athanasius, Contra gentes 2 (PG 25, 5-8). Th. Camelot has pointed out that this theology, though it can appeal to the Gospel (cf. Jn 14:9) as well as Genesis, rests on a Platonist philosophy whose language would for quite some time give Christian mysticism its most expressive formulas; but that these formulas had been sufficiently assimilated by Christian thought for Athanasius to use them without concern for their provenance; cf. Athanase d'Alexandrie: Contre les païens et Sur l'Incarnation du Verbe (Sources chrétiennes 18; Paris, 1946) p. 29.

Such, too, is man's destiny despite sin:

Just as they have turned from God in mind and have fashioned gods of non-existent things, so can they mount with the soul's mind and turn again to God. This conversion they can effect if they put off the filth of all the concupiscence they have put on, cleanse themselves until they have put away every accidental element foreign to the soul, reveal it only as it was made, so that in this way they can contemplate in it the Father's Word, after whom they were made in the beginning; for to the image and to the likeness of God was [the soul] made. . . . Consequently, when it puts from it all the sordidness of sin that has streamed over it, and keeps only the pure κατ' εἰκόνα, then, as is natural (for the κατ' εἰκόνα has been made brilliant), it contemplates therein, as in a mirror, the Word who is the Image of the Father, and in Him considers (λογίζεται) the Father whose Image the Savior is.[68]

In isolation, these texts present a perplexing mystique, a life of contemplation where faith, hope, and love are given no explicit place; a sort of heaven on earth, and all but static in its perfection.[69] In their context, and within the framework of Athanasius' theology, these texts are less startling and perhaps less significant, an apologetic preoccupation not destined to endure with him.[70] For our purposes, the passages are indicative of an approach to the image, to ἀφθαρσία, to holiness, substantially different from the perspectives of Cyril.[71]

[68] Athanasius, *Contra gentes* 34 (*PG* 25, 68–69). Bernard has indicated the Platonizing Alexandrian current which furnished Athanasius with the elements of his doctrine, while suggesting the religious, biblical, and Christian nuances; cf. *op. cit.*, pp. 74–79.

[69] Camelot, *op. cit.*, pp. 48–49, notes that this necessity of purification is a Platonist theme which Athanasius derived from Philo and the Alexandrian tradition. He concludes that "in our text there is no question of a knowledge in the supernatural order, not to say mystical, but simply of a purification of the soul which permits it, returning on itself, to perceive therein the Word, Image of the Father" (p. 50); precisely how this is achieved, Athanasius does not say. Bernard finds Athanasius much more difficult to interpret, perhaps even impossible; the expressions are excessive and seem to anticipate heaven; cf. *op. cit.*, pp. 79–81. As Bernard sees it (cf. p. 145), the knowledge in question is supernatural; I tend to agree.

[70] Cf. Bernard, *op. cit.*, pp. 79–83.

[71] It is regrettable that, whereas the preoccupations of the apologist kept Athanasius from a full development of his image doctrine in *Contra gentes* and *De incarnatione Verbi*, the Arian conflict concentrated his attention to such an extent on the theology of the Word that in his later works, though he dealt with adoption and grace, there is no studied link between these concepts and κατ' εἰκόνα. Cf. Bernard, *op. cit.*, pp. 145–46. Note the connection of likeness with holiness in *Contra Apollinarium* 1, 5 (*PG* 26, 1101–2).

A similar, perhaps more delicate problem arises if we search for anticipations of Cyril in Gregory of Nyssa. The peril lies in a simplistic rapprochement. In Gregory's theology, man "was made like God in all things."[72] As God's image he possesses in his finite way every excellence which is to be found in God. Implicitly, therefore, man is holy, somewhat as God is holy. True, Gregory sees no advantage in an exhaustive catalog of perfections; he is generally content with those qualities which are pertinent to a particular context—immortality, reason, freedom, individual virtues. Nevertheless, in view of his basic principle (man was made like God in every respect), man's holiness is a reflection of God's holiness.[73] There is, however, a fundamental divergence of approach in Gregory and Cyril. Cyril is relatively straightforward. He states flatly that the primary image and likeness is to be sought in sanctification; and the sanctification of his predilection is participation in God's nature, in the sanctifying Spirit, together with the godlike life of virtue which such a privilege entails. Gregory is far more nuanced, and his subtlety has been given synthetic expression by Leys in a paragraph remarkable for its insight:

This theme of the image is the soul of his admirable spiritual doctrine—a doctrine whose unity cannot be sufficiently underscored. The life of the mind (νοῦς) is to know God. And there is but one way to know Him, and that is to be like Him, to get to be in His image. To be sure, Gregory speaks also of "the ascent of the soul towards God by the ladder of creatures"; but he has little liking for this, perhaps because of its affinity with that knowledge of God (scarcely unitive) which even the wise of this world can achieve. Rather, the knowledge of God to which he gives preference in his thinking is that of participation in His virtues, in His holiness—that knowledge which is essentially union. The gaze of purity, of goodness, of rectitude, is undoubtedly a gaze "on" God, but primarily it is the gaze "of" God which communicates His divine presence to us. And how participate in that holiness of God? By following Him through faith, eyes closed, wherever He leads; by opening one's heart always to a further and deeper submissiveness; by divesting oneself of every favor already received through unceasing yearning for what is always beyond; in a word, by the ecstasy which is a going out of oneself. The image of God is not, therefore, static reality but continual growth; and far from being an object of clear vision, it keeps sinking deeper into God's unknown. No, "the mirror and the cloud" are not, as G. Horn believed, "two methods of knowing God in Gregory of Nyssa." They form but one: the image is holiness, and holiness is ecstasy, in the night.[74]

---

[72] Gregory of Nyssa, *Oratio catechetica magna* 5 (*PG* 45, 24).

[73] Cf. Muckle, *art. cit.*, pp. 60–70; Leys, *op. cit.*, pp. 67–78.

[74] Leys, *op. cit.*, pp. 139–40.

It should be obvious that, despite inevitable affinities in their theology of holiness, Gregory's orientation is not Cyril's. They are divided by all the difference between mystical theology and speculative, or, perhaps better, between the mystic and the theologian. And though the ways of the one are not inimical to the ways of the other, in Gregory and Cyril they do not meet.[75]

A summary is expedient. For Cyril, man's resemblance to the divine, in its most proper sense, is a matter of sanctification (ἁγιασμός). At times the image actually is denominated ἁγιασμός; at times the image is effected through ἁγιασμός.[76] In some passages ἁγιασμός is apparently a process; in other passages it is obviously a state. With reference to man and his destiny, ἁγιασμός has two prime facets. One facet is ontological, man's participation in God's nature, whereby the Holy Spirit, by a communication of Himself, fashions man to the Son whose Spirit He is, and so to the Father whose Image the Son is. To share God's nature *is* holiness; and to share God's nature, to be holy, is to be like God. The other facet is dynamic, man's conscious imitation of God through virtue. Briefly, man is holy, and he lives holily. It is (a) his emphasis on ontological holiness, (b) his unmistakable identification of ontological holiness with the image of God in man, and (c) his insistence that in holiness lies man's most significant resemblance to God—this it is that distinguishes Cyril from his Alexandrian predecessors. It is a question of stress, yes; but the difference in stress is striking.

[75] It should be observed that Gregory, like Cyril and the Alexandrians in general, insists on the necessity of purification (κάθαρσις) if God's image is to be realized in the soul; cf. J. Daniélou, *Platonisme et théologie mystique: Essai sur la doctrine spirituelle de saint Grégoire de Nysse* (Paris, 1944) pp. 17–123.

[76] I do not consider the fluctuation significant; cf. note 8 above.

# CHAPTER 7

# INCORRUPTIBILITY

In his *Replies to Tiberius* Cyril insisted that the primary and most proper way in which man images God is by sanctification and virtue.[1] In the *Commentary on John* he apparently assigns the same primacy to another aspect of God's image in man:

So then, this rational animal upon the earth, I mean man, was made in the beginning "to the image of the Creator," as Scripture has it (Col 3:10). Now, the idea of the image is a varied one; for there is not just one way of being an image; there are many. Nevertheless, the part of the likeness (ἐμφερείας) to God the Creator which is most remarkable (διαφανέστατον) is incorruptibility and imperishability (τὸ ἄφθαρτον καὶ ἀνώλεθρον). But I do not think that the [rational] animal was ever sufficient of itself, by reason of its own nature, to achieve that state of things; for how would the man from the earth have been able to boast of incorruptibility (ἀφθαρσίας) in his own nature, and not have received this blessing, like all the rest, from the God who is incorruptible and imperishable by nature? For "what do you have that you have not received?" (1 Cor 4:7). ... And so, in order that what had been brought into being from nonbeing might not return to its own origin and go back to nothingness, that it might rather be preserved perpetually—for this was the Creator's purpose—God made him partaker (μέτοχον) of His own nature; for "He breathed into his face the breath of life" (Gn 2:7), that is, the Spirit of the Son; for He is Himself Life with the Father; He holds all things in being. In Him, you see, the beings that are capable of life move and live, as Paul says (cf. Acts 17:28).[2]

Adam, therefore, was naturally corruptible; his nature, if left to itself, was perishable. It had come from nothingness; it would return to nothingness. To prevent this, God let man share in a divine prerogative, incorruptibility, by letting him share in the divine nature. Man's incorruptibility is an image of God's; that much is clear. Nevertheless, the significant problems remain. What is Cyril's concept of incorruptibility? To what extent is incorruptibility alien to man's nature? In what sense is human incorruptibility a reflection of God's? A satisfying synthesis

---

[1] Cf. *Responsiones ad Tiberium* 10 (Pusey, *In Ioannem* 3, 593).

[2] *In Ioannem* 9, 1 (Pusey 2, 484). It is possible that διαφανέστατον means "most conspicuous" rather than "most remarkable." Cf. also *In Hebraeos*, Heb 1:9 (Pusey, *In Ioannem* 3, 376): God "made man to His own image and likeness, superior to corruption (φθορᾶς), a practitioner of justice."

of ἀφθαρσία in Cyril demands a preliminary analysis of several aspects of his anthropology and an insight into his soteriology and eschatology.

Man is essentially mortal (θνητός); mortality belongs to Cyril's concept of man; it is usually included, with rationality, in the definition of man's essence.[3] What is mortality, this subjection to death? It is the departure of the human soul from the body.[4] It is a "common end" which is only "human."[5] Man dies because he is a man and has a body from the earth.[6] Bodily death is a law of nature, of man's nature.[7] More fundamentally still, man is mortal because he is a creature, because he is brought into being from nonbeing.[8]

For the same reasons man is corruptible (φθαρτός). He is corruptible "because of the nature of the flesh," somewhat as water is cold by its nature.[9] "This perishable body from the earth" is "rottenness and a worm and nothing else."[10] In the last analysis, everything created is subject to change; subject to change, it is subject to corruption. The power of God may preserve it from actual corruption, but by reason of creation itself the creature is corruptible.[11]

Man as a whole, therefore, is mortal and corruptible: soul will leave body, and body will dissolve—ultimately because man is a creature. Does this argumentation imply that the essential part of the human composite which we call man's soul is itself naturally mortal and corruptible? The question, as phrased, cannot be answered with a simple yes or no. There is one sense in which, for Cyril, the soul is indisputably mortal and corruptible by nature; I mean, where "natural" is equivalent to "not received." In this sense God alone is naturally immortal

[3] Cf. *In Ioannem* 6 (Pusey 2, 128).

[4] Cf. *ibid.* 7, fragmenta (Pusey 2, 268–69); also *In Lucam* hom. 112 (*PG* 72, 828): death is "freedom from the body"; *In Abacuc* 2 (Pusey 2, 125): death consists "in a putting aside, a casting off, of the soul."

[5] *In Ioannem* 4, 2 (Pusey 1, 516).

[6] Cf. *ibid.* 6 (Pusey 2, 120); also *ibid.* (Pusey 2, 123): Abraham and the prophets died "because they were earthborn of mortal parents."

[7] Cf. *ibid.* (Pusey 2, 118); also *ibid.* 10, 1 (Pusey 2, 527–28).

[8] Cf. *ibid.* 6 (Pusey 2, 130).

[9] *Ibid.* 4, 2 (Pusey 1, 531); cf. *ibid.* 9, 1 (Pusey 2, 480, 486, 487); *ibid.* 12 (Pusey 3, 107): corruptibility is one of "our nature's laws." Even Christ's flesh is spoken of as "naturally corruptible," superior to corruption and death only because of its union with the Word; cf. *Glaphyra in Exodum* 1 (*PG* 69, 413); *In Ioannem* 4, 3 (Pusey 1, 550).

[10] *In Ioannem* 5, 4 (Pusey 2, 25).

[11] Cf. *ibid.* 5, 5 (Pusey 2, 68–69); also *ibid.* 1, 6 (Pusey 1, 75); *ibid.* 6 (Pusey 2, 124, 133); also *Contra Iulianum* 6 (*PG* 76, 800): everything brought into existence in time is subject to corruption by the very laws resident in its nature.

(ἀθάνατος), properly immortal, because He alone does not receive immortality, immutability, as a gift. Even an angel is naturally mortal in this sense, because even an angel is immortal only by the will and favor of its Creator.[12] Similarly, in this sense God alone is naturally incorruptible (ἄφθαρτος, ἀνώλεθρος), properly incorruptible; for no being but God is "sufficient of itself, by reason of its own nature, to achieve that state of things"; everyone save God receives this blessing from another.[13] In this sense, we must conclude, the soul itself is mortal and corruptible; for a created nature has nothing of itself; it has everything from its Creator.[14] Whatever blessings, whatever possessions we have, these are "entirely God-given, and the nature neither of men nor of the holy angels is adorned by its own benefits; for together with existence each existing thing has from God its nature as well." There is nothing essentially in creatures which is not a gift (δῶρον) from a prodigal God; it has its root in His free giving (χάρις).[15] Here Cyril's guiding principle is, "What do you have that you have not received?" (1 Cor 4:7).[16]

And yet, the soul is immortal.[17] But is the soul's immortality natural to it in the sense that it is a property inseparable from it? It must be conceded that on occasion Cyril attributes the soul's immortality to a positive disposition on God's part. Thus, he tells us of a

true doctrine (δόγμα), which we believe and the churches value; I mean, the fixed idea that the rational soul of man is immortal (ἀθάνατον); that death does not corrupt the soul together with (συγκαταφθείρει) the bodies of earth; that, on the contrary, the Maker releases it, lets it go free, withdraws it from the experience of death, making it share in life. The fact is, man was made in the beginning into a living soul, when God inspired in him the breath of life; for so it is written. In my opinion, you see, we shall be ascribing feebleness to the Life that endues all things with life, if we say that what was made by Life for life perishes together

---

[12] Cf. *Thesaurus* 20 (*PG* 75, 345); also *De sancta et consubstantiali trinitate* dial˙ 7 (*PG* 75, 1116): God alone has immortality "of Himself (οἴκοθεν) and in His own nature"; *In Ioannem* 1, 9 (Pusey 1, 138): only God has incorruptibility οὐσιωδῶς. Note that, for Cyril, the angels "are in incorruptible and indestructible bodies"; *In epistolam 2 ad Corinthios* 3, 2 (Pusey, *In Ioannem* 3, 349).

[13] *In Ioannem* 9, 1 (Pusey 2, 484); cf. *ibid.* 1, 9 (Pusey 1, 138); also *De sancta et consubstantiali trinitate* dial. 7 (*PG* 75, 1081): incorruptibility is proper to the divine nature.

[14] Cf. *In Ioannem* 1, 7 (Pusey 1, 88). It is in this sense that we must interpret the statement that "nothing besides [God] is incorruptible and indestructible"; *In Hebraeos*, Heb 1:10 ff. (Pusey, *In Ioannem* 3, 381).

[15] *In Ioannem* 1, 9 (Pusey 1, 110).

[16] Cf. *ibid.* 1, 7 (Pusey 1, 88).

[17] Cf. *Adversus Nestorii blasphemias* 5, 7 (*ACO* 1, 1, 6, 105; *PG* 76, 244).

with the bodies that are transient. On the other hand, we shall crown Life with intelligence (συνέσει), if we believe that the soul is immortal, since the Maker of the universe, in whom we live and move and are, thinks it good that it be so.[18]

It must be remembered, however, that a natural immortality of the soul is not incompatible with a positive ordinance of God. In fact, the former is genuinely dependent on the latter, in Cyril's system and in any acceptable psychology. At any given moment it can be said that life is a gift,[19] even if the soul has within itself no principle of corruption. Of itself, therefore, the text just quoted does not weigh either for or against the soul's natural immortality.

This same tendency to regard the soul's immortality not from a negative, deistic standpoint, but positively, from the perspective of God's activity on and within the soul, is perhaps the key to another pertinent passage. Cyril relates that in consequence of Adam's transgression the Spirit of Him who is Life departed, and man descended to death; but it was "death of the flesh alone, the soul being preserved in immortality (ἀθανασίᾳ)," because it was only at the flesh that Gn 3:19 was leveled.[20] It is significant, of course, for Cyril's thought, that the soul remains immortal despite the departure of the Holy Spirit; for this deprivation argues that it was not the indwelling of the Spirit that conferred immortality on the soul in its original creation. It may be even more significant that Cyril calls attention explicitly to the soul's preservation in immortality after Adam's sin, whereas the Scholastic theologian would tend to take it for granted. Cyril is not implying that the human soul is naturally mortal; he does not imply an extraordinary activity on God's part to save the soul from the fate of the body; he does seem to suggest that, as the flesh lost its incorruptibility when the Spirit ceased to dwell in man, in similar fashion the soul would have lost its immortality if God had ceased to preserve it. How it could have been lost, how it was preserved, Cyril does not say.

Immortality as an innate prerogative of the soul emerges with clarity from those passages where a contrast is introduced between the soul and a body characterized as τὸ φθείρεσθαι πεφυκός, "naturally corruptible." Thus, in a striking sentence whose purpose is to demonstrate that Christ had to rise with the body that had died, Cyril asserts that victory over death and corruption could not have been achieved unless that precise element rose from the dead which is "naturally corruptible,"

[18] *De adoratione* 10 (*PG* 68, 697).
[19] Cf. *In Ioannem* 1, 7 (Pusey 1, 80–81).
[20] Cf. *ibid.* 1, 9 (Pusey 1, 138–39).

the flesh; not, therefore, through the death and resurrection of a soul, or an angel, or even the sheer Word of God.[21] The conclusion seems inescapable: unlike the body, the soul does not have within itself the seeds of its own destruction. Immortality is a gift, yes; once given, however, it is natural to man; it is an essential element in the soul's make-up.[22]

How, concretely, does man escape corruption, defeat death? How does he keep alive, even for an instant? What prevents him from returning to the nothingness from which he sprang? In its most general formulation Cyril's answer is this: by some sort of participation in the nature that is incorruptible, in the Word who is the expression of the Father's fulness of life.[23] It is basically the insight of St. John, that the life of creatures is the Word (cf. Jn 1:3–4):

[The Word] not only gives to the creature its existence; once it has come to exist, through Himself He keeps it from falling apart, mingling Himself, so to speak, with those beings which do not have perpetuity by their own nature, and becoming life for those beings which exist, in order that they may abide in existence when once made, and be preserved each according to the measure of its own nature. That is why [John] says of necessity, "Whatever was made, in it was Life." He says not merely, "Through Him all things were made," but also, "If anything has been made, in it was the Life," that is, the only-begotten Word of God, the origin of all things and their principle of consistency (σύστασις), things visible and invisible, in heaven, on earth, and beneath the earth. The reason is this: since He is Himself Life by nature, He bestows being, life, and movement on existing beings in varied ways. It is not that He spreads Himself among all the naturally different creatures by some sort of division and alteration; rather, creation in its own self is diversified by the inexpressible power and wisdom of its Maker. All things have the one Life, which comes to each as befits it and according to its capacity to participate (μετασχεῖν). . . .[24]

Here we confront, as Weigl has pointed out, a natural participation in the Logos which looks to the creature's continuation in existence on a natural niveau. It is the presence of the Logos in creatures, to give them being and life, and to sustain them in being and life.[25] Although Cyril's ideas are reminiscent of the Stoic λόγος σπερματικός and perhaps the Logos of Philo, they have been thoroughly Christianized. He rejects

[21] Cf. *ibid.* 12, 1 (Pusey 3, 128); also *ibid.* 10, 2 (Pusey 2, 542).

[22] E. Weigl has come to essentially the same conclusion; cf. *Die Heilslehre des hl. Cyrill von Alexandrien* (Mainz, 1905) pp. 32–33.

[23] Cf. *ibid.*, p. 17.

[24] *In Ioannem* 1, 6 (Pusey 1, 74–75).

[25] Cf. *ibid.* 1, 7 (Pusey 1, 80).

any explanation of participation which involves pantheism or emanationism; he repudiates specifically a Stoic ramification of the Logos. The Logos is not divided, not changed; the creature itself leads an autonomous existence in the power of the one Demiurge.[26]

So then, the creature exists and owns a certain duration; man lives and continues in life. But this is participation on a relatively low level.[27] Cyril speaks of a richer participation in God's life, which involves a larger measure of incorruptibility. It is the consequence of a share in the Spirit of the Logos, a participation which raises man above his own nature and its exigencies. This extraordinary ἀφθαρσία was first given to Adam. In the *Commentary on John*, for example, Cyril reminds us that man, a composite being fashioned of soul and a perishable body, does not possess incorruptibility and indestructibility (τό τε ἄφθαρτον καὶ ἀνώλεθρον) of his own nature; only God is incorruptible and indestructible of His very essence (οὐσιωδῶς). So God sealed man with the Holy Spirit, the Spirit of life, and in this relationship to the divine, man acquired a blessing "above his nature."[28] And the restoration of this ἀφθαρσία is intimately intertwined with the Incarnation of God's Son:

for the nature that lay subject to corruption (φθορᾷ) could not spring up to incorruptibility (ἀφθαρσίαν) unless the nature that was superior to all corruption and change had come down to it, in some fashion elevating the ever-fallen to His own prerogative (τὸ ἴδιον ἀγαθόν), and by communion and mingling with itself [i.e., the divine nature] all but withdrawing it from the limits proper to created nature, and refashioning to [the divine nature] what was not so of itself.[29]

This supernatural participation, as Weigl saw, builds harmoniously upon the natural:

What we have here, properly speaking, are three specifically different, superposed categories. There is the category of the sheer creature; it is pure potency, its essence is finiteness and nonentity. To this is joined the revelation and communication of God in the creation of the creature. Nonentity enters into natural actuality. A step higher lies the second revelation and communication. All three categories interlock and, where they exist, form a unity. From a purely theo-

[26] Cf. Weigl, *op. cit.*, pp. 18–19.
[27] Cf. *In Ioannem* 1, 6 (Pusey 1, 75) for the increased perpetuation of a creature by propagation of species.
[28] *Ibid.* 1, 9 (Pusey 1, 138).
[29] *Ibid.* 11, 12 (Pusey 3, 3). Cf. *Homiliae paschales* 10, 1 (*PG* 77, 609) for a strikingly similar passage, where instead of "the nature that lay subject to corruption" Cyril speaks of τὸ φθείρεσθαι πεφυκός.

logical point of view, the latter revelation and communication appears as a supernatural one, in contrast to the initial revelation and communication which underlies it. This underlying category presents itself from this standpoint as natural, although in another direction it is itself a grace. As often as Cyril speaks of participation in the Logos, what he regularly has in view is primarily the supernatural—just as in general the whole development of his theological doctrine deals with the supernatural relations of God with the creature, man more particularly, in whom the spiritual and material world is concentrated. . . .[30]

A summary at this point may help. Man, as Cyril sees him, is a fascinating blend of the mortal and immortal, the corruptible and incorruptible. (a) If we regard man as a human being and nothing more, his body will necessarily be abandoned by the soul and will dissolve; for dissolution is innate in flesh. Man, the composite, is mortal and corruptible. Human life must end. (b) The soul's status is paradoxical. In one sense it is naturally impermanent: since it is a creature, whatever permanence it has is a free gift of God. In another sense it is naturally permanent: God has freely elected to root permanence in the soul's constitution, in its very texture. The soul's life cannot end. (c) The transitory life of the flesh and the endless life of the soul are each the consequence of a participation in God's nature, specifically in the Word who is Life. Since this participation does not lift man above the level of the human, it can be denominated natural. (d) In an excess of graciousness God gave to Adam, and through Christ has given to us, a richer participation in His life, in His incorruptibility, a sharing in the Spirit of life which constitutes a divinization of the human. It is this ἀθανασία, this ἀφθαρσία, which remains to be analyzed. The task is imperative, because here we touch the core of the resemblance to God which is incorruptibility; but the task is difficult indeed, because Cyril's concept is complex and his expression is confusing.

It seems advisable to approach this aspect of ἀφθαρσία from the standpoint of redeemed human nature, for two reasons: (a) this is the approach which Cyril prefers, and (b) the condition of Adam will emerge with sufficient clarity from such a methodology. From this viewpoint I submit that the image of God which Cyril finds in ἀφθαρσία stresses the incorruptibility of the body; that it concerns the body's continuation in

---

[30] Weigl, op. cit., pp. 20-21. Weigl indicates how Cyril's scriptural basis (consortium divinae naturae, communicatio Spiritus sancti, etc.) divides his thought radically from Platonist participation in subsisting ideas, and from a Philonic prototype-copy system; cf. ibid., pp. 21-22. He recognizes, however, that Alexandrian philosophy, especially Logosophy, may well have been divinely destined to play the role of praeparatio evangelica.

existence for eternity; but that there is a fuller, richer concept of incorruptibility for which the notion of mere duration in existence is little more than an indispensable foundation.

The first broad proposition: Cyril emphasizes the body's incorruptibility rather than the soul's. It would be tedious and pointless to document this statement mathematically. Persuasive enough for our purpose is Cyril's expression of the methodology of the Incarnation as far as ἀφθαρσία is concerned. Man, this composite being of soul and perishable body, was originally gifted with incorruptibility beyond the exigencies of his nature. With the advent of sin the Spirit departed, and man became subject once more to death—but "death of the flesh alone, the soul being preserved in immortality (ἀθανασίᾳ), because it was to the flesh alone that it was said, 'Earth thou art and into earth shalt thou return' (Gn 3:19). Therefore, that in us which was especially in danger had to be rescued the sooner, and by being intertwined with Life-by-nature be recalled to incorruptibility (ἀφθαρσίαν)." That is why the body which had fallen was united to the life-giving Word, and flesh partook of immortality.[31]

The second broad proposition: Cyril sees in this corporal incorruptibility the body's continuation in existence for eternity, its immunity from death and dissolution. Admittedly, the exact meaning of ἀφθαρσία is not always clear;[32] but there are many instances where φθορά is best interpreted as physical death and bodily dissolution, while ἀφθαρσία is man's victory over both. In this sense of the word, Cyril maintains that the entire human race, no man excepted, was refashioned in Christ to ἀφθαρσία, just as in Adam's transgression the whole race was condemned to φθορά.[33] But two important distinctions must be remembered. The first is the distinction between hope and realization, between promise and fulfilment, between first fruits and final harvest. Incorruptibility has indeed been communicated to redeemed humanity; in fact, it was

[31] *In Ioannem* 1, 9 (Pusey 1, 138–39). On Adam, cf. *Contra Iulianum* 3 (*PG* 76, 637): his body, before sin, was superior to death and corruption, because God so willed it "and the nature of things follows His will."
[32] Cf., e.g., *Thesaurus* 15 (*PG* 75, 281–84).
[33] Cf. *In Ioannem* 6, 1 (Pusey 2, 220–21); also *Homiliae paschales* 27, 4 (*PG* 77, 940–41): as the whole race died in Adam, so did we come alive in Christ; He refashioned human nature in Himself to ἀφθαρσία and immortal life. Cf. *De adoratione* 9 (*PG* 68, 617); *In Ioannem* 11, 2 (Pusey 2, 657); *In Romanos*, Rom 5:11 (Pusey, *In Ioannem* 3, 182); *Thesaurus* 25 (*PG* 75, 405); *Epistolae* 1, 26 (*ACO* 1, 1, 1, 23; *PG* 77, 37).

communicated to man in the Incarnation. Victory over corruption was given initially to flesh when God's Son took flesh:

Since the Word of God is Life by nature, He made what was naturally corruptible His own body, in order to transform it to incorruptibility by disabling the power of deadness (νεκρότητος) within it; for, just as iron, when vigorous fire is applied to it, changes its color so as to assume immediately the form of the fire, and gives birth to the power of the prevailing fire, so the nature of the flesh, having welcomed within it the incorruptible and life-giving Word of God, remained no longer in the same condition but became thereafter superior to corruption.[34]

And the victory was communicated at that moment to human nature as a whole:

So then, in order to free from corruption and death the man who had been condemned through that ancient curse, He became man, inserting Himself as it were in our nature, He who is Life by nature; for it was in this way that the domination of death was defeated and the power of the adventitious corruption in us was destroyed; and, inasmuch as the divine nature is absolutely free from inclination to sin, He bore us through His own flesh—in Him, you see, all of us were, in so far as He became man—in order to put to death the "members which are on earth" (Col 3:5), that is, the passions of the flesh, and nullify the law of sin that tyrannizes in our members. . . .[35]

Incorruptibility is achieved likewise through the Eucharist. If we partake of it, we come to share in the divine nature; we are restored "to incorruptibility and life," to our primeval state.[36] Moreover, in His own resurrection the Incarnate Word raised human nature with Him[37]—the

[34] *Homiliae paschales* 17, 4 (*PG* 77, 785–88).

[35] *In Ioannem* 10, 2 (Pusey 2, 618); cf. *ibid.* 5, 2 (Pusey 1, 692–93): Christ had our whole nature, all humanity, in Himself in the Incarnation, to restore it to its primitive condition. It is the opinion of Gross that Cyril, Athanasius, and Gregory of Nyssa are the most brilliant representatives of "the physical concept of divinization"; *op. cit.*, p. 284. But he admits—and rightly—that, for Cyril, the Incarnation would have been useless without the death of Christ; cf. *ibid.*, p. 285. He recognizes that Cyril's recourse, now to the Incarnation, now to the passion, to explain our deification, is done according to the needs of the moment, with no attempt to reconcile the two points of view. In the next chapter we shall deal more intimately with Cyril's concept of the inclusion of all men in Christ.

[36] Cf. *In Ioannem* 3, 6 (Pusey 1, 479); also the long passage *ibid.* 4, 2 (Pusey 1, 529–32); *Adversus Nestorii blasphemias* 4, 5 (*ACO* 1, 1, 6, 87; *PG* 76, 197). For Cyril's conception of the vivifying power of the Eucharist, cf. du Manoir, *Dogme et spiritualité*, pp. 185–95; Weigl, *op. cit.*, pp. 203–20.

[37] Cf. *In Ioannem* 6, 1 (Pusey 2, 233). Cf. *ibid.* 12 (Pusey 3, 106): The "new tomb" (Jn 19:41) in which Christ was laid signifies something more profound than an

whole of human nature; for resurrection is "common to saints and sinners."[38]

The flowering of this seed, however, the full realization of our hope, the fulfilment of the promise, is reserved for the consummation of the world. It is a distinction which Cyril indicates often enough. He does so, for example, when he resolves the problem, whether image and likeness are identical concepts or, as some claimed, the image was received concurrently with creation, while the likeness is delayed till the world to come. Cyril defends the identity of image and likeness; he insists that we possess both image and likeness now; and yet he confesses that there is an aspect of our resemblance to divinity whose actualization has been temporarily withheld. We *shall* be like Christ in incorruptibility and in superiority to death, as evidenced by Col 3:3–4 and Phil 3:21.[39]

The second distinction has been tersely phrased by Cyril: all the dead will rise in ἀφθαρσία, but not all will rise in δόξα.[40] The universal resurrection has for its basis a physical relationship, a physical oneness, with the Incarnate Word, who in His own resurrection raised all men with Him; the glorious resurrection is grounded in a mystical relationship,

---

unused vault; it symbolizes something new, a return from death to life, the innovation contrived by Christ against φθορά. The death which had been king from Adam's time was changed into a sleep. By His death Christ bought life for us; by coming to life again He destroyed the power of corruption. In consequence, "we have been transformed into His image; we undergo a new kind of death, which does not dissolve us in endless corruption but injects a sleep full of good hope, quite obviously in the likeness of Him who inaugurated this way for us, that is, Christ." Here incorruption is life in hope.

[38] *Ibid.* 6, 1 (Pusey 2, 220).

[39] Cf. *De dogmatum solutione* 3 (Pusey, *In Ioannem* 3, 555–57). In interpreting 2 Cor 3:18, Cyril distinguishes the divine glory which we possess here and the glory reserved for the hereafter; we image God now, we "are most assuredly in glory," if we have come to know Christ and are counted among His children, but at the time of the resurrection Christ, who has already given us the Spirit as a pledge, "will add what is wanting," will conform our bodies to His own glorified body; cf. *In epistolam 2 ad Corinthios* 2, 1 (Pusey, *In Ioannem* 3, 339); cf. *ibid.* 3, 2 (Pusey, *In Ioannem* 3, 351). See also *In Romanos*, Rom 8:24 (Pusey, *In Ioannem* 3, 218): the superiority of our bodies to corruption and death is a gift "laid up for us in hope"; cf. also *Homiliae diversae* 9 (*PG* 77, 1013); *Homiliae paschales* 25, 3 (*PG* 77, 912); *ibid.* 24, 4 (*PG* 77, 900); *De adoratione* 17 (*PG* 68, 1116–17); *In Ioannem* 9, 1 (Pusey 2, 474–75, 480); *ibid.* 10, 2 (Pusey 2, 571). True, these passages refer explicitly to the glorious resurrection, but they are applicable to the universal resurrection as far as the basic fact of resurrection is concerned.

[40] Cf. *In epistolam 1 ad Corinthios* 7 (Pusey, *In Ioannem* 3, 309); this statement is made by Cyril on the basis of 1 Cor 15:42–43.

a mystical oneness, with Christ, because some have "become conformed
to the image of [God's] Son" (Rom 8:29):

... it is not to all indiscriminately that the favor (χάρις) of honor and glory
such as this will be proposed. On the contrary, it is a question of selection; it
befits those who have been chosen in preference to others, who have "become
conformed to the image of His Son." The bodies of all, we admit, will come to
life again, completely clothed with the gift of incorruptibility (τῇ τῆς ἀφθαρσίας
χάριτι), "but not all will be changed" (1 Cor 15:51). The wicked will continue
in their dishonorable form, for one purpose: punishment. The just alone will be
changed so as to have the blessing of incorruptibility (τῷ τῆς ἀφθαρσίας ἀγαθῷ),
richly garbed in God's glory. Therefore, by His personal power and by an
operation that befits God He will Himself "refashion the body of our lowliness,
conforming it to the body of His glory" (Phil 3:21). What sort of body is the
body of our lowliness? It is this body from earth, held fast by death in consequence of that ancient curse which Christ destroyed, "becoming a curse for us"
(Gal 3:13). Our transformation will not be a transfer into some other nature—
for we shall be what we are, that is, men—but we shall be incomparably better.
The point is, we shall be incorruptible and imperishable (ἄφθαρτοι καὶ ἀνώλεθροι),
and besides this we shall have been glorified. . . .[41]

In his conception of incorruptibility, therefore, Cyril distinguishes a
universal ἀφθαρσία, the resurrection of the flesh, which is itself a gift
(χάρις) of God, and a selective ἀφθαρσία, the glorification of the flesh,
which is a blessing (ἀγαθόν) of God. It is in understanding the implications of this blessing, the difference between "the body of our lowliness"
and "the body of His glory," that we shall achieve some insight into
our third broad proposition: Cyril has a richer, fuller concept of incorruptibility for which the notion of mere duration in existence is little
more than an indispensable foundation.

In point of fact, the heart of this matter is our contention that, for
Cyril, the more profound significance of φθορά and ἀφθαρσία lies in their
moral implications. Cyril suggests as much in many different ways.
First, in his theology corruption implies not the naked fact of death,
but death as dominating, "tyrannizing savagely over us."[42] Second, he
states flatly that "death, properly so called, is not the death which

[41] *Ibid.* (Pusey, *In Ioannem* 3, 316–17). It is apparently with reference to the
latter form of incorruption that Cyril finds ἀφθαρσία inseparably linked to participation in the Spirit, and asserts that, if we are to escape corruption, adoptive
sonship is necessary; cf. *In Ioannem* 12, 1 (Pusey 3, 134–36); *ibid.* 1, 9 (Pusey 1, 133).
It may be noted that the expression, "mystical relationship," is applied even to
the kinship of man with God realized in the Incarnation; cf. *In Ioannem* 7, fragmenta (Pusey 2, 252).
[42] *In epistolam 1 ad Corinthios* 7 (Pusey, *In Ioannem* 3, 315).

separates the soul from the body, but the death which separates the soul from God. God is Life, and he who is separated from the Life is dead. . . ."[43] Third, he contrasts man's corruption with life in Christ.[44] Fourth, he opposes human corruption to sanctification.[45] Fifth, he contrasts with death and corruption an eternal life which is salvation.[46] Sixth, the moral implications of ἀφθαρσία are insinuated by an abundance of phrases like "corruption and impurity,"[47] "incorruptibility and the new life of the Gospel,"[48] "life in sanctification and incorruptibility,"[49] "holy and incorruptible,"[50] "incorruptibility and life,"[51] "life in incorruptibility and blessedness and sanctification."[52]

[43] *Homiliae diversae* 14 (*PG* 77, 1088–89). This is one of the homilies which demand further investigation before they can be confidently ascribed to Cyril; cf. du Manoir, *Dogme et spiritualité*, p. 58.—Cyril's concept of life and death is not simplistic. He is aware of a problem in the promise of Christ that some will not see death at all (cf. Jn 6:51). He observes, in reply, that our Lord was accustomed to use the term "life" of the utterly happy, unending life reserved for the saints in hope; death in this context does not mean "the death of the body, but the punishment prepared for sinners"; *In Ioannem* 6 (Pusey 2, 115). Cf. *De adoratione* 8 (*PG* 68, 581): those who are in the trap of sin are "murderers of their own soul"; also *Epistolae* 86, fragmentum (*PG* 77, 384): on a Friday Adam died "in soul for sin," and on a Friday he died "in body."

[44] Cf. *Glaphyra in Genesim* 6 (*PG* 69, 329): Cyril represents David as all but exhibiting to the Father his death-possessed body and beseeching Him to release it through the Son from φθορά and to restore it to its original state, "that is, to blessed and undefiled life in Christ."

[45] Cf. *In Ioannem* 11, 11 (Pusey 2, 730–31): The image of Adam is evident in "the feebleness that is death and corruption," in fleshly lust, in an earth-bound frame of mind; the image of Christ is conspicuous "in cleanness and purity, in total incorruption (τῇ κατὰ πᾶν ὁτιοῦν ἀφθαρσίᾳ) and life and sanctification." This latter image was man's primal beauty; it can only be recaptured through participation in the Spirit, who communicates to us a share in His own holiness and "refashions to His own life the nature that fell subject to corruption, and thus restores to God and to God's semblance what had been deprived of this glory."

[46] Cf. *In Isaiam* 5, 2 (*PG* 70, 1216): "For we have been born not of corruptible seed but through the Word of the living and abiding God. This is the way in which Christ creates; He refashions believers to Himself through sanctification and brings them back to salvation; for He creates us not for destruction, that is, no more for corruption and death, but for long, unending life." Cf. also *Homiliae paschales* 2, 8 (*PG* 77, 448).

[47] *De adoratione* 15 (*PG* 68, 1008).

[48] *Ibid.* 16 (*PG* 68, 1049).

[49] *Ibid.* 17 (*PG* 68, 1093).

[50] *Quod unus sit Christus* (*PG* 75, 1273).

[51] *In Ioannem* 3, 6 (Pusey 1, 479); *ibid.* 10, 2 (Pusey 2, 571); *Contra Synousiastas* 12 (Pusey, *In Ioannem* 3, 488).

[52] *In Ioannem* 9 (Pusey 2, 409).

But these are, in themselves, suggestions. That such suggestions are actually revelatory of a more profound concept of ἀφθαρσία is rather clear from a deceptively simple passage:

... The Creator devised as it were a second root of our race, to bring us back to our former incorruptibility (ἀφθαρσίαν), in order that, just as the image (εἰκών) of the first man, the man from the earth, engraved on us the necessity of dying and involved us in the meshes of corruption (φθορᾶς), so, conversely, the second beginning, the one after him, that is, Christ, and the likeness (ὁμοίωσις) to Him through the Spirit, would stamp us with indestructibility (τὸ ἀνώλεθρον), and just as disobedience subjected us to punishment in the former, so in the latter compliance and complete obedience might make us partakers of the blessing from heaven and the Father.... The only-begotten Word of God came down among us of His own accord, not to have death rule over Him as well as over us, as though Adam transmitted deadness (νέκρωσιν) to Him as well; for He it is who gives life to all. His purpose was to show our form held fast by corruption (φθορᾷ) and transform it to life (ζωήν).... For it would be absurd to think that Adam, who was earthborn and a man, could send hurtling into the whole race, like some inheritance, the power of the curse that was leveled at him, while Emmanuel, who is from above, from heaven, God by nature, did not give on His part a rich participation in His own life to those who might elect to share His kinship through faith.[53]

It seems reasonably clear that, in this passage at least, φθορά is not simply subjection to physical death and subsequent dissolution. It is that, and more. Φθορά is the condition of a rational creature who is deprived of precisely that life which is divine and eternal; "the meshes of corruption" are opposed to "a rich participation in His own life." And if God's life has gone from man, human life itself is doomed to death and decay; it has no finality. Life left Adam's body because life had fled from his soul.[54] Similarly, ἀφθαρσία is a concept paradoxically simple and complex. It means that man, the whole man, is alive. Not with a double life, natural and supernatural, human and divine. Man, this composite creature of soul and body, has been divinized; *he* is alive with *God's* life. It is this incorruptibility that must be "the most remarkable part of the likeness."[55]

It remains true, however, that Cyril's preoccupation is with "that in

[53] *Glaphyra in Genesim* 1 (*PG* 69, 28–29). Note that "bring back" should perhaps be simply "raise up"; the Greek is ἀναβιβάζουσαν.

[54] Cf. *De dogmatum solutione* 7 (Pusey, *In Ioannem* 3, 563): "Having offended in Adam because of the transgression, we were placed in a state of aversion from God; and for this reason we returned to our own dust, having become cursed."

[55] *In Ioannem* 9, 1 (Pusey 2, 484).

us which was especially in danger," the naturally corruptible flesh. And it is from his conception of flesh (*a*) as it will be at the end, and (*b*) as it was in the beginning, that we gain a fresh insight into his theology of incorruptibility. An interesting passage in the *Commentary on John* discusses the problem of the glorified body in arresting terms:

> This too, I think, deserves investigation. Thomas felt the Savior's side and searched out the wounds from the soldier's lance; he saw the marks of the nails. And so someone may say: how was it that in the incorruptible body the signs of corruption were manifest? For the continued presence of perforations in hands and side, and the outward appearances of wounds and penetrations effected by a weapon, these are evidence of bodily corruption (φθορᾶς). On the other hand, correct reasoning argues that, if corruption is put off, everything that is a consequence of corruption must be put off as well. If someone has a limp, is he going to rise up again maimed in foot or leg? If someone has lost his eyes in this life, will he be raised bereft of vision? How, then, have we already thrown off corruption, one may ask, if the misfortunes (πάθη) consequent upon it are extant and dominate our bodies? I do not consider this inquiry impertinent. However, here is our answer to the difficulty proposed, as far as it can be answered. . . . At the time of the resurrection no remnant of adventitious corruption will survive in us. Rather, as the wise Paul said with reference to this body, "what is sown in weakness rises in power" and "what is sown in dishonor rises in glory" (1 Cor 15:43). This expectation that the resurrection of this body will be in power and glory, what else could it mean if not that [the body], having cast off all the weakness and dishonor that comes from corruption and passions, will return to its original creation? For it was made not for death and corruption. But, because Thomas demanded this too for full, unerring conviction, our Lord Jesus Christ, to afford no pretext for our lack of faith, found it needful to show Himself in the manner that Thomas required. . . .[56]

What ἀφθαρσία implied in man's "original creation" can be concretized to some extent if we summarize Cyril's understanding of Adam's incorruptibility. Because his body was not corruptible, "the passions of corruption" did not sprout in Adam; there was no law of sin in his members.[57] The flesh was not weak with the weakness which corruptibility entails.[58] Adam was not the slave of fleshly passions;[59] in fact, there seems to have been an inclination in the flesh itself towards God's

---

[56] *Ibid.* 12, 1 (Pusey 3, 146–47). Cyril adds that our Lord wanted to make the Incarnation, crucifixion, and resurrection an evident reality for the angels upon His ascension; cf. *ibid.* (Pusey 3, 147–48).

[57] Cf. *In psalmos*, Ps 6:3 (*PG* 69, 745).

[58] Cf. *In Ioannem* 2, 5 (Pusey 1, 294); *In psalmos*, Ps 67:29 (*PG* 69, 1157).

[59] Cf. *In Sophoniam* 2 (Pusey 2, 240).

will in preference to Adam's own.[60] The mind, in its turn, was not borne down by lusts that lead to sin.[61] On the contrary, the Spirit within Adam strengthened him to every form of virtue,[62] and established him against the devil and sinful desires.[63] Moreover, in that paradise of delight no curse was leveled at woman to bring forth children in sorrow;[64] grief had no grounds to tyrannize over man;[65] anything like suffering was simply unknown.[66]

In his polemic against Julian, Cyril attaches incorruptibility to Adam's body specifically. This body, he confesses, was framed of earth; still, it was superior to death and corruption (ἄμεινον θανάτου καὶ φθορᾶς), simply because God so willed it, simply because God implanted life in what was naturally corruptible (τὸ φθείρεσθαι πεφυκός). "Now, while it was beyond corruption, it had indeed innate appetites, appetites for food and procreation, but the amazing thing was that his mind was not tyrannized by these tendencies; for he did freely what he wanted to do, seeing that the flesh was not yet subject to the passions consequent upon corruption." It was only after sin entered in that corruption made its appearance and became a sort of "unholy root" of concupiscence.[67]

---

[60] Cf. In Ioannem 9, 1 (Pusey 2, 483).

[61] Cf. Glaphyra in Deuteronomium (PG 69, 656).

[62] Cf. In Ioannem 9, 1 (Pusey 2, 483).

[63] Cf. In psalmos, Ps 50:14 (PG 69, 1100-1101).

[64] Cf. In Lucam hom. 2 (PG 72, 489; CSCO 70, 11-12; Lat. tr. 140, 3).

[65] Cf. In Ioannem 7, fragmenta (Pusey 2, 280).

[66] Cf. In Lucam hom. 153 (Smith, Eng. tr. 2, 719).

[67] Contra Iulianum 3 (PG 76, 637). This passage is not in contradiction to Cyril's remarks on 1 Cor 15:45; cf. In epistolam 1 ad Corinthios 7 (Pusey, In Ioannem 3, 313): Paul "called Adam ψυχικόν; for this, I think, is the meaning of 'he was made into a living soul (ψυχήν)': he was not entirely free from concupiscence of the flesh. For the appetites (ὀρέξεις) which are concerned with the passions of the flesh, even though they may have a law to plead for them, may still be truthfully charged with fleshly weakness, at least if we regard the nature of the things that are done." An example is marriage and the procreative appetite. If we look at the end in view, the desire is beyond accusation; but if we consider the nature of the action itself, we are faced with a passion which is σαρκικόν, ψυχικόν; "and so it is with all the other passions which are unassailable." Cyril simply attributes to Adam's original state a certain imperfection, in the sense that he had desires of the flesh, howsoever licit; he does not suggest that Adam was dominated by these desires. For a synopsis of Cyril's use of ψυχικός and πνευματικός cf. Weigl, op. cit., pp. 41-42. In one sense Christ has already made the ψυχικόν body πνευματικόν, in that He "condemned sin in His own flesh, commanding it to be idle, and remodeling it so that it would be stirred to do God's good pleasure rather than self-will"; In Ioannem 9, 1 (Pusey 2, 483). In the next world the body will be πνευματικόν in that it will have laid aside entirely what is "of flesh and earth"; cf. In Romanos, Rom 8:23 (Pusey, In Ioannem 3, 217-18).

A corruptible body, then, is not merely flesh destined to wither. It is that, of course; but, more importantly, it is the raw material of sinful concupiscence.[68] For the Bishop of Alexandria, therefore, ἀφθαρσία and φθορά are not problems purely of physical life and physical death; they are not, in their richer significance, the logical consequence of ἀθανασία and θάνατος. Incorruptibility and corruption frequently have connotations absent from immortality and death; they engage the spiritual, they touch sanctity and sin. Not, indeed, as necessary causes—psychological necessity is foreign to Cyril's perspectives of freedom—but as the "root" from which a godlike ἀπάθεια or a godless πάθος are born and flower.[69] If we must say in brief what corporal ἀφθαρσία means for Cyril, it is this: the body will know neither physical nor moral imperfection, neither physical weakness nor fleshly concupiscence.[70] The process was initiated when the Son of God quickened corruptible flesh with His Incarnation; it is individualized and heightened through Christian living; it will be consummated when our bodies participate definitively in Christ's life and glory.[71]

It cannot be sufficiently stressed, however, that, despite certain emphases, Cyril's outlook is holistic. It is sinful man, and not simply the body, that is φθαρτός, because it is man who is dominated by concupiscence and is a rebel against God; and it is sanctified man, and not simply the body, that is ἄφθαρτος (inchoately now, consummately later),

[68] Cf. also De dogmatum solutione 5 (Pusey, In Ioannem 3, 559): in the next life there will be no passions, because no corruption; the body will be πνευματικόν, "that is, it will have in view only the things of the Spirit."

[69] Cf. Contra Iulianum 8 (PG 76, 928) for God's merciful design to "forge man . . . anew to incorruptibility and put him beyond passions." Cf. also In epistolam 1 ad Corinthios 7 (Pusey, In Ioannem 3, 316): Christ Himself will transform creation, will make the universe new, will deliver it from "slavery into the freedom of the glory of the sons of God" (Rom 8:21). This being so, man too must be made new; it is for his sake that creation exists. "He too must prove to be new, not tyrannized by his former corruption, not led fraudulently to sin by lusts of the flesh, but rather awakened in incorruptibility, firmness, and honor, and clothed in a certain divine glory. . . ." Cf. In Ioannem 9, 1 (Pusey 2, 483): the image of Christ means that one is in ἀπάθεια and ἀφθαρσία; also ibid. 11, 12 (Pusey 3, 15): by His passion (πάθος) Christ purchased ἀπάθεια for all.

[70] Cf. In epistolam 1 ad Corinthios 7 (Pusey, In Ioannem 3, 310-12); In Matthaeum, fragmentum (PG 72, 471-72); In Lucam, Lk 24:38 (PG 72, 948). On the light of glory in the body cf. Weigl, op. cit., pp. 337-39.

[71] Cf. In epistolam 1 ad Corinthios 3 (Pusey, In Ioannem 3, 266); also In epistolam 2 ad Corinthios 3, 1 (Pusey, In Ioannem 3, 347). A restricted but useful study of Cyril's conception of incorruptibility is the recent article by G. Langevin, "Le thème de l'incorruptibilité dans le commentaire de saint Cyrille d'Alexandrie sur l'Evangile selon saint Jean," Sciences ecclésiastiques 8 (1956) 295-316.

because it is man who is lord of his passions and one with his God.[72] It is here that the image which is ἀφθαρσία joins hands with the image which is ἁγιασμός; for humanity has "sprung back to incorruptibility through sanctification in the Spirit."[73]

One problem persists: is Cyril guilty of contradiction? On the one hand, he has asserted categorically that the image of God in man is not to be sought in the body; it is the soul that resembles God. On the other hand, he makes it clear that the immortality and incorruptibility recovered for us by the Incarnate Word in His resurrection and definitively communicated to us in our resurrection includes the body as an essential element: the participated incorruptibility of the whole man, soul and body, is a reflection of the incorruptibility that is native to God. Cyril makes no effort to resolve the conflict; apparently he is not even aware of a conflict. This unawareness is excusable to some extent. When Cyril maintains that the image of God is not to be sought in the body, his precise meaning is generally to be gathered from his apologetic preoccupation: anthropomorphism. Man does not image God in the sense that man's bodily make-up somehow reflects a similar physical struc-

[72] Weigl has come to much the same conclusion as we; cf. *op. cit.*, p. 42: "The basic meaning of φθορά is best given etymologically: that which, in its inner structure as a creature, is subject to a dissolution in the sense of nonbeing or not-being-such (φθείρεσθαι πεφυκός). In a more restricted sense the concept often concerns the body, especially since in consequence of sin dissolution and disorder affect our corporal powers in particular fashion. The opposite of φθορά is ἀφθαρσία, and the concept designates natural as well as supernatural integrity. The expression is not seldom restricted to bodily integrity. Elsewhere, however, it has a wider comprehension and comes to mean the totality of supernatural glory, the fulness and imperishability of God's being, as well as every participation therein."— Cyril tells us that the soul itself will be transfigured, because the mind of man will see the glory of God directly, will "see Him just as He is" (1 Jn 3:2); cf. *In Ioannem* 9, 2 (Pusey 2, 647–48). For a more detailed analysis of this glorification in soul cf. Weigl, *op. cit.*, pp. 332–35. Cyril considers it obligatory doctrine that after death the soul receives reward or punishment without delay; cf. *In Ioannem* 12 (Pusey 3, 96): "Our mind, I think, must be . . . that the souls of the saints, once they have gone from their earth-sprung bodies, are by God's goodness and benevolence committed, as it were, into the hands of the Father who loves us so tenderly. They do not, as some unbelievers have supposed, haunt the monuments, waiting for the libations that are poured over the tomb. Neither are they brought down into the place of limitless punishment, that is, into hell, like the souls of those in love with sin. On the contrary, they hasten into the hands of the universal Father. . . ."

[73] *De sancta et consubstantiali trinitate* dial. 3 (*PG* 75? 853); cf. the same idea in *De recta fide, ad augustas* 5 (*ACO* 1, 1, 5, 28; *PG* 76, 1341): Christ has become "the head, that is, the principle, of those who are reformed through Him to Him unto incorruptibility by sanctification in the Spirit."

ture in God. In this sense the image is not in the body. Nevertheless, there is a defect in Cyril's presentation. He (a) insists stoutly that the image is to be found exclusively in the soul, and (b) he does not relate to this thesis his belief that the body of man shares here and now in the image which is incorruptibility, and that the incorruptible body of man will be modeled on the glorified body of Christ. Briefly, the image of God *is* in the body, but not as the anthropomorphists would have it. This distinction Cyril fails to make.

I would suggest that in the Greek theology of the first four centuries there are recognizable anticipations of Cyril, even his richer vision of incorruptibility. Ἀφθαρσία plays an important part in the anthropology of the second-century Apologists, all of whom intimate what Theophilus enunciates: participation in the immortality and incorruptibility that is proper to God implies an assimilation to God, a divinization.[74] More striking still, the ideological rapport between Cyril and Irenaeus—perhaps even a dependence of Cyril on Irenaeus—will be evident to anyone who follows the careful analysis which M. Aubineau has recently made of incorruptibility and divinization in the Bishop of Lyons.[75] This study of ἀφθαρσία and ἀθανασία, at once lexical and theological, reveals that in Irenaeus the successive stages of man's journey to God, his progressive resemblance to the divine, can be traced on the lines of incorruptibility. Aubineau's concluding summary of Irenaeus' position will recall much of Cyril:

On the level of the body, incorruptibility appears as emancipation from the biological process which sweeps it to its destruction. But this liberation is the expression of a more radical transformation. The incorruptibility which penetrates the whole man, body and soul, is a participation in the incorruptibility of God, in His perfect, uncreated, immortal nature—not that which the philosophers of antiquity dreamed for the soul, but that which the Father bestows on His adopted sons.

Man reaches incorruptibility by stages; for God's pedagogy respects man's freedom and the law of progress written in his nature. Adam received a fragile incorruptibility, without deep roots, proportioned to his imperfection as a child. He lost it, Irenaeus says, more through carelessness and surprise than through malice. If sin disturbs God's plan, it does not alter its essential lines. Christ, in His coming, brings humanity a firm, stable incorruptibility, which is disseminated in the Church, through the sacraments [baptism and the Eucharist], under the

[74] Cf. Gross, *op. cit.*, pp. 133–43; for Theophilus cf. *Ad Autolycum* 2, 27 (*Sources chrétiennes* 20, 164–66).

[75] Cf. M. Aubineau, "Incorruptibilité et divinisation selon saint Irénée," *Recherches de science religieuse* 44 (1956) 25–52.

breath of the Spirit. Received by Christians in harmony with the whole scale of participations, incorruptibility ascends like sap in each of them, to make them produce and mature the fruits of immortality. It is in vision, finally, that perfect incorruptibility finds its full bloom. There is no break in the continuity of this movement. In each stage of his growth man possesses, in his soul and in his body, one same homogeneous principle which makes him kin to God—not a divine fragment that has escaped from the pleroma, but incorruptible life communicated gratuitously.[76]

For Clement of Alexandria, to become like God (καθ' ὁμοίωσιν) is equivalent to divinization (ἐκθεοῦσθαι); and this takes place primarily through participation in God's ἀφθαρσία, the incorruptibility in which antiquity recognized God's proper reality and glory in contrast to mortal man. The stages in human divinization are three: life, good life, eternal life.[77]

In the matter of incorruptibility Bouyer discovers a striking illustration of Athanasius' originality.[78] For Athanasius, there are two, and only two, modes of existence which are radically distinct. One is God's, and it implies ἀφθαρσία; the other is the creature's, and it implies φθορά. 'Αφθαρσία is not merely the fact of not dying; it is the property of a life which has in itself no reason for ever ceasing to be. As such, it is strictly proper to God. Φθορά is man's natural condition, sin or no sin; he is ephemeral as well as dependent. It is only in consequence of incredible generosity, it is only by God's self-communication, that creatures can

[76] Ibid., p. 52. Whether Irenaeus regarded the human soul as naturally immortal is a debated point. Some scholars conclude that, for Irenaeus, the soul's physical subsistence for eternity depends on its conduct in time; so Quasten, op. cit. 1, 310; J. Lawson, The Biblical Theology of Saint Irenaeus (London, 1948) p. 208. Others prefer to distinguish. In one sense the soul is naturally immortal: God has endowed it with immortality. In another sense it is not immortal by nature: it does not have of itself the power to continue in existence. The elect will have immortality not only of being but of blessedness as well; the damned will have the former alone. So Vernet, "Irénée, Saint," DTC 7, 2498-99.

[77] Cf. Mayer, op. cit., pp. 11-12, 88-89. Cf. ibid., p. 89, note 47: "According to Clement, all men belong to the perishable realities (τὰ θνητά) in so far as in virtue of their nature they are merely 'to the image' of God; imperishability (ἀφθαρσία, ἀθανασία) is a free gift of God's grace (χάρις), and it is allotted to those who fashion themselves in God's likeness, as far as this is possible for created nature." Gross is of the opinion that immortality plays a secondary role in Clement—"not astonishing in a disciple of Plato who recognizes in the soul a natural incorruptibility and sees in the gnosis which is vision the last end of man"; op. cit., p. 174.

[78] Cf. L. Bouyer, L'Incarnation et l'Eglise-Corps du Christ dans la théologie de saint Athanase (Paris, 1943) pp. 36-45. I am indebted to Bouyer's analysis for this aspect of Athanasius' thought.

*become* incorruptible. How is this achieved? Through knowledge—the knowledge whereby the purified soul contemplates the eternal God in the image which the Word impresses on it. By the indwelling of the Word, man contemplates God in the mirror of his soul. Contemplating the incorruptible God as He is, man participates in God's incorruptibility. It is here that the two primary aspects of the Athanasian image make contact. As long as man is λογικός, he is ἄφθαρτος ; as long as he participates in God's Word, he shares in God's life—unending life. This is the realization of the biblical declaration, "You are gods" (Ps 81:6).[79]

Gregory of Nyssa likewise sees an aspect of the divine image in man's immortality (τὸ ἀθάνατον, τὸ ἀΐδιον).[80] But Gregory is absorbed not by the immortality which concerns Socrates in the *Phaedo*, not by the incorruptibility of the *Enneads*. His perspective is totally theological; he is engrossed in the immortality (ἀθανασία) which transforms us, by God's free giving, to the image of the Immortal,[81] the incorruptibility which is a participation in the God who "is Incorruptibility" (ἀφθαρσία).[82] Daniélou has recaptured Gregory's preoccupation:

[For Gregory] there is not a natural state of the incorruptible spirit, to which the divine life would come to be added. There is only the real, true state, that of divinized man, who is ἄφθαρτος, and the state of fall, φθαρτός, the state where he is not physically corruptible but immersed in corruptible realities. And it is this positive corruption which is significant. The term ἀθανασία, which we find beside ἀφθαρσία to designate the state of "image" . . . , calls for the same remarks. The opposition is not between existence and nothingness; for we are on the human level, where the spirit is endowed with a radical immortality. The opposition is between the state of mortality, that is to say, the condition of man

[79] Cf. Athanasius, *De incarnatione Verbi* 4 (*PG* 25, 104); *Contra gentes* 2 (*PG* 25, 5–8). This is the life which the angels live, blessed life, a life of familiarity with God, here and now. As for the restoration of the image, the fundamental principle of Athanasian soteriology is that the Word took on Himself our φθορά in order to consume it by His ἀφθαρσία. As Bouyer puts it, "the life which emerges triumphant from the tomb on Easter morning, and which is to become our life, is no longer the life subject to the φθορά of sheerly human beings—which we had become by sin; it is divine life, ἀφθαρσία in us"; *op. cit.*, p. 43. It should be observed that Athanasius does not, as is sometimes alleged, stress deliverance from death at the expense of deliverance from sin; for him, death includes sin, and life includes holiness. On this latter point cf. G. Aulén, *Christus Victor*, tr. A. G. Hebert (London, 1931) pp. 59–60.

[80] Cf. Gregory of Nyssa, *Oratio catechetica magna* 5 (*PG* 45, 21–24).

[81] Cf. Gregory of Nyssa, *In Canticum canticorum* hom. 12 (*PG* 44, 1020–24); cf. Leys, *op. cit.*, p. 77.

[82] Cf. Gregory of Nyssa, *Adversus Apollinarem* 55 (*PG* 45, 1257).

separated from God—which is the real, true death—and consequently invested with an animal nature subject to mortality, and the state of ἀθανασία, which is at once life of the soul united to God and liberation from biological mortality.[83]

On the level of incorruptibility, at least two basic insights link the more distinguished of the Alexandrians. The first insight is that ἀφθαρσία is perhaps the most significant facet of the divine image in man. The second insight is that ἀφθαρσία is only secondarily biological (life); it is primarily theological (God's life).

[83] Daniélou, *Platonisme et théologie mystique*, pp. 55–56. He notes that the same idea is to be found in Athanasius; cf. *ibid.*, p. 56, note 1. Leys is willing to assert "boldly" that Gregory never speaks of "radical immortality" but always of the other; cf. *op. cit.*, p. 77.

# CHAPTER 8

# SONSHIP

A final aspect of Cyril's image, at once a consequence of sanctification and a basis for incorruptibility, is divine sonship. The question of sonship arises naturally from Cyril's consideration of Jn 1:12: "To as many as received Him He gave the power of becoming sons of God—to those who believe in His name." A prerogative which belongs properly and by nature to God the Son, and to Him alone, He makes a common possession of men, out of love:

> Those who bore the image of the earthy (cf. 1 Cor 15:49) could not escape corruption, had not the beauty of the image (εἰκόνος) of the heavenly been stamped on us through the vocation to adoptive sonship (υἱοθεσίαν); for, made partakers of [Christ] through the Spirit, we have been sealed to His likeness (ὁμοιότητα) and we mount to the archetypal form of the image, according to which, Scripture says, we have been created as well. Once we have recovered in this fashion and with difficulty the primeval beauty of our nature, we shall be superior to the evils that have struck us in consequence of the transgression. And so we rise to this supernatural dignity (τὸ ὑπὲρ φύσιν ἀξίωμα) by reason of Christ. It is not, however, exactly as He is (κατ' ἐκεῖνον ἀπαραλλάκτως) that we too shall be sons (υἱοί) of God, but rather in relation to Him through the grace that is imitation (πρὸς ἐκεῖνον διὰ τῆς κατὰ μίμησιν χάριτος). The reason is that He is true (ἀληθινός) Son sprung from the Father, while we are adopted sons (θετοί) from His loving kindness; it is as a favor (χάριτος) that we receive the [scriptural] "I have said, 'You are gods, and sons of the Most High' " (Ps 81:6). For the creature, fashioned and a slave, is called to the supernatural (τὰ ὑπὲρ φύσιν) by the mere nod and will of the Father. . . . Nature and adoption, imitation and truth, are different ideas. Since, then, we have been called sons by adoption and imitation, surely He is Himself Son by nature and in truth; for in being sons we are contrasted with Him: we enjoy this blessing as a favor (χάριτος) and not as a natural dignity.[1]

Our divine sonship, therefore, achieved as it is through participation in the Son of God, is an imaging of the Son, and consequently of the Father; it is the refashioning of our nature to the divine nature in whose likeness man was created in the beginning. It is the communication of a prerogative properly God's, elevates us above human nature to the

---

[1] *In Ioannem* 1, 9 (Pusey 1, 133–34). Cf. *ibid.* (Pusey 1, 153): sons of God are not made like the natural Son ἀπαραλλάκτως. On the fact of adoptive sonship as an aspect of the image, cf. also *ibid.* 2, 1 (Pusey 1, 219).

sphere of the divine, and makes it possible for man to escape φθορά.
Nevertheless, our sonship differs from Christ's. For Him, sonship is
inseparable from His essence, and He is Son par excellence; we are sons
of God in imitation of Him, by God's uncompelled favor, a participation
on our part, an adoption on His.[2] What we achieve in sonship is likeness,
not identity, of nature. To prevent any confusion, Cyril believes, our
Lord did not say, "Everything which the Father has, I too have" (cf.
Jn 16:15). He did not wish to be taken for "some sort of mere image,"
similar in form to the Father, fashioned after the archetype "by adornments from without—as we are; for we have been made to God's image."
Rather, He says, "they are mine," and so He shows that He and the
Father are perfectly one, consubstantial, with identical properties.
Between Father and Son there is equality of essence, substantial likeness,
in all things; therefore, they have the same nature.[3]

In a compact passage Cyril has grouped the essential ideas: the fact
of our adoptive filiation, its origin in the Incarnation, and its relation to
the natural sonship of the Word:

[The Word] lowered Himself, in order to lift to His own height that which
was lowly by nature; and He bore the form of the slave, though by nature He
was Lord and Son, in order to transport what was slave by nature to the glory
of adoptive sonship, after His own likeness (ὁμοιότητα), with reference to Him.
Therefore, just as He became like us, that is, man, in order that we might become
like Him, I mean gods and sons, He takes to Himself what is properly ours and
gives us in return what is His. . . . We mount to a dignity which is supernatural
(ὑπὲρ φύσιν) through our likeness (ὁμοιώσεως) to Him; for we have been called

---

[2] Cf. also *Thesaurus* 32 (*PG* 75, 540): not φύσις but χάρις has procured sonship
for us; He is Son "properly and by nature," we "by imitation"; *In Ioannem* 11,
12 (Pusey 3, 5): "we have been loved as sons after the likeness of the natural, true
Son"; it is not equality, but it is a very exact imitation; cf. also *ibid.* 3, 4 (Pusey 1,
423-24). Cyril argues that our adoptive sonship is a proof of Christ's natural sonship; cf. *Homiliae paschales* 24, 3 (*PG* 77, 896): "If there is no real (κατὰ ἀλήθειαν)
Son, after whom are we adopted sons fashioned? Whose distinctive mark (χαρακ-
τῆρα) do we have? Where is the imitation (τὸ κατὰ μίμησιν), if we say that the truth
(τὴν ἀλήθειαν) does not subsist?" Cf. *Thesaurus* 32 (*PG* 75, 525); *De sancta et consubstantiali trinitate* dial. 2 (*PG* 75, 749–52). A basic principle for Cyril is that
adoptive sonship is always compared with natural sonship; cf. *In Ioannem* 10,
2 (Pusey 2, 579); *Thesaurus* 32 (*PG* 75, 477). Sonship by adoption and grace always
bears a likeness (ὁμοίωσις) to sonship by nature and in truth; cf. *Quod unus sit
Christus* (*PG* 75, 1296); *Thesaurus* 12 (*PG* 75, 205).

[3] Cf. *In Ioannem* 11, 2 (Pusey 2, 637–38). That is evidently why Cyril can say
that Scripture "misuses language" when it applies υἱότης and θεός to adopted sons;
cf. *ibid.* 11, 12 (Pusey 3, 14).

sons of God, even though we are not sons by nature. . . . By nature and in reality the Father of Christ is the God of the universe; but that does not make Him our Father by nature; rather is He God, as Creator and Lord. But the Son, as it were mingling Himself with us, bestows on our nature the dignity that is properly and peculiarly His own, giving the name of common Father to His own Begetter. . . .[4]

This is the sense in which Christ is "the first-born of every creature" (Col 1:15): "because all of us are called in the Son and through the Son to an equal form ($\iota\sigma\sigma\nu$ $\sigma\chi\hat{\eta}\mu\alpha$) with Him, made sons of God by grace. And He Himself is the origin ($\dot{\alpha}\rho\chi\dot{\eta}$) of the grace given us, likening to Himself . . . those who were made through Him. . . . It is through Him that all things have been made and rational creatures are called to adoptive sonship."[5]

All this is theologically unexceptionable, and genuinely Cyril. But Cyril's conception of adoptive sonship (and implicitly of God's image in man) is too complex to be comprehended from isolated quotations; it is a rounded theory built solidly on the Incarnation.[6] The basic fact is that the Incarnation established between the enfleshed Word and human beings a twin relationship: exchange and solidarity. First, the Incarnation is an exchange: the Son of God became man in order that men might become sons of God. He took what is ours, to give us what is His.[7] Second, the condition of this exchange is the solidarity of all humanity with Christ. The significance of the solidarity lies in this: in virtue of it the Father has restored human nature to its primeval state. The origin of the solidarity is the human nature of Christ.[8]

[4] *Ibid.* 12, 1 (Pusey 3, 122–23).

[5] *Thesaurus* 25 (*PG* 75, 412–13).

[6] For much of what follows I am indebted to the stimulating article of L. Janssens, "Notre filiation divine d'après saint Cyrille d'Alexandrie," *Ephemerides theologicae Lovanienses* 15 (1938) 233–78. Janssens is very much taken by Cyril's approach to our divine filiation in terms of the Son's natural filiation, in contrast to the more juridical springboard (legal adoption) of the manuals. His presentation of Cyril's theology of filiation is so well organized, and almost invariably so accurate, that I have thought it best in more than a few instances to simply digest his analysis; my several reservations will emerge clearly enough. So careful a Cyrillan scholar as du Manoir has recognized the value of Janssens' work, and he gives little more than an abridged version of it in the pertinent section of *Dogme et spiritualité*, pp. 171–81.

[7] Cf. *In Ioannem* 12, 1 (Pusey 3, 122–23); *In Lucam* hom. 71 (*PG* 72, 688; *CSCO* 70, 284; Lat. tr. 140, 195).

[8] Cf. *De adoratione* 8 (*PG* 68, 552); *In Ioannem* 8, fragmenta (Pusey 2, 318): "for what has not been assumed has not been saved."

More concretely, solidarity and exchange between Christ and us are reducible to the consubstantiality of Christ with the Father and with men. This twofold consubstantiality was imperative: consubstantiality with the Father, if men were to participate in the divine nature;[9] consubstantiality with men, if the Incarnation was not to be a spurious thing, and an exchange between humanity and divinity impossible.[10] The former is clear enough: the Word in flesh remains God, of identical substance with the Father;[11] that is why the Incarnation can be presented as the source of gifts divine. It is the consubstantiality of Christ with men that is a theological tinder-box for Cyrillan scholars—not so much on the essential fact (that much is undeniable), as rather because it involves philosophical presuppositions whose truth or falsity affects seriously the strength or weakness of the soteriological structure built upon them.

In what sense, as Cyril understands it, are human beings consubstantial, one in substance? What does Cyril mean when he insists so often that Christ had all humanity in Himself by the sheer fact of His Incarnation? For scholars like Weigl the answer is to be sought in an Aristotelian unity of "second substance": there is but one species "man."

There is no doubt that [Cyril's expressions] have a very realistic ring. On no account, however, does he teach a universal man, who assumed objective reality in Christ; the only nature he knows is an individual nature. He does indeed emphasize, repeatedly and vigorously, that which is common (τὸ κοινόν), that which in all things is alike; the difference lies [for Cyril] in the accidents. But this is not to say that this "common" somehow has independent reality and is the same in all things, that is, numerically one, as Gregory of Nyssa thought. It simply teaches the so-called *substantia secunda*, which is alike in all things of the same species. The point is, Cyril's primary concern is to demonstrate against the Arians the consubstantiality of the Son with the Father (through generation). This he does by pointing out that things of one and the same species have the same essence, not specifically different essences. When he writes further, "He [Christ] has us in Himself, inasmuch as He bore our nature, and the Word's body was called our body" (*In Ioannem* 9, 1 [Pusey 2, 486]), this is by no means an affirmation that Christ bore human nature as universal; it merely predicates an individual nature which is the same as that of the species. Moreover, since Cyril's viewpoint elsewhere is not sheerly Platonist, and since the objections to the Platonist doctrine of ideas were evidently known to him, it is antecedently unacceptable that he would have been en-

---

[9] Cf. *Adversus Nestorii blasphemias* 3, 3 (*ACO* 1, 1, 6, 66; *PG* 76, 144).
[10] Cf. *Quod unus sit Christus* (*PG* 75, 1288).
[11] Cf. *In Ioannem* 1, 9 (Pusey 1, 142).

tangled in such extreme realism. On the contrary, we have every reason for including him with the moderate Aristotelian realism. Were Cyril teaching a universal nature, two questions would remain forever unresolved: How could so sharp a mind, which speculates so profoundly on the relationship of grace and Christology, fail to notice that with such an assumption the doctrine of grace is rather superfluous? How, in point of fact, was something special to happen to the individual, if the whole of humanity had become divine in Christ? Further, why did the numerous enemies of Cyril, the Antiochenes with opposed philosophical views, fail to lay hold of this error, although they picked from his writings everything that was speciously shocking? Such a doctrine could not escape them, because it is important for Christology and is sufficiently touched on even in the controversial treatises. Precisely on this point they had the same views as Cyril.[12]

On the other hand, Malevez has concluded that "for Cyril, as for Gregory [of Nyssa], human nature is an ideal reality which is numerically one, immanent in each individual according to its unmultipliable and indivisible totality."[13] Nor is Janssens convinced by Weigl's presentation of an Aristotelian Cyril. He argues persuasively that for Cyril, as for Athanasius and the Cappadocians, consubstantiality is numerical unity not of the second substance but of the concrete substance.[14] The substance whose numerical unity makes men consubstantial among themselves and Christ consubstantial with us as man, is the flesh.[15] This is the consubstantiality which is the basis of our solidarity with Christ. This is why Cyril insists that the Word had to take our flesh if we were to be in Him;[16] that He dwelt in all "through one";[17] that it is through the flesh that He is one with us, has all of us in Himself.[18] This is why he can say that Christ conquered sin in His own flesh and transmitted

[12] Weigl, *op. cit.*, pp. 67–68. As Weigl sees it (cf. pp. 68–69), Cyril is presenting Christ's activity as representative *per modum capitis*; though Cyril does not define its nature, Weigl interprets it as not merely juridico-moral but physical in a broad sense.

[13] L. Malevez, "L'Eglise dans le Christ: Etude de théologie historique et théorique," *Recherches de science religieuse* 25 (1935) 286. Malevez' attempt (in his second essay, *ibid.*, pp. 418–39) to transpose the Platonic realism which he discovers in Gregory and Cyril into the more moderate realism of Aristotelian-Thomistic philosophy can perhaps best be summed up as a brilliant failure.

[14] Cf. Janssens, *art. cit.*, pp. 237–38.

[15] Cf. *Apologeticus pro duodecim capitibus adversus orientales episcopos* 96 (*ACO* 1, 1, 7, 59; *PG* 76, 373).

[16] Cf. *Quod unus sit Christus* (*PG* 75, 1268).

[17] Cf. *In Ioannem* 1, 9 (Pusey 1, 141).

[18] Cf. *ibid.* 9, 1 (Pusey 2, 486).

this grace to us;[19] that in Him our whole nature was withdrawn from corruption, because in Him the common πρόσωπον of humanity rose from the grave;[20] that the prayers, actions, and even affections of Christ have meaning for humanity as such.[21]

How do these principles and conclusions affect Cyril's conception of our divine sonship? First, in virtue of the Incarnation men assume a relationship of brotherhood (ἀδελφότης) with the Son of God. Simply as only Son of the Father, the Word does not have natural brethren; become flesh and blood, He has become Brother of all who have flesh and blood. He was incarnate to bestow on us the dignity of brethren, by uniting us physically with Himself through kinship of the flesh.[22]

Second, through the flesh of Christ we assume a new relationship to the Father: brothers of the Son, we are sons of the Father.[23] A striking application of this insight is discoverable in the ascension of Christ, which is the ascension of all humanity, an adoption of human nature, a sonship of all men with reference to the Father that is akin to the oneness achieved in the Incarnation:

Christ did not ascend to exhibit Himself to God the Father; for He was and is and always will be in the Father. . . . He ascended on this occasion as man, for a strange and unaccustomed manifestation, the Word who of old was without humanity. For us and for our sakes He did this, in order that, man that He was, He might hear addressed to Him in His wholeness, as Son in power and with flesh, the words, "Sit at my right hand" (Ps 109:1), and transmit the glory of sonship (υἱοθεσίας) to the whole race through Himself. . . . He manifested Himself as man, in order to set us once more in the sight of the Father, we who had gone from His gaze by reason of the primeval transgression. He sat down as Son, that we too might be called sons (υἱοί) through Him and children (τέκνα) of God. . . .[24]

In the divine and human consubstantiality of the Incarnate Word we have the ultimate reason of our new relationship to the Father. In consequence of our kinship with the Word, who united human nature to Himself in the body which He took from us, we are sons of God, in imita-

[19] Cf. *In Matthaeum*, Mt 11:18 (*PG* 72, 401).

[20] Cf. *In Ioannem* 1, 9 (Pusey 1, 141).

[21] Cf., e.g., *Thesaurus* 20 (*PG* 75, 333); *ibid.* 23 (*PG* 75, 384); *In psalmos*, Ps 2:8 (*PG* 69, 724).

[22] Cf. *Adversus Nestorii blasphemias* 3, 2 (*ACO* 1, 1, 6, 58–59; *PG* 76, 125); *Thesaurus* 23 (*PG* 75, 384); *In Ioannem* 1, 9 (Pusey 1, 141); for more ample documentation on this point cf. Janssens, *art. cit.*, p. 240.

[23] Cf. *In Lucam*, Lk 2:7 (*PG* 72, 485).

[24] *In Ioannem* 9 (Pusey 2, 404).

tion of the relation of filiation which the Son bears to the Father. We are sons like the Son.[25]

Third, in virtue of our solidarity with Christ we receive the Holy Spirit—the Spirit whom Christ as God gave to Himself as man, for this reason alone, that human nature might receive the Spirit in Him.[26]

But if the consubstantiality of men among themselves and with Christ is explained by the identity of the concrete substance, does this not implicitly exclude the efficacious, particularized sanctification of the individual, seeing that the whole of humanity has already participated in the divinity of Christ? Does it not, as Weigl put it, make grace superfluous? Cyril, replies Janssens, has forestalled the objection.[27] He does not abandon his theory of consubstantiality. Because the flesh of the Word enfleshed is our flesh, all men contract a radical relationship to the Son and so belong to the Savior's flock. But all men are found in the flock with their subjective, personal dispositions; and here we have two categories. There are those who stubbornly refuse to believe; for them, consubstantiality with the Son becomes an inexorable accusation. And there are the faithful, who comply with the words and commands of Christ; for them, the radical kinship is the principle of an efficacious kinship, by participation and grace, which implies special prerogatives.[28] It is through grace that believers are efficaciously oriented to the dignity of the Son; it is here that we have the real reason why they are called sons of God.[29] What is this grace which makes us sons of God? As Cyril has it, Christ sanctifies us in two ways: corporally, as man, through the Eucharist; and spiritually, as God, by the communication of His Spirit in baptism.[30] This twofold form of grace is what determines our strictly supernatural relations; this is how Christ reaches us in the supernatural order.

What is the relationship between this twofold communication of the

[25] Cf. *ibid.* 1, 9 (Pusey 1, 141–42).

[26] Cf. *ibid.* 2, 1 (Pusey 1, 185).

[27] Cf. Janssens, *art. cit.*, p. 243.

[28] Cf. *In Ioannem* 6, 1 (Pusey 2, 230–35). One of the requisites for the resemblance which is sonship is faith in Christ; cf. *De sancta et consubstantiali trinitate* dial. 4 (*PG* 75, 889): "Is it not true that through the Son we who have received faith in Him have been called to adoptive sonship and have been formed to Him like images to an archetype?" Cf. *Homiliae paschales* 10, 1 (*PG* 77, 612): "Christ is formed in you no otherwise than through blameless faith and the Gospel way of life. . . ."

[29] Cf. *In Ioannem* 7, fragmenta (Pusey 2, 252).

[30] Cf. *In epistolam 1 ad Corinthios*, 1 Cor 6:15 (Pusey, *In Ioannem* 3, 263–64); *In Matthaeum*, Mt 26:27 (*PG* 72, 452); *In Ioannem* 11, 12 (Pusey 3, 2–3).

divine and our adoptive sonship? First, participation in the Holy Spirit makes us temples of the Spirit; and in consequence of our union with the substantial, personal Spirit Cyril concludes to a new relation of the faithful to the Son. Because we participate in the divine nature of Christ and are conformed to Him by the presence of the Spirit, we are brothers of the Son by grace. This superior relationship emerges splendidly from a passage which we have discussed when dealing with sanctification—Cyril's reply to Nestorius' ironic question, "Surely you do not mean to say that God the Word had brethren (ἀδελφούς) who were like the divinity?" Cyril maintains that, beyond the common privilege of brotherhood conferred on all men by the Incarnation, by our kinship with Christ in flesh, there is another basis for brotherhood which confers a resemblance to our Lord's divinity. Some men bear "the image of the heavenly," and that image is "utter absence of slavery to passion, ignorance of sin, superiority to death and corruption, holiness, justice. . . . These, I think, are possessions that befit the divine, undefiled nature; for it is superior to sin and corruption; it is holiness and justice." And so, in answer to Nestorius' objection, Cyril presents man's primary conformity to Christ, his supernatural brotherhood:

[Christ] has, therefore, brethren like Himself, who bear the image of His divine nature by way of sanctification; for that is the way Christ is formed in us, inasmuch as the Holy Spirit as it were transforms us from what is human to what is His. . . . On those who have been made partakers of His divine nature through participation in the Holy Spirit, there is somehow stamped the suprasensuous likeness to Christ, and the beauty of the inexpressible divinity gleams in the souls of the saints. How, then, can you attribute to us, without blushing, sheer likeness of the flesh, and that alone, with utter disregard for the divine, suprasensuous formation?[31]

Brothers of the Son, we are at the same time sons of the Father. Conformed to the Son, we participate in His relationship to the Father; our divine sonship is, in the realm of grace, an imitation of the real, substantial generation of the Son by the Father. Inasmuch as "God the

---

[31] *Adversus Nestorii blasphemias* 3, 2 (*ACO* 1, 1, 6, 59–60; *PG* 76, 128–29). This sonship by grace would not have been achieved, were it not for the Incarnation of the Son, "to whom we are ourselves formed through participation in the Spirit and so are called children (τέκνα) of God and gods"; *In Ioannem* 11, 9 (Pusey 2, 695); cf. *Homiliae paschales* 28, 4 (*PG* 77, 952). In fact, the purpose of the Incarnation was "that we might be above ourselves, beyond the limits of humanity, called children (τέκνα) of God, with Him for Brother who is above all creation"; *ibid.* 22, 2 (*PG* 77, 861).

Word makes His home in us through the Spirit and is in us, we mount to the dignity of sonship (υἱοθεσίας), having the Son Himself in us, to whom we are refashioned by participation in His Spirit, and rising to a boldness of speech equal to His we dare to say, 'Abba! Father!' "[32] In fact, this sonship of ours is a new birth.

The second form of grace is the Eucharist, by which we participate in the flesh and blood of Christ in a fashion that is somehow physical; and through this contact with the life-giving body of Christ we participate in His divinity. As Janssens synthesizes it:

> It is in this way that the Word sanctifies us, by using His Eucharistic body as an instrument; it is in this way that, through our quasi-physical participation in the Eucharistic body of Christ, we contract an intimate union—though relative and accidental—with the Word, to whom this body is substantially united. The Eucharist consummates our kinship with the Word, our communion with the Father, our participation in the divine nature, by adding to these supernatural relations which already exist a special nuance and a superlatively intimate character, because it realizes them by means of a very real contact between our body and that of the Word.[33]

There are, then, two stages in our sonship: a radical kinship with God, realized by humanity at the moment of the Incarnation; and a properly supernatural relationship, achieved in the individual by participation in the divine nature and by the Eucharist. Startlingly, the fact that the radical kinship is an indispensable condition for the supernatural relationship would imply that the grace of adoption, and therefore the image under this aspect, is limited to the Christian era. Did Adam, who shared so intimately in the Spirit of sanctification and incorruptibility, somehow lack the grace of adoptive sonship? If so, can our redemption

---

[32] *Thesaurus* 33 (*PG* 75, 569). Cf. *In Romanos*, Rom 1:3-4 (Pusey, *In Ioannem* 3, 175-76): It is through Him who is Son by nature that we are adopted as sons (υἱοποιούμεθα); for we have received His Spirit through baptism and can therefore cry, "Abba! Father!" (Rom 8:15). "Therefore, as images are to an archetype, so is our relation, we who are sons by adoption, to Him who is Son by nature, in power, and in truth. . . ."

[33] Janssens, *art. cit.*, p. 253. On the Eucharist in Cyril cf. du Manoir, *Dogme et spiritualité*, pp. 185-218; J. Mahé, "L'Eucharistie d'après saint Cyrille d'Alexandrie," *Revue d'histoire ecclésiastique* 8 (1907) 677-96, on the efficacy of the Eucharist and on the Real Presence; E. Michaud, "Saint Cyrille d'Alexandrie et l'Eucharistie," *Revue internationale de théologie* 10 (1902) 599-614, 675-92, severely criticized by Mahé for its "fantastic exegesis" and, on one occasion, for "bad faith"; and A. Struckmann, *Die Eucharistielehre des heiligen Cyrill von Alexandrien* (Paderborn, 1910), for Cyril's doctrine before 429 and then against Nestorius.

be genuinely denominated a restoration, a return to the original condition of humanity? In this matter several texts are highly significant. One is Cyril's comment on Jn 11:49–52:

Caiphas said that the death of Christ would be for the sake of the Jews alone; but [John] says that it was for all humanity. The point is, all of us are called God's race and children (γένος καὶ τέκνα), inasmuch as He is Father of all in that He engendered us by way of creation and brought into existence what did not exist. Still more, because we have the honor of having been made from the beginning after His image, and [the honor] of having obtained dominion over the creatures of earth. . . . But Satan scattered us . . . and led man astray. . . . However, Christ gathered us together once more and brought us all through faith into the one enclosure that is the Church, and put us under one yoke: all have become one . . . and are refashioned into "one new man" (Eph 2:15) and adore one God.[34]

The text mentions two senses in which Adam, like any man, could be called a child of God: he was created by God and he was an image of God. It does not justify the conclusion that Adam enjoyed a sonship equivalent to that given by Christ to Christians in the Church.

A second significant text occurs in the *Commentary on Isaiah*. When Is 43:6 speaks of sons and daughters hurrying from the four regions of the earth, it is "making manifest the time of Christ's coming, when the grace of adoption (υἱοθεσίας) through sanctification in the Spirit was given to those on earth."[35] Cyril does not say that adoptive sonship was restored—as we might expect from the context and from Cyril's insistence elsewhere on the restoration of humanity to its primeval state; he simply asserts that the gift was "given." Moreover, in the same context he had already declared that the Word's purpose in taking flesh was "to gather [Greeks and Jews] into spiritual oneness through faith and sanctification, make them worthy of that kinship with Him which is finely perfected (τελουμένης εὖ μάλα καὶ τῆς πρὸς αὐτὸν οἰκειότητος), and in this way link them through Himself to the Father."[36] With the Incarnation Cyril appears to envision a divine sonship which is unique; it was not part of humanity's aboriginal dowry, man's primeval resemblance to the divine. Where precisely does the distinction lie?

In the first place, Cyril maintains that the situation of humanity since the Incarnation is superior in several respects to the primitive

[34] *In Ioannem* 7, fragmenta (Pusey 2, 295).
[35] *In Isaiam* 4, 1 (*PG* 70, 889).
[36] *Ibid.* (*PG* 70, 888–89).

state of Adam. That primitive period of human existence in Adam was, Cyril admits, a holy (ἅγιος) period; but holy too, and "far greater" (πολὺ μείζων), is the period of human life "in Christ, who is the second Adam, renewing the race . . . to newness of life in the Spirit."[37] Concretely, our advantage over Adam is determined by the respective bases on which his condition and ours have been constructed: creation and Incarnation. In Janssens' paraphrase of Cyril's thought:

It is from God, in so far as He is Creator, that Adam received the Spirit; and by reason of his instability he could lose the Spirit, and he actually did lose Him for our whole nature. It is in our Savior, in so far as He is Word Incarnate, that we have obtained the Spirit as a stable gift, because Christ initially gave His immutability to our nature in His divine person. In the new economy the communication of the Spirit exhibits a character of stability which it does not possess in the case of Adam, because our human nature is found more intimately united to the divinity by the mystery of the Incarnation than by the fact of creation. Here we have the deep-seated reason for the basic difference between man's primitive situation and his state within the New Testament.[38]

It is recapitulation, but with increase, addition: a root kinship with God effected by the physical entrance of the Incarnate Word into humanity.

Is there increase in our properly supernatural kinship as well? To begin with, it is important to clarify Cyril's distinction between the intervention of the Holy Spirit in the New Testament and His intervention in the Old. "The Spirit was in the prophets for the requirements of prophecy, but now He dwells in the faithful through Christ—and first of all in Him, when He became man."[39] What we confront here is the profound difference between "illumination" (ἔλλαμψις) and "complete and perfect indwelling" (κατοίκησις).[40] The latter came only with the

---

[37] De adoratione 17 (PG 68, 1076). Cf. also In Ioelem 2 (Pusey 1, 338): In consequence of sin, the Spirit originally given to Adam did not remain with humanity; but, seeing that the Spirit remained upon Christ (cf. Jn 1:32), the second Adam, we have been established in a condition that is "incomparably better (τὸ ἀσυγκρίτως ἄμεινον)." In another passage, Homiliae paschales 16, 6 (PG 77, 765), Cyril asserts that the Father sent the Son "to transport our condition to a state incomparably better than it was of old"; but the context suggests strongly that this text (employed without reservation by Janssens, p. 257, to support his thesis that, for Cyril, our situation is superior to that of Adam in several respects) is actually contrasting our Incarnational condition not with the state of primitive justice but with the situation of humanity between the sin of Adam and the coming of Christ.

[38] Janssens, art. cit., p. 259; cf. In Ioannem 5, 2 (Pusey 1, 693-94).

[39] In Ioannem 5, 2 (Pusey 1, 697).

[40] Cf. ibid. (Pusey 1, 696, 698).

glorification of Christ; for, as Cyril claims when dealing with Mt 11:11, "when Christ rose up with the spoils of hell, then it was that the Spirit of adoption (υἱοθεσίας) was given. But blessed John [the Baptist] departed from life before the Spirit was given; therefore, though we be inferior to those who practiced justice successfully under the Law, nevertheless we have been put in a superior state (ἐν μείζοσι) through Christ."[41] It is simply a specific application of a consistent thesis, namely, that the gift of adoption was conferred only after the resurrection of Christ:

> Blessed John [the Baptist], together with all those who existed before him, is indeed born of woman, but they who have welcomed faith are no longer born of women; they are called sons of God. . . . For when Christ rose up with the spoils of hell, then it was that He gave the Spirit of adoption to those who believed in Him—and before all others to His own disciples; for "He breathed upon them, saying, 'Receive the Holy Spirit'" (Jn 20:22). . . . [It was then that] they became sharers completely (ὅλως) in the divine nature. . . . That the Spirit of adoption was not in men before His return (ἀναφοιτήσεως), the very wise evangelist John makes clear when he says, "For not yet was the Holy Spirit, seeing that Jesus had not yet been glorified" (Jn 7:39). By "glory" he means the resurrection from the dead and the ascent to heaven; for the only-begotten Word of God, upon His return there, sent us the Paraclete in His own stead, and He is in us through Him. . . . Therefore, the fact remains that, though we be inferior to those who had the justice of the Law, I mean in goodness of life, nevertheless because of Christ we are superior (ἐν μείζοσι) to those born of woman.[42]

The Spirit of adoption is given by the risen Christ, who has become through His resurrection the consummated principle of a new humanity. It is in baptism, concretely, that Christ confers on us the Spirit of

[41] *In Matthaeum*, Mt 11:11 (*PG* 72, 400). Cf. *In Isaiam* 4, 2 (*PG* 70, 936): When Christ is fashioned in us through the Spirit, we are fashioned into God's παῖς. "But since the name παῖς is a common name—for it is used of servants (οἰκετῶν) and of sons and daughters (υἱῶν)—we say that for those who are fashioned in the Law a formation rather to servants (οἰκέτας) is fitting; for a spirit of servitude was upon Israel. . . . But if one be fashioned in Christ, he is fashioned into a son (υἱόν) of God. . . ."

[42] *In Lucam* hom. 38 (*PG* 72, 617-20; compare *CSCO* 70, 86-87; Lat. tr. 140, 55-57). Cyril does not deny υἱοθεσία to the Old Testament; but Israel's adoption was a matter of type and external form (ἐν τύπῳ καὶ σχήματι), like Israel's circumcision in flesh; it was not the reality (κατ' ἀλήθειαν), which is given only through the indwelling Spirit of the Word enfleshed; cf. *In Ioannem* 1, 9 (Pusey 1, 135). For the significance of the "breathing" of Christ upon the apostles (not simply a parallel with the original communication of the Spirit in Gn 2:7, but an aspect of the instrumental role of Christ's humanity in the bestowal of the Spirit), cf. Janssens, *art. cit.*, pp. 262-64.

adoption whom He gave the apostles the day of His resurrection, and so continues in us the task of sanctification which opened with the Incarnation. In this New Testament grace of adoption Janssens justifiably sees what the contemporary theologian calls *gratia Christi capitis*.[43]

But the more profound reason which limits adoption in the Spirit to the Christian economy is not quite the instrumental causality of Christ's humanity; it is rather the mediation of Christ as contrasted with the mediation of Moses:

> Therefore, as far as the image of mediation is concerned, Moses of old should be considered a type of Christ: he ministered well to the sons of Israel what God had decreed. But the mediation of Moses was that of a servant (διακονική), while the mediation of Christ was that of a freeman (ἐλευθέρα) and it was more profound (μυστικωτέρα); for He touched by nature (φυσικῶς) those between whom He mediated: He reached both, humanity for whom He was mediator, and God the Father. On the one hand, He was God by nature, inasmuch as He was God's only Son, not separated from the Father's substance, and existing in it, just as He proceeds from it. On the other hand, He was man as well, inasmuch as He became flesh, likening Himself to us, in order to unite to God what was by nature far distant from God.[44]

It is to this physical mediation of the God-Man that Cyril links our supernatural kinship with God; it is this which confers adoption on us:

> ... it was in type that Israel was called to adoption through the mediation of Moses. That is why they were baptized into him, as Paul says, "in the cloud and in the sea" (1 Cor 10:2). . . . But they who mount to God's adoptive sonship by faith in Christ are baptized not into some created being but into the holy Trinity itself through the mediation of the Word, who links what is human to Himself through the flesh which is united to Him, and who is linked naturally to the Father inasmuch as He is God by nature. That is how the slave rises to sonship: through participation in the true Son he is called, and as it were ascends, to the dignity that belongs by nature to Him. That is why we are called, and are, begotten of God; through faith we have received the regeneration that comes through the Spirit.[45]

Here we discover the ultimate reason why Cyril calls our radical kinship with God "in Christ" the principle of our supernatural kinship with God "through Christ": it is the physical mediation of the Incarnate Word. If He were not man, He would have transmitted nothing to man's

---

[43] Cf. Janssens, *art. cit.*, p. 264.
[44] *In Ioannem* 3, 3 (Pusey 1, 393).
[45] *Ibid.* 1, 9 (Pusey 1, 135-36).

nature; if He were not God, He would not have transmitted a participation in God's nature.

On the basis of this analysis Janssens has synthesized admirably Cyril's vision of the analogy between our redeemed condition and the primitive state of Adam:

The economy of the Incarnation is a recapitulation: it restores the supernatural privileges which Adam had received at the time of his creation, i.e., participation in the divine nature through the Holy Spirit, incorruptibility, and domination of the passions; our divine sonship contains all these prerogatives. But, beyond that, it involves an increase. In point of fact, Adam did not have the radical kinship with God: though partaker of the divine nature, he found himself, in his capacity of creature, at an infinite distance from the Creator. It is only in Christ that this distance is filled up, since the moment of the Incarnation. In consequence, our first father had received the Spirit of his Creator without the physical mediation of Christ. Now it is only the Spirit given by Christ as humanity's new principle, and therefore communicated as a privilege of the economy of the Incarnation, that Cyril calls the Spirit of adoption. It is not astonishing, therefore, to read nowhere in Cyril's writings that Adam received the Spirit *of adoption*. Between the original union with God and ours there is, for difference, all the soteriological signification of the mystery of the Incarnation: we cannot speak of divine sonship of men before they are united to God through a physical mediator who is the link between humanity and divinity.[46]

[46] Janssens, *art. cit.*, p. 269. One difficulty persists; Janssens has not taken cognizance of it. It is true that we "read nowhere in Cyril's writings that Adam received the Spirit *of adoption*" (*ibid.*). It is, however, pertinent to point out that Cyril introduces Gn 1:27 into a context of adoptive sonship on more than one occasion—so much so that it is possible to conclude, at least from these passages in isolation, that our adoptive sonship is a return to Adam's original condition—incomparably better now because of Christ, but essentially the same sonship. Cyril asserts, e.g., that we would not have escaped corruption, "had not the beauty of the image of the heavenly been stamped on us through the vocation to adoptive sonship (υἱοθεσίαν); for, made partakers of [Christ] through the Spirit, we have been sealed to His likeness and we mount to the archetypal form of the image, according to which, Scripture says, we have been created as well. Once we have recovered in this fashion and with difficulty the primeval beauty of our nature, and have been refashioned to that divine nature, we shall be superior to the evils that have struck us in consequence of the transgression. And so we rise to this supernatural dignity by reason of Christ. . . ."; *In Ioannem* 1, 9 (Pusey 1, 133). Cf. also *De sancta et consubstantiali trinitate* dial. 3 (*PG* 75, 837): "we have been sealed to sonship (υἱότητα) through the Son in the Spirit; for the image of the Son is sonship, while the image of the Father is paternity. . . . We are God's image and likeness, molded thus to the whole supreme nature in the beginning." Again, interpreting Gn 1:26 of the whole Trinity, he says that "we have been

The profound difference between our divine sonship and the Word's is reducible to this: our filiation is participated, His is natural.[47] In Christ divinity is present substantially; our participation in divinity is an accidental thing, analogous to iron sharing in fire without ever becoming fire. Christ's sonship is "truth," ours is likeness, imitation.[48] It is imitation because it resembles the natural filiation of the Word; but in this very resemblance lies its grandeur. Cyril never compares our sonship with the juridical notion of adoption; its exemplary cause is invariably the relation of the natural Son of God to His Father. Nor is there any trace of adoptianism in Cyril's theology, if we remember his distinction between the gift of the Spirit as given by God and as given by the Word Incarnate. With reference to Christ our Lord, "it is the Word who Himself communicates His Spirit to His humanity; as for the faithful, it is through the mediation of Christ, new head of humanity—therefore, as *gratia Christi capitis*—that the Spirit is communicated to them, and it is only as such that Cyril calls Him the Spirit of adoption."[49]

In Cyril, as Janssens has concluded, we discover a new concept of our

made to the divine image, shaped as our nature is to God. But if we must say something not improbable, we who were about to be called sons of God (ἡμᾶς μέλλοντας υἱοὺς ὀνομάζεσθαι θεοῦ) had to be made rather to the Son's image, in order that the distinctive mark of sonship (υἱότητος) too might be conspicuous in us"; *De dogmatum solutione* 4 (Pusey, *In Ioannem* 3, 558). It is possible that the expression, "we who were about to be called sons of God," refers to the Christians to come, and to that extent supports Janssens' thesis; but it may well be that "we" refers to human nature, to all men, that "about to be" looks forward simply to the next verse, Gn 1:27, and that consequently the sinless Adam as well as the redeemed Christian is a son of God. However, Janssens might justifiably reply (a) that *adoptive* sonship—and it is the Spirit *of adoption* that makes the difference—does not receive specific mention save in the first of these three texts; and (b) that even in the first text Cyril does not state explicitly that the recovery of sonship is a return to a primitive *adoption*, a recovery of the Spirit *of adoption*.

[47] Cf. *Thesaurus* 12 (*PG* 75, 189): Cyril takes wing from an objection posed by heretics: If the fact that the Son is called the Father's Image makes Him one in nature with the Father, why are not men like God in essence, seeing that we have been called His sons and have been made to His image? Cyril's answer is simple: the Word is Son by nature, we are sons by grace; His dignity is natural, ours is adventitious; unless we are careful to avoid evil, we can easily lose what we have received. Moreover, we are called God's image because the Image of God dwells in us. For this image through indwelling cf. *De sancta et consubstantiali trinitate* dial. 5 (*PG* 75, 949).

[48] Cf. *In Ioannem* 1, 3 (Pusey 1, 37): "true" sonship means to be from the Father's substance; cf. *Thesaurus* 10 (*PG* 75, 136-37): true generation means consubstantiality.

[49] Janssens, *art. cit.*, pp. 274-75.

divine sonship. God's only Son became the first-born among many brethren, "in order that in Him and through Him we might be sons of God by nature and by grace (φυσικῶς τε καὶ κατὰ χάριν) : by nature, in Him and in Him alone; by participation (μεθεκτῶς) and by grace, through Him in the Spirit."[50] Our divine filiation—and, implicitly, our resemblance to God, the image of God in us under this aspect—is achieved in two stages. The first stage is a radical kinship with God for all men, in Christ, at the moment of the Incarnation. With this as foundation, the second stage is a properly supernatural filiation in the individual, in so far as Christ by His unique mediation communicates to human beings the Spirit of adoption.[51]

It is in connection with this aspect of the image, adoptive sonship, that Cyril confronts on several occasions a dilemma which, I suspect, disturbs him more than he will admit. Do we image the divine nature as such, or is there a specific resemblance which we bear to one or other of the Persons? On one point he is adamant. He will not tolerate the thought that we image one divine Person and not three. This fundamental thesis is stated unmistakably in the *Contra Iulianum*. There he refuses to entertain the theory that in Gn 1:26 the Father could have been addressing inferior gods. Such a theory is outlawed by sound exegesis and by theology; it does not harmonize with the text and it will not square with a correct concept of God. Moses simply wanted to leave the impression that man's creation was not an unconsidered thing on

---

[50] *De recta fide, ad Theodosium* 30 (*ACO* 1, 1, 1, 61; *PG* 76, 1177). Cf. the same text in *De incarnatione Unigeniti* (*PG* 75, 1229). Janssens' "fondamentalement" is not a literal translation of Cyril's φυσικῶς; it is interpretation, though justified, I believe, by the exhaustive analysis he has made of sonship in Cyril. However, it is one of the rare instances where Janssens translates an important word without reproducing the Greek original; it might leave the impression that Cyril had actually used some derivative of ῥίζα, "root," "foundation." It is worth mentioning, because "natural sonship" is unusual in Cyril to express our basic kinship with God in Christ.

[51] Cf. Janssens, *art. cit.*, p. 275; also pp. 275–77, where he concludes that, for Cyril, the formal cause of the radical kinship is the hypostatic union; the formal cause of the supernatural kinship is the Spirit of adoption, i.e., the Spirit as communicated by the risen Christ. In both cases it is *gratia Christi capitis.*—Janssens indicates (p. 278) how Cyril's approach to adoption saves him from having to confront the problem which concerns later Christologists: is adoptive sonship a formal effect of sanctifying grace? In fact, Cyril finds it absurd to suppose that He who is Son by nature became Son by grace; cf. *De sancta et consubstantiali trinitate* dial. 4 (*PG* 75, 909): "for where or what sort will the archetype be, if He to whom we have been formed descends with us to that which is by adoption and imitation (τὸ κατὰ θέσιν καὶ μίμησιν)?"

God's part; "man's nature was honored with what I might call previous deliberation."[52] Moreover,

since in Father, Son, and Holy Spirit, that is, in the consubstantial Trinity, the one, ineffable, and incomprehensible nature of God is to be understood—that no one might be carried away by excessive stupidity to the unbefitting statement that man was made to the image and likeness of God, but not of the Son as well —and, I suppose, there would be also the probability of the contrary conjecture, and the declaration that man was made to the likeness of the Son, but not of the Father as well—anticipating, as I said, such sophistical language from somebody or other from time to time, he said that the holy Trinity itself said to itself, "Let us make man to our image and likeness," to have it understood that he was formed, I mean spiritually (νοητῶς), to the whole inexpressible nature of the divinity. . . . Therefore . . . we must concede that in the holy and consubstantial Trinity the fulness of the ineffable divinity is to be understood; while we, on our part, have been formed to the true, perfectly exact Image of the Father, that is to say, to the Son, and on our souls His divine beauty is stamped through participation of the Holy Spirit; for He is in us, just as the Son Himself is.[53]

[52] *Contra Iulianum* 1 (*PG* 76, 536). Cyril recognizes, in the same passage, that we cannot properly speak of reflection, doubt, or inquiry when treating of God's mind; "for, as soon as it has willed anything, this is correctly and faultlessly done." Cf. *ibid.* 2 (*PG* 76, 585): the "previous deliberation" implies that man's creation was different from the rest; "it was as though God gave deep thought to this thing." On the Trinity in Gn 1:26 cf. also *ibid.* 4 (*PG* 76, 725); *ibid.* 8 (*PG* 76, 909): "let us make" shows the fulness of the Trinity; "to our image" indicates their natural identity.—Most of the Fathers who interpret Gn 1:26 see in it "words addressed by the Father to the Son; others, words addressed to the Son and to the Holy Spirit; still others, a kind of deliberation of the divine Persons among themselves"; J. Lebreton, *Histoire du dogme de la Trinité des origines au concile de Nicée* 1 (7th ed.; Paris, 1927) 553, note 1; the same note contains a number of patristic references. The semi-Arian Council of Sirmium in 351 anathematized those who claimed that the Father spoke to Himself and not to the Son; cf. Concilium Sirmiense, can. 14, in Athanasius, *De synodis* 27 (*PG* 26, 737); cf. J. Mansi, *Sacrorum conciliorum nova et amplissima collectio* 3 (Florence, 1759) 258. In this matter Philo had little, if any, influence on the Christian Greek tradition. We gather from him that "let us make" was addressed by God to a fair-sized audience of co-workers, that God was "holding parley with His powers." Why did God solicit the cooperation of inferior agents? First, that human vice might be referred back to subordinate powers, human virtue to God; second, it was fitting that the sovereign faculty of the soul, reason, be fashioned by the Sovereign, the subject part by subjects; cf. *De opificio mundi* 72–75 [24] (Cohn-Wendland 1, 19–20); *De confusione linguarum* 168–79 [33–35] (Cohn-Wendland 2, 251–54); *De fuga et inventione* 68–70 [13] (Cohn-Wendland 3, 110).

[53] *Contra Iulianum* 1 (*PG* 76, 537–40). Cf. *De sancta et consubstantiali trinitate* dial. 3 (*PG* 75, 804–8), where Gn 1:26–27 is used by Cyril to show the trinity of

Briefly, in being fashioned to God, to the Son who is God's Image, man was fashioned to the whole divine nature, not to some one Person to the exclusion of another.[54]

But the problem is posited in more challenging fashion on other occasions. In the *Dialogues on the Trinity*, for example, an initially profitable line of reasoning ends in sudden surrender. Cyril knows that we "are formed to sonship (υἱότητα) inasmuch as the Son refashions us to, as it were, His own glory, and stamps [on us] the distinctive marks of His own form." Moreover, he believes that the power to adopt (υἱοποιεῖν) is to be ascribed "as a natural operation (ἐνέργεια)" to the Son—and solely because He is Son. He maintains, however, that the indwelling of the Father does not effect something different than does the Son; otherwise the Father would make His image a father and not a son. The question is then asked: this divine resemblance of which Genesis speaks, is it a likeness to the Son alone, or is the Father to be included as well? Should we say that we have been formed to the whole divine nature, even though we are called, and actually are, sons? Cyril's answer:

> . . . our complete faith, on this point at any rate, has in view one nature in divinity, and that in three proper hypostases, which are conformed and identical in nature, and together form the one supreme beauty, to which we too have been fashioned. But we have been sealed to sonship (υἱότητα) through the Son in the Spirit; for the Son's image is sonship, while the Father's is fatherhood. Therefore, we are sons by sonship, but we are God's image and likeness, molded in this way to the whole supreme nature in the beginning.[55]

At this point, however, just as his literary foil interjects, "you are right," Cyril gives up this line of reasoning as idle and unprofitable. We are left with two items of information and one unanswered problem. We are told that we image the one divine nature, identical in all three Persons; and we are told that there is a specific resemblance to the Son, at least in the sense that, like Him, we too are sons. The problem which haunts

---

Persons in the one godhead; man was made to the image of all three Persons; the same must be true now, if the work of Christ is to be genuinely a restoration. Cf. also *ibid.*, dial. 4 (*PG* 75, 881, 893). It is striking how frequently we meet, especially in the Eastern authors, the argument for the unity, the unicity, of the divine nature from Gn 1:26-27: there must be one only divine nature, because the divine image impressed on man is one, the image of Father, Son, and Holy Spirit.

[54] More frequently Cyril is concerned to prove that man resembles not one specific Person but all three. His scriptural basis is Gn 1:26: "In the expressions, 'let us make' and 'in our likeness,' the holy Trinity is signified"; *In Ioannem* 11, 7 (Pusey 2, 682); cf. *Thesaurus* 1 (*PG* 75, 25); *De sancta et consubstantiali trinitate* dial. 4 (*PG* 75, 881, 893); *Contra Iulianum* 1 (*PG* 76, 536).

[55] *De sancta et consubstantiali trinitate* dial. 3 (*PG* 75, 837).

him, which he never answers, which he never quite formulates, is this: In imaging the Trinity, do we have a resemblance to the Father which corresponds in any way to the resemblance we bear the Son in being sons?

In the *De dogmatum solutione* Cyril is presented with the same problem in different terms. The difficulty has been proposed to him that apparently we are not properly images of God; we are rather images of an image. The proper Image of God the Archetype is the Word of God; man is image of the Word, of the Son, of the Image. The justification is Genesis: God did not make man His image; He made man to His Image. Cyril's solution opens in promising fashion, but once again he finds speculation flat and profitless, and prefers to close the discussion on a note of theological simplicity:

> The divine and consubstantial Trinity is superior to every form and corporeal representation. Now we must believe that the Father is in the Son, and the Son is in the Father, and that he who has seen the Son has seen the Father. Further, the Son is seen in the consubstantial Spirit. . . . Where there is complete identity of essence, there surely we find no difference. What you understand the Father to be, that the Son is too, save only for being Father; and what you assume the Son to be, that the Spirit is too, save only for being Son. On the one hand, each of those named subsists independently and is actually what He is said to be; on the other, the complete likeness (ὁμοιότης) of the holy Trinity is an exact likeness. Therefore, even though man was made to the image of the Son, even in this way he is to the image of God; for the distinctive marks of the whole consubstantial Trinity shine forth in him, inasmuch as there is the one godhead by nature in Father, Son, and Holy Spirit. It is true, the remarkable Moses writes: "And God said, 'Let us make man to our image and likeness.'" But the "our" does not signify one Person, because the fulness of the divine, ineffable nature is had in three hypostases. It is unprofitable, therefore, to waste one's efforts in subtle disputes, useless to say that we are not images of God, are not images of the Archetype, but are images rather of God's Image. On the contrary, it is sufficient to believe with simplicity that we have been made to the divine image, shaped as our nature is to God. But if we must say something not improbable, we who were about to be called sons of God had to be made rather to the Son's image, in order that the distinctive mark of sonship too might be conspicuous in us.[56]

Once again, the basic, undeniable, significant fact for Cyril is that we have been fashioned in such a way that we resemble the one divine nature and consequently all three divine Persons. Again, speculation is abandoned as fruitless. Again, there is a strong suggestion that we image the

[56] *De dogmatum solutione* 4 (Pusey, *In Ioannem* 3, 557-58).

Son in His proper personality; for we resemble Him in the sonship which is His to the exclusion of Father and Holy Spirit.

To conclude this chapter, it may be observed that the conception of sonship as a facet in the divine image is recognizably present in the earlier Alexandrians; for example, in Clement, Origen, Athanasius, and Didymus. For Clement, to obtain salvation, to achieve divine sonship, to become a heavenly and holy man, to have been made after God's image and likeness, all mean the same thing.[57] As Mayer summarizes it, adoption (υἱοθεσία)

denotes the final perfection possible for Christians, because it is awarded to those alone who have achieved the ideal godlikeness. . . . If it is certain that for Clement divine sonship is granted in baptism, he prefers to call Christians as such merely children (παῖδες), while he reserves the title of son (and the likeness to God) for the perfect Christian, the "gnostic," who has become godlike after the model of Christ and has become man (ἀνήρ). In fact, Clement seems even to have in mind the perfection of the next life (admission to the vision of God).[58]

Perfect ὁμοίωσις θεοῦ means υἱοθεσία, ἀφθαρσία.[59]

In Origen's eyes, "the saints, being image of an image (for the Image is the Son), express (ἀπομάττονται) sonship"—and they do so not simply by conformity to Christ's glorified body; renewed in mind, they are conformed to the Christ who is in that body.[60] Interpreting the opening words of the Lord's Prayer, he assures us that "it is not possible to see among the ancients the stability and unchangeableness of sonship." Adoption comes fully with the coming of Christ.[61]

In his later works Athanasius speaks frequently of υἱοθεσία, a supernatural condition whereby the just, sanctified by divine grace, are called and are sons of God.[62] On one occasion he appears to identify divinization

[57] Cf. Mayer, op. cit., pp. 8–9; cf. also pp. 83–85; Clement of Alexandria, Stromata 6, 14 (GCS 15, 489).

[58] Mayer, op. cit., pp. 8–9, note 13. Cf. K. Prümm, "Glaube und Erkenntnis im zweiten Buch der Stromata des Klemens von Alexandrien," Scholastik 12 (1937) 45; W. Völker, Der wahre Gnostiker nach Clemens Alexandrinus (Berlin and Leipzig, 1952) pp. 109–15.

[59] Cf. Mayer, op. cit., p. 20.

[60] Origen, De oratione 22, 4 (GCS 3, 348–49); cf. ibid. 22, 3 (GCS 3, 347–48): the genuine sons of God are joint heirs with Christ; they flee sin and pursue good works. Cf. also Origen, In Ioannem 20, 23 (GCS 10, 356–57).

[61] Origen, De oratione 22, 2 (GCS 3, 346–47).

[62] Cf. the many references in G. Müller, Lexicon Athanasianum (Berlin, 1952) cols. 1464–65. See, e.g., Athanasius, Epistola 1 ad Serapionem 19 (PG 26, 576): adoption comes through the Spirit; Oratio 3 contra Arianos 9 (PG 26, 340): Christ

and adoption: it is in the Holy Spirit that the Word leads men to the Father "by divinizing and adopting (θεοποιῶν καὶ υἱοποιῶν) them."[63] Our divine filiation was the purpose of the Incarnation: "the Son of God became Son of man, that the sons of man, that is, of Adam, might become sons of God."[64] It is a matter of imitation (μίμησις), adoption (θέσις), and grace (χάρις), not of nature (φύσις) and essence (οὐσία).[65] Nevertheless, Athanasius makes no studied effort to link the reality which is sonship with the image of God in man.[66]

Didymus argues that the Spirit must be God "if together with God the Father and His Son the Holy Spirit renews us through baptism to the first image and so is responsible for our adoptive sonship (υἱοθεσίας) and our divinization," whereas "no creature can adopt (υἱοποιεῖν) or divinize in this way."[67] For Didymus, adoption is divinization, a return to man's original resemblance to his God.

The early indications are not insignificant; still, Cyril remains unrivaled among the Alexandrians for his bold effort to fathom the depths of our divine sonship and to link it intelligibly to its archetype, the Christ who is God's only Son and yet the first-born of many brethren.[68]

---

is called first-born, to show that it is through the Son that all are made and all are adopted; Oratio 1 contra Arianos 39 (PG 26, 94): there is no adoption independently of the true Son.—Regrettably, I have not seen the article signed T. M., "Redenzione e filiazione adottiva in s. Atanasio e s. C. Alessandrino," Scuola cattolica 67 (1939) 728–37.

[63] Athanasius, Epistola 1 ad Serapionem 25 (PG 26, 589). Gross remarks that "these two terms are here obviously synonyms"; op. cit., p. 212, note 1.

[64] Athanasius, De incarnatione Dei Verbi et contra Arianos 8 (PG 26, 996). Despite the doubts that have been raised, we are justified in regarding this work as authentic; cf. Altaner, op. cit., p. 232.—Athanasius tells us that our adoption is effected in baptism; cf. Epistola de decretis Nicaenae synodi 31 (PG 25, 473).

[65] Cf. Athanasius, Oratio 3 contra Arianos 19 (PG 26, 364).

[66] So Bernard, op. cit., p. 146.

[67] Didymus, De trinitate 3, 2 (PG 39, 801–4); cf. also ibid. 2, 12 (PG 39, 680–81).

[68] For some of the patristic background on the problem of filiation before the Incarnation, cf. the stimulating study (patristic, scriptural, and theological) of G. Philips, "La grâce des justes de l'Ancien Testament," Ephemerides theologicae Lovanienses 23 (1947) 521–56; 24 (1948) 23–58; specifically, in the first essay, pp. 534–56. He finds that, for Irenaeus, the Incarnation alone introduces sonship, and our gifts of adoption surpass the privileges of Adam. Athanasius has no hesitation in seeing sanctity and sonship in antiquity, but men as a whole remained corruptible, slaves to their passions; and Philips does not dare to conclude that, for Athanasius, the Incarnation brings more than a quantitative difference, a quibusdam ad omnes. In Chrysostom's eyes, filiation and inhabitation are reserved for the Christian era. On Cyril, Philips is in agreement with Janssens. For Augustine and Leo the Great among the Latins, cf. Philips, pp. 547–54.

# CHAPTER 9

# WOMAN

In speaking of man as God's image, we have been using the term "man" in its widest application: a human being, a member of the human race. Anyone who has read Cyril extensively will not consider impertinent the question: did Cyril actually include the female of the species in his theology of the image? Does woman, as well as her male counterpart, resemble God in rationality, freedom, dominion, holiness, incorruptibility, and even "sonship"? If for no other reason, the question is relevant because of Cyril's ambivalent attitude towards woman. To see the problem in proper perspective, it is advisable to summarize (a) Cyril's psychology of woman and (b) his theology of woman.

Of some significance for Cyril's psychology of woman is his symbolism of woman; it is significant because it is so consistent. Woman is, in Cyril's eyes, a type (τύπος) or a symbol (σύμβολον) or a sign (σημεῖον) of two things especially: weakness or softness (ἀσθένεια, μαλακισμός) and sense pleasure (ἡδονή).[1] The weakness is, at least in one context, a weakness of nature.[2] At times it appears as a weakness of the mind;[3] elsewhere it embraces the will;[4] it even includes a facility for sin.[5] Usually, however, the weakness is not defined or circumscribed. The sense pleasure in question is still less accurately identified; it has, nevertheless, a distinctly odious flavor.

More significantly, in Cyril's psychology what woman symbolizes epitomizes what woman is. Although she has the same essential nature as man,[6] there are important differences.[7] Cyril maintains that the male,

---

[1] Cf. *In Zachariam* 2 (Pusey 2, 353); *In Oseam* 1 (Pusey 1, 34–35); *Glaphyra in Exodum* 2 (*PG* 69, 437); *Homiliae paschales* 10, 4 (*PG* 77, 624); *De adoratione* 3 (*PG* 68, 300), where Cyril adds that "all iniquity is committed through these two."

[2] Cf. *De adoratione* 16 (*PG* 68, 1053). For the male as type of spiritual manliness cf. *Glaphyra in Exodum* 1 (*PG* 69, 396); *Glaphyra in Leviticum* (*PG* 69, 552–53).

[3] Cf. *De adoratione* 1 (*PG* 68, 181); specifically, Cyril is speaking of Lot's wife.

[4] Cf. *In Oseam* 1 (Pusey 1, 34–35).

[5] Cf. *De adoratione* 16 (*PG* 68, 1053); *Glaphyra in Exodum* 2 (*PG* 69, 437). It is only just to mention that Cyril sees the Law (Dt 24:5) depicting the virtue of the saints under the form of a woman; cf. *De adoratione* 5 (*PG* 68, 377).

[6] Cf. *De sancta et consubstantiali trinitate* dial. 3 (*PG* 75, 852); *Thesaurus* 34 (*PG* 75, 585).

[7] Cf. *In epistolam 1 ad Corinthios* 4, 4 (Pusey 3, 283).

in obvious distinction from the female, is "a fair fetus" and the object of a prospective mother's longing; "for mothers prefer to bear a male child rather than a female."[8] Dealing with the Leviticus legislation on the purification of women after childbearing (Lv 12:1 ff.), Cyril remarks: "The experts tell us that, if it is a male child that is deposited in the womb, it just about receives its specific nature (εἰδοποιεῖσθαι) when forty days have elapsed; but if it is a female, the process is slower, since the female is weak and impotent. They say it needs twice forty days, that is, eighty, for its specific nature (εἰδοποίησιν) to emerge clearly."[9]

[8] *In Isaiam* 5, 6 (*PG* 70, 1436).

[9] *De adoratione* 15 (*PG* 68, 1008). Previously, *ibid.* 8 (*PG* 68, 545), Cyril had not distinguished between the sexes: "They tell us that the embryo in the womb is just about in human shape (ἀνθρωποειδές) when the fortieth day is completed; it is then that it assumes the general form (τύπον) of our body."—That the male embryo was formed more quickly than the female was the common view of ancient Greek medicine; cf. J. H. Waszink, *Tertulliani De anima* (Amsterdam, 1947) p. 422, and the references there to Hippocrates, Galen, Empedocles, Diogenes of Apollonia, Asclepiades, and Athenaeus. Tertullian, writing his *De anima* between 210 and 213 A.D., and greatly dependent on the physician Soranus, is simply reproducing the physiology of his time when he asserts, "masculus temperies effingitur . . . femina aliquanto serius"; *De anima* 36, 4 (ed. Waszink, p. 52). The difference was attributed, by Galen for example, to the superior heat and dryness of the male germ; cf. J. Needham, *A History of Embryology* (Cambridge, 1934) pp. 11, 54–55. The respective dates for male and female vary with the authors; Aristotle has forty days for the male, ninety for the female, but it is not clear whether he means that the rational soul is infused when he says that "about this period the embryo begins to resolve into distinct parts, it having hitherto consisted of a fleshlike substance without distinction of parts"; *Historia animalium* 7, 3 (tr. D. W. Thompson, in J. A. Smith and W. D. Ross, *The Works of Aristotle* 4 [Oxford, 1910] n. 583b); cf. the same dates in Pliny, *Naturalis historia* 7, 6 (*LCL*, Pliny, *Natural History* 2, 533), but with reference to initial movement in the womb. The general theory was long-lived; "the ancient belief that male embryos were formed twice as quickly as female ones . . . lingered on until Goelicke took the trouble to disprove it experimentally in 1723"; Needham, *op. cit.*, p. 58.—The medical opinion was of philosophical and theological interest because it was so closely allied with the question: when is the embryo a human being? For this aspect cf. R. J. Huser, *The Crime of Abortion in Canon Law* (Washington, D.C., 1942) pp. 1–78; I. Palazzini, *Ius fetus ad vitam eiusque tutela in fontibus ac doctrina canonica usque ad saeculum XVI* (Urbania, 1943); and especially F. J. Dölger, "Das Lebensrecht des ungeborenen Kindes und die Fruchtabtreibung in der Bewertung der heidnischen und christlichen Antike," *Antike und Christentum* 4 (1934) 1–61. As late as June 8, 1771, the Sacred Congregation of the Council referred to the 40–80 norm as the more common and accepted opinion of theologians on the time of animation; cf. Huser, *op. cit.*, pp. 64–65.—The influences on Cyril in this matter are primarily two. There is the LXX version of Ex 21:22–23, which, unlike the Hebrew, incorporates a physiology of the third century B.C. with

Cyril insists—often enough to be at once monotonous and indicative of a consistent outlook—that woman is inferior to man. Frequently he contents himself with the sheer enunciation of his thesis: man is superior, woman inferior;[10] man holds the chief place, woman is subject and subordinate;[11] man has the greater honor and glory, even before God, whereas woman is of less esteem.[12] But on occasion Cyril bares a few details. The inferiority is not purely a question of physical size or physical strength.[13] What is more momentous, woman falls short of man in "natural ability."[14] She has not the strength to achieve the virtue of which the male is capable.[15] She is of imperfect intelligence.[16] Unlike her male complement, she is dull-witted, slow to learn, unprepared to grasp the difficult and the supernatural;[17] for her mind is a soft, weak,

reference to the formed and unformed embryo. And there is the background of the famous medical school of Alexandria, where all earlier traditions met, and which had not yet lost its glory when Galen visited it in the middle of the second century A.D. The fusion of the Jewish and Hellenic streams of thought is apparent in Philo; cf. *Quaestiones et solutiones in Genesin* 1, 25 (*LCL*, Philo, Supplement 1, 15), so very much like Cyril: "Inasmuch as the moulding of the male is more perfect than, and double, that of the female, it requires only half the time, namely forty days; whereas the imperfect woman, who is, so to speak, a half-section of man, requires twice as many days, namely eighty." Cf. *ibid.* 2, 14; 4, 154 (*LCL*, Philo, Supplement 1, 90; 1, 438). It is interesting to find the Babylonian Talmud reporting the ruling of R. Išmael in the first half of the second century: "a male is fully fashioned on the forty-first day and a female on the eighty-first day. The sages, however, maintain that both the fashioning of the male and the fashioning of the female take the same course, each lasting forty-one days"; *Niddah* 3, 7 (tr. I. W. Slotki, in *The Babylonian Talmud: Seder Ṭohoroth*, ed. I. Epstein (London, 1948) p. 207. Note there, pp. 209–10, the story (adduced by both sides in support of their respective positions) that Cleopatra the Ptolemaic queen (perhaps confused with the gynecologist Cleopatra who was a contemporary of Soranus and Galen) had investigated fetal development, apparently at Alexandria, by the dissection of slaves at known intervals from conception.

[10] Cf. *De adoratione* 15 (*PG* 68, 953); *Glaphyra in Genesim* 3 (*PG* 69, 128).

[11] Cf. *De adoratione* 15 (*PG* 68, 968); *ibid.* 17 (*PG* 68, 1068); *Glaphyra in Numeros* (*PG* 69, 628).

[12] Cf. *De adoratione* 10 (*PG* 68, 712); "nature," Cyril says darkly, "testifies to this." Cf. also *In Isaiam* 3, 1 (*PG* 70, 584).

[13] On size and strength cf. *De adoratione* 16 (*PG* 68, 1037); *In Malachiam* 1 (Pusey 2, 570); perhaps *Glaphyra in Leviticum* (*PG* 69, 545).

[14] Cf. *De adoratione* 16 (*PG* 68, 1037).

[15] Cf. *ibid.*

[16] Cf. *ibid.* 4 (*PG* 68, 308, 344).

[17] Cf. *In Ioannem* 12 (Pusey 3, 113, 115–16); cf. *ibid.* 2, 4 (Pusey 1, 272): woman is incapable of keen perception, unlike the male, who is quicker to learn.

delicate thing.[18] Briefly, "the female sex is ever weak in mind and body."[19] Moreover, there is a softness in woman which precludes vigorous purpose.[20] She is a peaceable creature, with an aversion to war[21]—apparently a regrettable characteristic. She is timid and cowardly, naturally enervated, easily dispirited,[22] with a penchant for insatiable grief and unrestrained tears.[23] "Woman is a twittering, loquacious creature, with a gift for contriving deceit."[24] She is enamored of honor and show, of dress and golden ornaments; she revels in the body's beauty.[25] On the other hand, "the male sex is ever elect of God, because it is a warrior breed, because it is capable of coming to spiritual vigor, capable of sowing seed, of teaching the rest, of tracing its steps to the mature measure of the fulness of Christ" (cf. Eph 4:13).[26] From Paul's declaration to the Corinthians, "man was not created for woman, but woman for man" (1 Cor 11:9), Cyril concludes that Adam was (and, implicitly, every man is) more perfect (τελειότερος) than the woman who was fashioned for his sake.[27]

[18] Cf. *ibid.* 2, 4 (Pusey 1, 272); 12 (Pusey 3, 90–91); *In Malachiam* 1 (Pusey 2, 570).

[19] *Homiliae paschales* 28, 3 (*PG* 77, 948).

[20] Cf. *In Ioannem* 3, 6 (Pusey 1, 470); *In Oseam* 3 (Pusey 1, 111).

[21] Cf. *De adoratione* 4 (*PG* 68, 308); *In Isaiam* 2, 3 (*PG* 70, 401).

[22] Cf. *Glaphyra in Exodum* 1 (*PG* 69, 389); *In Isaiam* 2, 4 (*PG* 70, 465, 485); *In Lucam* hom. 152 (*PG* 72, 936; cf. English tr. from Syriac by R. Payne Smith, *op. cit.* 2, 716: "of a disposition ready to sink at the approach of aught that is sorrowful"); cf. also *Homiliae paschales* 10, 3 (*PG* 77, 621): the female sex is "cowardly and feeble, found wanting as far as battle and boldness go."

[23] Cf. *In Ioannem* 12 (Pusey 3, 89–90, 111); *ibid.* 7 (Pusey 2, 282); *In Lucam*, Lk 23:27 (*PG* 72, 936); *In Michaeam* 3 (Pusey 1, 717); *In Zachariam* 3 (Pusey 2, 375); *In Ioelem* 1 (Pusey 1, 299); *In Oseam* 3 (Pusey 1, 111); *In Isaiam* 2, 4; 2, 5 (*PG* 70, 485, 525).

[24] Cf. *De adoratione* 1 (*PG* 68, 205); *Contra Iulianum* 7 (*PG* 76, 845).

[25] Cf. *In Isaiam* 1, 3 (*PG* 70, 120). But cf. *In Nahum* 1 (Pusey 2, 53) for a slighting reference to the "ugliness" of the female body unclothed. Cyril does admit that good, decorous women scorn adornment and harlotry, anything that would result in loss of dignity; they prefer to seek their glory in good deeds; cf. *In Isaiam* 1, 3 (*PG* 70, 121).

[26] Cf. *In Matthaeum*, Mt 14:21 (*PG* 72, 417); also *De adoratione* 17 (*PG* 68, 1064): the reason why, according to Ex 23:17, all the men folk had to present themselves thrice each year before God was "because the male sex is worthy of God's heavenly inspection." Cf. *ibid.* 4 (*PG* 68, 320).

[27] Cf. *Thesaurus* 15 (*PG* 75, 257); also *In epistolam 1 ad Corinthios* 4, 4 (Pusey, *In Ioannem* 3, 283), where woman "differs a little in nature" because she is in God's image and likeness "as by means of the man." We shall discuss this passage in greater detail later in the present chapter.

. This pessimistic psychology of woman has influenced Cyril's conception of the woman who played so prominent and so lofty a role in his polemic against Nestorius: the Mother of God.[28] In his *Commentary on John* Cyril pictures our Lady and the other holy women weeping beneath the cross. "The female sex, you see, is ever given to tears and falls very easily into lamentation, especially when there is rich reason for tears." And he adds: "In all likelihood, even the Lord's Mother was scandalized by the unexpected passion." Christ's death on the cross, the mockery of the Jews, the soldiers jeering and dividing His garments, all this "almost drove her out of her mind." Cyril has Mary doubting her Son's claim to divinity, "because she did not know the mystery. So dreadful were the things which took place that they were enough to upset [even] cool, dispassionate reasoning." Nor is it surprising in a woman. Look at Peter's scandal (Mt 16:22)—and he was the leader of the apostles. Nothing incredible, therefore, if "the delicate mind of this woman" was carried away to weaker thoughts. Cyril's scriptural basis is the Simeon scene in Lk 2:34–35. The "sword" is the sharp assault of the passion cutting Mary's mind and causing strange thoughts; it is through temptation that souls are tested and their thoughts laid bare.[29] And yet, if the immediate basis is biblical, the root of Cyril's version of the Sorrowful Mother is a pessimistic psychology of the feminine. Despite his undeniably exalted idea of the θεοτόκος and of her part in the Christian economy, Cyril is persuaded by his theory of womanly weakness, emotional and intellectual, to cast Mary in a role beneath the cross that ill accords with his Marian theology.

This synthesis of woman's capacities on a natural level, and the application of these principles to the Mother of Christ, would lead us to expect rather little of woman in the order of redemption; it is a psychology which presages a pessimistic theology. In point of fact, such a presumption, so broad a conclusion, does not do justice to the ramifications of Cyril's thought. The labyrinthine ways of that thought will emerge more clearly if we consider briefly two aspects of Cyril's theology of woman: (a) the curse of God on woman and (b) the sanctification of

[28] For a comprehensive picture of Cyril's Mariology cf. A. Eberle, *Die Mariologie des heiligen Cyrillus von Alexandrien* (Freiburg, 1921).

[29] Cf. *In Ioannem* 12 (Pusey 3, 89–91). Cf. *ibid.* (Pusey 3, 93): Jesus gave Mary to John; John would explain to her in detail "the depth of the mystery"; also *Homiliae diversae* 12 (*PG* 77, 1049): "by the sword he may have meant the grief which she experienced over Christ, when she saw Him crucified to whom she had given birth, and had no idea at all that He would be superior to death and would return to life from the dead."

woman. This will supply useful background for the problem which concerns us more intimately: the image of God in woman.

First, then, the curse of God on woman. By inducing Adam to sin, woman had become, in Cyril's fine phrase, "death's deaconess."[30] In consequence, God laid a curse upon woman: "In sorrow shall you give birth to children" (Gn 3:16). In what did this curse, this sorrow, consist? For Cyril, "the goad of grief" at issue here is reducible to this, that until the coming of Christ women bore children εἰς θάνατον: life was a door only to death.[31] That was woman's reproach, woman's sorrow. That is why her sex was "especially dishonored."[32]

But God became man "to destroy the curse that lay upon the first woman."[33] How did He accomplish His objective? Cyril has two explanations, but they are not incompatible. The first explanation centers in the divine maternity. "Because they gave birth with death in prospect (εἰς θάνατον), women felt the goad of grief; but when a woman gave birth after the flesh to Emmanuel, who is Life, the power of the curse was destroyed, and together with death was extinguished the sorrow-laden bearing that lay upon earth's mothers."[34] In a word: before Christ, birth meant death; after Christ, birth led to life.

The second explanation—and the more common in Cyril—focuses on the appearance of the risen Christ to the women in the garden (cf. Mt 28:9-10). With His "do not be afraid," our Lord "casts out their fear and paves the way for belief."[35] His "welcome" (χαίρετε), pronounced by the same God who had thundered the curse, "is for the female sex the deliverance from reproach and the overthrow of the curse."[36] Moreover, the holy women, not the disciples, are the first to learn of the resurrection, the first to see the risen Christ's glory, the first invited to announce the glad tidings. Why? The Word took flesh

to heal the sick and to deliver man from his primeval guilt. It was therefore quite necessary for woman first to be favored with the task of announcing the resurrection's glad tidings; for, since the first and more ancient woman had induced Adam to transgress along with herself, seconding the serpent's speech, and became herself death's procurer, was it not imperative that the guilt of

---

[30] *In Lucam*, Lk 24:9 (*PG* 72, 941).
[31] Cf. *In Lucam* hom. 2 (*PG* 72, 489; *CSCO* 70, 11-12; Lat. tr. 140, 3).
[32] *In Matthaeum*, Mt 28:9 (*PG* 72, 469).
[33] *In Lucam* hom. 2 (*PG* 72, 489; *CSCO* 70, 11; Lat. tr. 140, 3).
[34] *Ibid.*
[35] *In Matthaeum*, Mt 28:9 (*PG* 72, 469).
[36] *In Lucam*, Lk 24:9 (*PG* 72, 941).

such dread charges be removed by the apostolic mission? For "where the offense has abounded," it says, "grace has abounded yet more" (Rom 5:20). The gospel of salvation was given to woman, who had been deaconess of death; for "welcome" was said to them of necessity by Him who had imposed the curse in the beginning. . . . The latter, therefore, have atoned for the former; what had sickened has been healed.[37]

Briefly, χαίρετε is the antidote to ἐν λύπαις. Woman, who had ministered to the tempter's words in the Garden of Eden, ministered to the words of angels (and of God) in another garden. This is the honor of the sex dishonored, this her good hope, this her healing: "welcome!" This is the end of her primal sorrow.

Second, the sanctification of woman. Despite his dismal picture of woman on a natural niveau, there is a striking absence of anti-feminism when Cyril considers woman's capacities specifically "in Christ Jesus." Thus, apropos of Lv 6:27 ff., he remarks: "Tell me: did the Law prescribe the rejection of the female sex from the blessing? We do not say this; for the female sex is sanctified (ἁγιάζεται) along with us. The truth is, these things are types and shadows. By the male and holy sex the Law cleverly indicated those who are spiritually manly and holy (ἱερούς) in Christ . . . ; for in Christ Jesus there is not male and female, but we are all of one, inasmuch as we partake of the one bread . . ." (cf. Gal 3:28; 1 Cor 10:17).[38] Again, interpreting Jl 2:28, Cyril believes that the words, "the sons and daughters will prophesy," reveal the universality of God's grace and the equality of all in this respect. "For the female sex, in the eyes of God, is not something to be cast aside, provided it is eager to do His will and elects to be wise. Nor is it unrewarded, or without share in sanctification (ἀμέτοχον ἁγιασμοῦ), if it is distinguished for faith and good works; for it, too, has been thought worthy of grace and

---

[37] In Isaiam 3, 1 (PG 70, 608). Cf. In Ioannem 12, 1 (Pusey 3, 120–22), where, commenting on Jn 20:17, Cyril proposes essentially the same doctrine, but with reference specifically to Mary Magdalene, because she was the first to weep for Christ, the first to reach the tomb, a more ardent lover of Christ, and because results are usually ascribed to leaders rather than co-workers. The contrast is again made between Eve's service to Satan and Magdalene's service to Christ. An interesting variation on our theme occurs in Cyril's comments on Cana, In Ioannem 2, 1 (Pusey 1, 200–201): Christ came to Cana (a) to work a miracle; (b) to sanctify the beginning of man's production in the flesh and extend His blessing to those not yet born; and (c) to destroy the curse of Gn 3:16 by honoring marriage with His presence. Cyril makes no effort to reconcile his two versions (Cana and the garden) of the destruction of the curse.

[38] Glaphyra in Leviticum (PG 69, 552–53).

of mercy, receives from God 'the pledge of the Spirit' (2 Cor 1:22), and has been reckoned among the children."[39]

In this matter Cyril feels impelled on one occasion to combine theological doctrine and pastoral advice. Obviously disturbed by a sacerdotal misogyny which parades as piety, he notes that our Lord's disciples were amazed at His kindness and condescension towards the Samaritan woman:

> For, unlike some who have been coarsened by an excess of piety, He does not think it well to shrink from conversation with a woman, but unfolds to all His love of humankind. By this act He shows that, since there is only one Creator, it is not to men (ἀνδράσι) alone that He imparts the life that comes through faith; He catches in His net the female sex as well. Let this serve as a model for the teacher in the churches, and let him not refuse to be of service to women; for it is surely not his own inclinations that he must follow but the advantage of the gospel preaching (κηρύγματος).[40]

So then, woman as well as man can be sanctified; she can receive the Holy Spirit; to her the Creator communicates His own life; she is God's child. Logically implicit in all this is the conclusion that woman, too, reflects divinity, is an image of God. And the most impressive proof that Cyril accepts the conclusion is the fact that almost without exception he does not make a special issue of woman in the hundreds of texts which deal with God's image. The rare exception is not of Cyril's own making; it has been forced upon him by Paul's lecture to the Corinthians on the God-Christ-man-woman hierarchy: "I would have you know that the head of every man is Christ, and the head of the woman is the man, and the head of Christ is God. . . . A man indeed ought not to cover his head, because he is the image and glory of God; but woman is the glory of man; for man is not from woman, but woman from man; for man was not created for woman, but woman for man" (1 Cor 11:3, 7–9). Two of Cyril's comments on this passage, in so far as they concern the image, deserve to be reproduced in extenso. One occurs in the *Commentary on 1 Corinthians*:

> By "head" here he means the archetypal beauty, with whose image (εἰκόνα), we are justified in thinking, each of those mentioned [i.e., Christ, man, and woman] has been enriched; each of them has been given an essential nobility or else the same nature. For the first man, Adam, was made to God's image and likeness. . . . Man's head, therefore, is Christ. On the one hand, He is

[39] *In Ioelem* 2 (Pusey 1, 339–40).
[40] *In Ioannem* 2, 5 (Pusey 1, 287).

archetype as God; on the other, by the law of our nature He was of our species too when He appeared as man. . . . Further, the woman was made to the image and likeness of man, that is, of Adam—by no means alien to him; on the contrary, of the same nature and species. . . .

Ugliness in the image is with perfect justice regarded as outrage to the archetype. If man (ἀνήρ) is God's image and glory . . . let him maintain the freedom (παρρησίαν) fit for God and keep his head uncovered . . . ; for the Deity is free (ἐλεύθερον). . . . And, seeing that woman is in man's likeness, image of an image, and glory of glory, and that nature legislates long hair for her, why does that which is first emulate what is inferior in grace (τὸ ὑστερίζον ἐν χάριτι)? Woman, too, is indeed in God's image and likeness, but as by means of the man, so that in some way she differs a little in nature. . . .

[Paul] said that the man (ἄνδρα) had been made to God's image and likeness. And that the female has, as it were, been hurled behind the male's honor and glory, he affirmed confidently and clearly when he added: "woman is the glory of man; for man was not created for woman, but woman for man." Then, covering over nicely what was likely to distress the female sex, he added: "yet neither is woman independent of man, nor man independent of woman" (1 Cor 11:11). Admittedly, woman came into being from man. . . . Nevertheless, woman is a contributing factor in man's production. Nature has brought the two together to form one; in nature's providential arrangement, theirs is a mutual need, theirs a link of love.[41]

The passage is complex, at times needlessly intricate, but for our purposes the essential idea is sufficiently clear. Both the male and the female have been fashioned to God's image; for both, the ultimate archetype is Christ as God. But the male was formed immediately to the image of God; the female was formed immediately to the image of man

---

[41] *In epistolam 1 ad Corinthios* 4, 4 (Pusey, *In Ioannem* 3, 281–84); ὑστερίζον could mean "comes later" rather than "comes short of," "is inferior," but the context suggests the latter version. On man as woman's "head" cf. *De sancta et consubstantiali trinitate* dial. 3 (*PG* 75, 852–53): it means (a) that man has the same nature as woman; (b) that his condition is better, corresponding to the honorable, glorious condition of the head in the human body; and (c) that woman came from man in the beginning and was formed to his image, whereas he had God for archetype. Cf. also *De recta fide, ad dominas* 52 (*ACO* 1, 1, 5, 76; *PG* 76, 1236): "man is woman's head because she was taken from his flesh and has him as her origin (ἀρχήν)."—On the question of their "mutual need" and "link of love" cf. *In Ioannem* 2, 4 (Pusey 1, 273): "What makes marriage blameless is not union that springs from lustful desire, but lawful consent and a bond of union that arises from pure love." Cf. *In Malachiam* 1 (Pusey 2, 589): According to God's creation, husband and wife are one body and one soul (the bond is love and God's law); in fact, the wife is part of her husband's soul. But cf. *In Oseam* 6 (Pusey 1, 256): Jacob's reward for serving Laban was "quite small: marriage. . . ."

(for she was originally fashioned from his substance), therefore to the
image of God mediately, through the image of God that is the male. In
consequence, she "differs a little in nature"; but this difference is apparently not in the content of the image but simply in the mediacy of her
resemblance to the divine.[42] What that image content is substantially,
comes to light from another exegesis of the Pauline passage in Cyril's
*Thesaurus*:

> ... first ... let us examine how [the male] is God's image and glory. I think
> it is initially clear that the male (ἄνδρα) is the first to be spoken of in this way
> because he participated in the Spirit of God, and through Him came to share
> in the divine nature, with the result that he has been filled with the glory that
> comes from God. Therefore, he has been called God's image and glory inasmuch
> as he has in himself the Spirit that proceeds from God's substance, and through
> this communion with the Spirit has been formed to the likeness of the Creator.
> We may learn the force of the phrase no less clearly from the fact that the woman
> too was given the same title. Paul says that she is man's glory because she came
> into being from his substance. ... Therefore, just as the woman has been called
> the glory of the man because part of his members was taken for her own constitution, so has the man been called God's glory because he has been made partaker of His substance through the indwelling of the Holy Spirit in him.[43]

The passage is not transparent, partially because Cyril's concern here
is not human beings but the Holy Spirit. From the fact that participation in the Spirit makes man an image of God, Cyril will conclude that
the Spirit must be God. The divine image is a premise, and the argument
is hastily concatenated. As for the image itself, this much seems a defensible interpretation of Cyril's thought. To image God means to participate in God's nature through the inhabitation of the Spirit. In this
sense the male of the human species is God's image and is filled with
God's glory. Woman is likewise God's image (this we know from the
*Commentary on 1 Corinthians*) and consequently she too is filled with
God's glory; but, in Paul's polemical preoccupation and Cyril's use of
Paul, what is accentuated is Eve's immediate archetype, the Adam from
whose substance she was framed.

---

[42] That Eve's creation was unique, that this manner of fashioning woman no
longer obtains, does not strike Cyril as an element to be considered in a discussion
of woman's resemblance to God, specifically in determining her immediate archetype.

[43] *Thesaurus* 34 (*PG* 75, 585). When Cyril says that woman "was given the same
title," I suspect that he is thinking only of δόξα (not of εἰκών), as the context goes
on to indicate.

At this point a brief summation is in order. First, with respect to woman's potentialities on a properly human level, Cyril betrays a surprising pessimism. Intellect, emotions, will—in all these, woman is decidedly inferior to man. In fact, Cyril recognizes in woman less natural aptitude for the acquisition of virtue in its broad sense, and even at times for achieving supernatural perfection. His attitude recalls inevitably the thanksgiving maxim that was current among Persians, Greeks, and Jews in the environment of the New Testament: Thank God I am "not an infidel, an ignoramus, a slave, or a woman."[44] Frankly, Cyril's ideal of woman sheerly as a human being does not touch the heights achieved by the pre-Christian Greek with his Niobe and Penelope, Andromache and Antigone, Cassandra and Clytemnestra, Iphigeneia and Eurykleia.[45]

Where grace enters in, however, Cyril leaves the general impression that "there is neither male nor female" (Gal 3:28). Granted, we may be

[44] Cf. A. Oepke, "γυνή," in G. Kittel, *Theologisches Wörterbuch zum Neuen Testament* 1, 776-77, with the references given on p. 777, note 4. For the situation of woman in Palestinian Judaism in Christ's time, cf. J. Bonsirven, *Le Judaïsme palestinien au temps de Jésus-Christ: Sa théologie* 2 (Paris, 1935) 9-10 ("a certain misogyny"), 211-16. In the *Letter* of Ps.-Aristeas, the Hellenized Jew who gives us so much information on Egyptian and Palestinian affairs in the second or even the third century B.C., we read: ". . . the female sex is rash, energetic in pursuing every object of its desires; it changes its opinion with sudden ease through fallacious reasoning; it was fashioned weak by nature"; *Epistola Aristeae* 250 (ed. H. St. J. Thackeray, in H. G. Meecham, *The Letter of Aristeas* [Manchester, 1935] p. 34).

[45] Cf. Oepke, *art. cit.*, p. 777. Much research is imperative if we are to understand the influences which molded Cyril's conception of woman, and the extent to which his attitude represents fifth-century thinking. Some of the introductory work on the early Christian writers has been done; cf., e.g., G. Cortellezzi, "Il concetto della donna nelle opere di Tertulliano," *Didaskaleion* (1923) 1:5-29; 2:57-79; 3:43-100. Too often, however, contemporary appraisals of the ancient Christian attitude are broad generalizations without the necessary qualifications. F. A. Wright, "Position of Women," *Oxford Classical Dictionary* (Oxford, 1949) p. 960, observes: "With the rise of Christianity in Rome women were put back into a position of relative subservience. . . . St. Augustine and St. Jerome were convinced that woman was the weaker vessel; and the Church followed their lead." J. Fitzsimons, *Woman Today* (London and New York, 1952) p. 170, sums up the patristic tradition in the words of John Milton: "Oh! why did God / Creator wise that peopl'd highest Heav'n / With Spirits Masculine, create at last / This noveltie on Earth, this fair defect / Of Nature?" (*Paradise Lost* 10, 888 ff.). On the other hand, L. Bender, "Donna," *Enciclopedia cattolica* 4, 1873, insists that "Christianity, by preaching that in the family the husband is head . . . has greatly elevated woman's personality, putting her . . . on the same spiritual level as man."

justified in concluding from his psychology that grace will experience greater difficulty in perfecting woman's nature; still, Cyril usually preaches a universality and an equality "in Christ Jesus" which leave little room for distinctions based on sex. Here the remote influences on Cyril are several. There is the attitude of Christ our Lord, who called all human beings indiscriminately to the freedom of the children of God. There is the tradition of the Christian community: from its beginning, the woman (ἀδελφή) belonged to the community as fully as the man (ἀδελφός). There is, nevertheless, in Cyril as in Paul, a certain tension between the progressive and the reactionary.[46] Paul insists that in Christianity there is no invidious distinction between male and female; and yet he can declare that in virtue of creation woman is a step further removed from God than is man. In similar vein, Cyril finds man and woman equally images of God; and still he can maintain that woman images God indirectly, by imaging man. His stimulus is Paul; for the thesis appears only under the impact of 1 Corinthians. But it is his own psychology that prepares him for Paul and permits the conclusion: "Woman, too, is indeed in God's image and likeness, but as by means of the man, so that she differs a little in nature."[47] What softens the picture, in Cyril as in Paul, is the realization that, whatever position of pre-eminence God has conferred on man, whatever subordination God has decreed for woman in point of fact, man is to exercise his prerogative not selfishly but in selfless, enduring love.[48]

That woman as well as man has been fashioned in God's image is quietly assumed rather than expressly proved in the early Alexandrian tradition—even where an author's psychology of the feminine is tinged with a masculine bias. Clement of Alexandria, for example, refuses to distinguish woman from man on the basis of human nature. Because her soul is the same as his, she is expected to achieve the same virtue; because her body is different, she is destined for childbearing and housekeeping.[49] And still Clement can say that "the males are better and first

[46] On Paul cf. Oepke, *art. cit.*, pp. 785–86.

[47] *In epistolam 1 ad Corinthios* 4, 4 (Pusey, *In Ioannem* 3, 283).

[48] Cf. *ibid.* (Pusey, *In Ioannem* 3, 284); cf. also 1 Cor 11:10; Col 3:18; Eph 5:22 ff.

[49] Cf. Clement of Alexandria, *Stromata* 4, 8 (*GCS* 15, 274–79). This difference, he claims, does not touch human nature; it is a question of womanhood. Despite his realization of the depths to which many women had sunk (cf. *Paedagogus* 3, 3 [*GCS* 12, 244–51]), Clement has a more optimistic approach than Cyril to the problem of the feminine; he uses Prv 31 to good advantage; cf. *ibid.* 3, 11 (*GCS* 12, 266–82). Cf. also *Stromata* 4, 19 (*GCS* 15, 300): perfection is equally possible to woman and to man.

in everything."[50] Even so, he will not deny woman the same resemblance to God, though she strive ever so incongruously for artificial beauty: "It is absurdly out of place for those [i.e., women] who have been made 'to the image and to the likeness of God' to dishonor the archetype by assuming a foreign embellishment, preferring the evil arts of men to the workmanship of God."[51]

Cyril's pastoral counsel with reference to the Samaritan woman[52] is redolent of Origen's observations on the same passage: "Even the disciples marvel when they come upon Christ. They have seen before this the magnitude of His divinity, and they marvel: how can such a person speak with a woman? But we ourselves, led by swaggering arrogance, disdain the more shabby of men, forgetful of the fact that 'Let us make man to our image and to our likeness' pertains to each human being (ἕκαστον ἄνθρωπον)."[53] The image of God is not applied expressly to woman, but the implication is unmistakable.

I cannot find that Athanasius ever introduces a distinction into human resemblance to the divine on the basis of sex, even when 1 Cor 11:7 offers an occasion for it.[54] In contrast with such silence, however expressive it be, the author of In verba: Faciamus hominem is splendidly outspoken. He is afraid that the feminine sex will argue from the masculine article (τόν) before ἄνθρωπον in Gn 1:26 that it was merely the male (ἀνήρ) who was fashioned to God's image. And he asserts that, precisely to forestall so mistaken an interpretation, Gn 1:27 added, "Male and female He created them." His own mind is unclouded: "Woman too was made to God's image, just as man was." Their natures are equal, their virtues are equal. Any differences are external; their souls are the same.[55]

In the indisputably authentic works of Gregory of Nyssa we do not

[50] Clement of Alexandria, Stromata 4, 8 (GCS 15, 277).

[51] Clement of Alexandria, Paedagogus 3, 11 (GCS 12, 273). If there seems a connotation here that the body itself is in God's image, this interpretation is outlawed by Paedagogus 3, 2 (GCS 12, 238), where, in a similar context, the image of God is undeniably within.

[52] Cf. note 40 above, with the corresponding text.

[53] Origen, In Ioannem 13, 28 (GCS 10, 252). Compare Origen's "they were amazed" (καταπεπλήγασιν; Jn 4:27 has simply ἐθαύμαζον) at His "goodness" (χρηστότητα), with Cyril's "they are amazed" (καταπλήττονται) at His "kindness" (ἡμερότητα).

[54] Cf. Athanasius, Oratio 2 contra Arianos 30 (PG 26, 209).

[55] Cf. In verba: Faciamus hominem 1 (PG 44, 276); cf. the same ideas in De hominis structura 1, 22-23 (PG 30, 33-36).

find as simple a solution to the problem of sex and the image. Nevertheless, however his thorny theory of a double creation is to be construed,[56] two pertinent theses of Gregory can scarcely be questioned. (*a*) In the "first creation" the image had nothing to do with sex; creation according to God's image is prior—logically at least—to sexual differentiation; "male and female He created them" is an addition to "God made man to His image."[57] (*b*) In the "second creation," with the human creature divided into male and female, it still remains true that the divine image is independent of sex.[58] However we interpret his states of humanity, ideal or real, paradisiacal or earthly, Gregory's theme is unchanging: sex is adventitious to the image.[59] "In Christ Jesus," he repeats after Paul, "there is neither male nor female."[60]

It is not surprising that some of the more Antiochene of the Fathers, whose image concept stresses the aspect of domination, are led to refuse the image to woman—influenced by the subjection of woman to man in biblical passages like Gn 3:16, 1 Cor 11:3 ff., and Eph 5:22. Diodore of Tarsus argues from 1 Cor 11:7 that the male alone is God's image; and, as we have seen, he places the image in dominion.[61] Isidore of Pelusium finds the image (dominion) in woman before sin, in harmony with Gn 1: 26; he finds it "diminished" (subjection to man) after sin, in harmony with 1 Cor 11:7.[62] Ambrosiaster concludes from 1 Cor 11:7 that woman is not God's image.[63] Why not? Because she is subject to her husband's

[56] Cf., e.g., E. V. McClear, "The Fall of Man and Original Sin in the Theology of Gregory of Nyssa," *Theological Studies* 9 (1948) 177–85; Leys, *op. cit.*, pp. 106–11; Daniélou, *Platonisme et théologie mystique*, pp. 57–58; H. von Balthasar, *Présence et pensée: Essai sur la philosophie religieuse de Grégoire de Nysse* (Paris, 1942) pp. 39–42; H. F. Cherniss, *The Platonism of Gregory of Nyssa* (Berkeley, 1930) pp. 25–33; E. F. Sutcliffe, "St. Gregory of Nyssa and Paradise," *Ecclesiastical Review* 84 (1931) 337–50.

[57] Cf. Gregory of Nyssa, *De hominis opificio* 16 (*PG* 44, 181).

[58] Cf. *ibid.* (*PG* 44, 184).

[59] Cf. Leys, *op. cit.*, p. 138; cf. the double creation in Philo, *De opificio mundi* 134 [46] (Cohn-Wendland 1, 38).

[60] Cf Gregory of Nyssa, *De hominis opificio* 16 (*PG* 44, 181).

[61] Cf. Diodore, *Fragmenta in Genesin*, Gn 1:26 (*PG* 33, 1564–65). In Chrysostom's observations on 1 Cor 11:3 ff., the subjection of woman is clear enough, but the image doctrine is vague; cf. *In epistolam 1 ad Corinthios* hom. 26, 1–5 (*PG* 61, 214–18).

[62] Cf. Isidore of Pelusium, *Epistolae* 3, 95 (*PG* 78, 801).

[63] Cf. Ambrosiaster, *Quaestiones veteris et novi testamenti 127*, 21 (*CSEL* 50, 48); cf. *ibid.* 106, 17 (*CSEL* 50, 243–44); *In epistolam b. Pauli ad Corinthios primam*, 1 Cor 11:7 ff. (*PL* 17, 253–54).

dominion and has no authority;[64] and because it is from the one man that all human beings have their origin upon earth.[65]

But this Antiochene orientation, despite its attachment to Paul, is not the approach of Cyril, who discovers the image of God in every human being regardless of sex, even though he is persuaded by his psychology of the feminine and by his exegesis of Paul to see in the male an intermediate archetype through whom woman resembles her Creator.

[64] Cf. Ambrosiaster, *Quaestiones* 45, 3 (*CSEL* 50, 82–83).
[65] Cf. Ambrosiaster, *In 1 Corinthios*, 1 Cor 11:7 ff. (*PL* 17, 253).

# CHAPTER 10

# SIN

In paradise the image of God that was man (Adam first, and Eve by way of Adam) was a many-splendored thing. First, he was λογικός. The light of reason is a participation in Him who is Light, who is Reason, the Logos; it means a mind germinally virtuous, open to the divine, in quest of God. Such was eminently the mind of Adam: "his mind was totally and continually absorbed in the contemplation of God";[1] he was "perfect in understanding."[2]

Second, he was ἐλεύθερος. Freedom is basically the power to elect one object in preference to another; the specific activity which the Giver of freedom has in view is deliberate choice of the good, rejection of the evil; to that end man is divinely oriented towards good by the indeliberate drive of his will. Such was Adam's situation: he was "entrusted with unrestricted movement towards his every desire,"[3] so that virtue might be "a matter of deliberate choice,"[4] though fed by his "natural appetite for everything that is good."[5]

Third, he was ἀρχικός. The dominion of which Gn 1:26 speaks is sovereignty over the fish of the sea, the beasts of the field, and the birds of the air. This Adam had: "God bestowed on man . . . empire over everything on earth."[6]

Fourth, he was ἅγιος. Holiness, ontologically, is a participation in God's nature, whereby the Spirit, by a communication of Himself, fashions man to the Son and so to the Father; dynamically, it is man's conscious imitation of God through virtuous living. Such was Adam's lot: "the primitive period of human life in . . . Adam was holy";[7] "the Creator implanted [in Adam], like some seal of His own nature, the Holy Spirit . . . through whom he was fashioned to the archetypal beauty, and

---

[1] *In Romanos*, Rom 5:18-19 (Pusey, *In Ioannem* 3, 186); unfortunately, Cyril does not explain θεοπτία here; but cf. *Contra Iulianum* 3 (*PG* 76, 637), quoted later in this chapter.

[2] *In Ioannem* 1, 9 (Pusey 1, 111).

[3] *Glaphyra in Genesim* 1 (*PG* 69, 24).

[4] *De adoratione* 1 (*PG* 68, 145).

[5] *De dogmatum solutione* 2 (Pusey, *In Ioannem* 3, 552).

[6] *Glaphyra in Genesim* 1 (*PG* 69, 20).

[7] *De adoratione* 17 (*PG* 68, 1076).

was perfected after the image of the Creator, strengthened to every form of virtue by the power of the Spirit who dwelt in him."[8]

Fifth, he was ἄφθαρτος. Human incorruptibility is an endless existence in which the whole man is superior not simply to physical dissolution but also to the concupiscence rooted in corruptible flesh. Such was Adam: "his body was superior to death, because the Maker of all things implanted life in it. Now, while it was beyond corruption, it had indeed innate appetites, appetites for food and procreation, but the amazing thing was that his mind was not tyrannized by these tendencies; for he did freely what he wanted to do, seeing that the flesh was not yet subject to the passions consequent upon corruption."[9]

Sixth, he was not θεός. Divine sonship on the human level is a participation in the Son through the Spirit; an imitation, by grace, of Him who is Son by nature. Adam was τέκνον, yes; for every human being can call God Father by the twin titles of existence and image.[10] Perhaps he was even υἱός in some sense; for he did have the Spirit of the Son. But θεός, no; for adoptive sonship is the privilege of the Christian, to whom alone the risen Christ communicates the Spirit of adoption.

In paradise, therefore, "human nature lacked nothing for its well-being and its happiness."[11] And Adam "would have abided in the original gifts of [human] nature" if he had not revolted.[12] Gifted with glory, however, and surrounded by delights, man had to realize that God was his King and Lord, lest prosperity engender independence; for unbridled freedom, in Cyril's view, leads but to pride and passion. And so, that man might ever be mindful of human subordination to the divine, God gave man "a law of self-control"—he was not to eat of the tree of life—and God threatened punishment for its transgression.[13] But Satan was envious (envious, Cyril hints, of man's immortal destiny[14]) and, "using as the tool of his villainy" the woman whom Adam had received as one flesh with himself,[15] he lured the latter by sophistry to eat of the for-

[8] *In Ioannem* 9, 1 (Pusey 2, 485).
[9] *Contra Iulianum* 3 (*PG* 76, 637).
[10] Cf. *In Ioannem* 7, fragmenta (Pusey 2, 295).
[11] *Glaphyra in Genesim* 2 (*PG* 69, 77). Cf. *De adoratione* 2 (*PG* 68, 248): "As long as the man who had been made to God's image was all but nursed in God's bosom and had not yet trampled on the command given, he was covered all round with His loving care and lived a pure and holy life, unaware of death."
[12] *In Ioannem* 9 (Pusey 2, 359).
[13] Cf. *Glaphyra in Genesim* 1 (*PG* 69, 20); *De adoratione* 1 (*PG* 68, 148); *In epistolam 1 ad Corinthios* 7 (Pusey, *In Ioannem* 3, 314).
[14] Cf. *In Lucam* hom. 142 (*PG* 72, 908; cf. Smith, Eng. tr. 2, 665).
[15] Cf. *De adoratione* 1 (*PG* 68, 148); *Glaphyra in Genesim* 1 (*PG* 69, 29).

bidden fruit.[16] Able to choose good or evil, Adam "was carried away by
bitter guile."[17] His transgression was an act of disobedience,[18] and his
disobedience offended God.[19]

What manner of whirlwind Adam reaped from his sin Cyril makes
frighteningly vivid in the fate of the image. Regrettably, he has not
synthesized his ideas in this respect; and his references are so frequent,
the individual treatments are so fragmentary, and his phraseology is at
times so puzzling, that a contrived synthesis runs the risk of adulterat-
ing his thought. Nevertheless, the effort should be made. And any reconstruction of Cyril's theology of sin and the image must begin with
two general principles. On the one hand, despite sin "we have lost none
of our essential components,"[20] no possession that is indispensable if man
is to remain human, if he is to be "a rational, mortal animal, capable of
understanding and knowledge." Or, as his literary foil phrases it in the
*Dialogues on the Trinity*, "we have suffered no injury to our nature; for
we have not by any means departed into nonbeing; we do exist, but
without virtue."[21] On the other hand, Adam's sin did affect the image
adversely: "sin ($\dot{\eta}$ $\dot{a}\mu a\rho\tau\iota a$) marred the beauty of the godlike image, and
Satan filled the radiant face of humanity with sordidness."[22] That much
prefaced, what was the specific impact of Adam's sin on each aspect of
the image?

First, rationality. In harmony with Cyril's postulate, it must be in-
ferred that Adam, if sin-scarred, remained rational, "capable of understanding and knowledge." Essentially, therefore, the image was unim-
paired. Nevertheless, Cyril knows a primeval perfection of wisdom whose
continuation was linked with the preservation of Adam's sinlessness; he
was "perfect in understanding ($\tau\epsilon\lambda\epsilon\iota os$ $\dot{\epsilon}\nu$ $\sigma\upsilon\nu\dot{\epsilon}\sigma\epsilon\iota$)—as long as he preserved pure and unsullied in himself the enlightenment given to his

[16] Cf. *Glaphyra in Genesim* 1 (*PG* 69, 20); *In Ioannem* 5, 2 (Pusey 1, 691); *In
epistolam 1 ad Corinthios* 7 (Pusey, *In Ioannem* 3, 314).

[17] *In Ioannem* 2, 1 (Pusey 1, 183–84).

[18] Cf. *In Lucam* hom. 142 (*PG* 72, 908; cf. Smith, Eng. tr. 2, 665); *In Lucam*
hom. 42 (*CSCO* 70, 113; Lat. tr. 140, 75; Smith, Eng. tr. 1, 171); *In psalmos*, Ps
6:3 (*PG* 69, 745).

[19] Cf. *In Romanos*, Rom 5:11–12, 18–19 (Pusey, *In Ioannem* 3, 182, 186).

[20] *Responsiones ad Tiberium* 10 (Pusey, *In Ioannem* 3, 594).

[21] *De sancta et consubstantiali trinitate* dial. 1 (*PG* 75, 676).

[22] *Responsiones ad Tiberium* 8 (Pusey, *In Ioannem* 3, 590). The effect was instantaneous; cf. *De adoratione* 1 (*PG* 68, 149): "Having bartered, therefore, the
grace that came from God and having been stripped of the blessings given in the
beginning, man's nature was cast out of the paradise of delight and instantly
($\epsilon\dot{\upsilon}\theta\dot{\upsilon}s$) transformed to ugliness. . . . "

nature by God, and did not prostitute the dignity of that nature."[23] It may well be this intellectual perfection that Cyril has in view when he develops his concept of Adam's original "completeness" ($\dot{\alpha}\rho\tau\iota\omega\varsigma\ \dot{\epsilon}\chi o\nu\tau a$) in soul and body:

> For his mind was made in such wise that it was capable of seeing God and divine things distinctly, in the measure allotted our nature. . . . It was filled with desire for every kind of admirable thing; it had a (so to speak) simple and uniform knowledge of all that was good, and looked to this without distraction, as though it saw only this. With the whole sweep of its volitions it tended to this indefatigably. . . .[24]

This unclouded contemplation was affected by sin and concupiscence;[25] and it seems consonant with Cyril's outlook to suggest that here sin makes contact with the image. Sin did not make the first man inhuman, did not make Adam irrational; but it did impair the preternatural perfection of reason ($\theta\epsilon o\pi\tau\iota a$) which is feasible when, by God's gracious giving, mind has dominion over passion.

Second, freedom. Self-determination was not destroyed by sin: "it is in our power to bend in either direction, towards the good and towards its opposite."[26] Cyril's proof, significantly, is here not drawn from Christianity; it reaches him from ill-starred Phaedra in Euripides' *Hippolytus*:

> Oft sleepless in the ling'ring hours of night
> Have I mused how the life of men corrupts.
> 'Tis not, I think, through nature's inborn will
> They act so ill—for wisdom dwells at least
> With many—, but consider this we must:
> The good we know full well and recognize,

[23] *In Ioannem* 1, 9 (Pusey 1, 111). The passage is confusing. From the contrast drawn between our progressive advancement to intellectual maturity (the intellect begins to function with the fifth year, according to *De adoratione* 16 [PG 68, 1037]) and the original state of perfect intelligence in Adam, the latter might appear to be nothing more than the adult wisdom to which the first man was entitled because of his unique creation. On the other hand, the dependence of this perfection on sinlessness, and the text we quote next from *Contra Iulianum* 3, argue to a wisdom preternatural not simply in the manner of its giving (instantaneous) but in content as well.

[24] *Contra Iulianum* 3 (PG 76, 637). True, the passage is, on the face of it, an effort to describe Adam's complete humanity; but the "completeness," the "perfection," is ambiguous—especially since Cyril declares that man at creation "lacked nothing that was good ($\kappa a\lambda o\hat{v}$)."

[25] Cf. *ibid.* (PG 76, 637–41).

[26] *De adoratione* 6 (PG 68, 453).

Yet practice not, now some from laziness,
While some a pleasure place before the fair.
And many are the pleasures of this life:
Long gossip, ease—delightful evils they. . . .[27]

True, Cyril does say, in connection with the difficult passage in Rom 7: 18 ff., that the flesh "forces" (καταβιάζεται) a reluctant mind to turn unwillingly from the good; but he modifies this when he denominates the tyranny of the flesh "hard to escape" (δυσδιάφυκτον) and reminds us that, despite all this, man "holds the reins of his own volitions."[28] There is a tension here between psychological and spiritual freedom. Man is not compelled to sin; still, the dominion of Satan did inhibit Adam's liberty, his openness to the divine, his response to the spiritual. This is the freedom which only an Incarnation would restore:

Men were free (ἐλευθέρους) upon the earth, finely fashioned to the divine image' and "created," as blessed Paul says, "for good works, which God made ready beforehand that we may walk in them" (Eph 2:10); but the discoverer of iniquity defrauded them beyond all measure. He withdrew them from their love for God and made them his own worshipers, hanging on them sin's yoke that was hard to escape (δυσδιάφυκτον). Pitifully as they fared . . . Christ rescued them and made them free (ἐλευθέρους) once more.[29]

Freedom in its larger sense is the unreserved response of the graced soul to the suggestions of grace, uninhibited by Satan without or by concupiscence within; the less inhibited, the greater the freedom. This is the freedom which Adam had when "with the whole sweep of [his] volitions" he "tended indefatigably" to all that was good.[30] This is the freedom which Adam lost.

Third, dominion. Adam "was made to the Creator's image and was appointed to rule over the things of earth"; but, once the devil deceived him, "he was stripped of the kingship (βασιλείας) and the glory which he had in the beginning. . . ."[31]

[27] Ibid. (PG 68, 456). The quotation is from Euripides, Hippolytus 375-84. (LCL, Euripides 4, 192, 194; translation mine).

[28] In Romanos, Rom 7:18 ff. (Pusey, In Ioannem 3, 206-7).

[29] In Isaiam 1, 5 (PG 70, 249).

[30] Contra Iulianum 3 (PG 76, 637).

[31] De adoratione 2 (PG 68, 244). Cf. also Responsiones ad Tiberium 10 (Pusey, In Ioannem 3, 593-94), where the context indicates, though not indisputably, that dominion, like sanctification and justice, is not essential to man, and that, unlike corporeity, it was lost through sin. See also chapter 6 above, where we treated briefly the loss of dominion.

Fourth, incorruptibility. In Cyril's exegesis, the "earthy" man of 1 Cor 15:49, whose image we bear, is Adam. Once sin entered in, therefore, Adam became the archetype of physical death,[32] of subjection to passions and corruption,[33] of frailty and facility in the face of sin.[34] Adam is as authentically the prototype of φθορά as Christ is the archetype of ἀφθαρσία.

Fifth, holiness. In consequence of his sin Adam lost holiness:

> Turn your mind to that ancient Adam, and in the first fruits and root of the race count the whole of humanity as it were in him. Ponder this fact as well, that he had been made to the Creator's image and had been appointed to rule over earthly things, and was as it were in God's hand through the life [that consisted] in holiness (ἁγιασμῷ). . . . But when, tricked by the serpent's bitterness, he was removed from his original state . . . then it was that, torn from his first root and position, he slipped from the hand that held him in holiness (ἁγιασμόν) and fell down to earth, that is, from the heights of virtue. . . . In this way he was stripped utterly of the kingship and glory he had in the beginning, and was cast from paradise and its delights. [The Holy Spirit fled from him, because] holiness and impurity (ἁγιασμὸς καὶ ἀκαθαρσία), light and darkness, justice and injustice, are irreconcilable. And so, the fact that the rod fell from Moses' hand (cf. Ex 4:1 ff.) might well signify that the man who had been made to God's image was originally a plant of paradise, with the glory of kingship and in the Creator's hand, and that he slipped to earth because he chose to be carnal-minded, and through his extreme bitterness was like some serpent in God's eyes. . . .[35]

Adam lost, therefore, the ontological as well as the dynamic: "the Holy Spirit fled from him" and "he fell from the heights of virtue."[36] When Adam "violated God's command, he sold the gift" that was his resemblance to God through sanctification.[37] In a word, Adam "was sanctified

---

[32] Cf. In Ioannem 12 (Pusey 3, 106); also ibid. 2, 1 (Pusey 1, 183); Contra Iulianum 8 (PG 76, 928); De recta fide, ad dominas 134 (ACO 1, 1, 5, 95; PG 76, 1281–84).

[33] Cf. In Ioannem 9, 1 (Pusey 2, 483); also ibid. 11, 11 (Pusey 2, 730); Thesaurus 33 (PG 75, 569–72).

[34] Cf. In epistolam 1 ad Corinthios 7 (Pusey, In Ioannem 3, 315); In Ioannem 11, 2 (Pusey 2, 657); Adversus Nestorii blasphemias 3, 2 (ACO 1, 1, 6, 60; PG 76, 128).

[35] De adoratione 2 (PG 68, 244). It is quite possible that Cyril here intends the loss not only of holiness but of dominion as well; but the latter loss is not as clear as the former.

[36] Cf. also In Ioannem 11, 11 (Pusey 2, 730): the image of Adam is to be seen in "the filth of sin"; cf. likewise Adversus Nestorii blasphemias 3, 2 (ACO 1, 1, 6, 30; PG 76, 128–29).

[37] Cf. De sancta et consubstantiali trinitate dial. 6 (PG 75, 1008); also ibid. (PG 75, 1013); ibid., dial. 7 (PG 75, 1088).

by being made partaker of the Holy Spirit; and he cast Him away through his sin."[38]

Sixth, sonship. If Janssens' synthesis of sonship in Cyril is correct, then Adam did not forfeit divine adoption, simply because he never had it to forfeit. Moreover, he remained τέκνον; he could still call God Father by title of creation, of existence.[39] What he did lose was the supernatural relationship, the unmerited kinship, which had accrued to him through the indwelling Spirit; for, as Cyril states so emphatically, it is only by participation in the Holy Spirit that man can "have that splendor which consists in sanctification and kinship (οἰκειότητι) with God."[40] Surely, he could no longer be called son in a supernatural sense, since he no longer possessed the Spirit of the Son.

But Cyril is interested in Adam primarily as "the first root of our race."[41] As Gaudel has observed, "whether he is treating of original sin by allusion or speaking of it ex professo, St. Cyril sees always, in the condemnation and fall of the first man, not the fall of an isolated individual, but the fall of human nature in its entirety."[42] A cardinal principle of his theology—to be complemented, of course, by his thesis of ἀνακεφαλαίωσις—is the simple statement: "we have become joint heirs of the evils that befell the first man."[43] The tragedy of Adam's sin is that "in Adam, in the one, Satan conquered the whole nature of man."[44] It is fascinating to follow the thread of this thought on the spindle of the image.

Even from the standpoint of rationality human nature did not escape from Eden unscathed:

... since the mind of man is intent on evil from his youth because he lacks the gifts that are from above, the entire (so to speak) race on earth was corrupted and something like a famine of heavenly knowledge consumed us. This we may see in the parable of the prodigal, who devoured in a foreign land the substance he inherited from his father, and longed to be filled with the carob which the pigs were eating (cf. Lk 15:16). That is why we have run to the things that are earthy; we have passed the better by, when we should have yearned for what was more profitable, through which we would likely not have lost God's favor

[38] De dogmatum solutione 2 (Pusey, In Ioannem 3, 554).

[39] Cf. In Ioannem 7, fragmenta (Pusey 2, 295).

[40] De sancta et consubstantiali trinitate dial. 4 (PG 75, 908).

[41] Cf. In Romanos, Rom 5:11-12 (Pusey, In Ioannem 3, 182); In psalmos, Ps 44:3 (PG 69, 1032-33).

[42] A. Gaudel, "Péché originel," DTC 12, 404.

[43] In Isaiam 2, 1 (PG 70, 313).

[44] In Ioannem 12 (Pusey 3, 63).

and would have been enriched with His intimate friendship. Having fallen, therefore, from everything that could sustain us in well-being, even with God, we have ceased to consider Him who is Lord by nature and in truth, as the master and dispenser of all that is ours.[45]

It would seem that not only Adam, but his descendants as well, lost that unclouded, undistracted contemplation of God and divine things, that "simple and uniform knowledge of all that was good," that perfection of intelligence, which was part of man's original "completeness."[46] In fact, Cyril maintains that, as time went on and sin multiplied apace, "the Spirit took His leave totally and rational man dropped to the depths of irrationality, ignorant of his very Creator."[47]

It was not simply Adam whom Satan defrauded of his original freedom; it was on men that he hung "sin's yoke that was hard to escape."[48] The pressure of that yoke, as reported by Cyril, is so heavy that one wonders whether the sinner is compelled to sin by forces beyond his control: "It is not an improbable idea that perhaps those who are hemmed in by sins are like some murderers of their own soul, and that they have sunk to such distressing depths not of their own will but forced, as it were, to transgress and to offend God, because the mind of man is intent on evil from his youth and because the law of untamable concupiscence tyrannizes in the members of the flesh."[49] But the harshness of Cyril's expression is tempered by the obscure adverb ὥσπερ, "as it were"; just as in another text the slender syllable πως, "somehow," softens a profound pessimism: "Just as God's gracious kindness makes us extremely stout of heart and nerves us to stand up against evil, in the same way, when we fall beneath God's anger, then it is that there is somehow every necessity that we fall down like slaves beneath wicked pleasures."[50] As the context makes clear, Cyril is simply asserting that with God's grace we are strong enough to resist sin, but without God's grace we are certain to fall. And he quotes the sobering sentence of Christ: "Without me you can do nothing" (Jn 15:5).[51]

In consequence of Adam's sin man lost his sovereignty over earth. It was to human nature that God spoke when he said to Adam, "Increase

---

[45] *Glaphyra in Exodum* 1 (*PG* 69, 389).

[46] Cf. *Contra Iulianum* 3 (*PG* 76, 637); *In Ioannem* 1, 9 (Pusey 1, 111).

[47] *In Ioannem* 2, 1 (Pusey 1, 183).

[48] *In Isaiam* 1, 5 (*PG* 70, 249).

[49] *De adoratione* 8 (*PG* 68, 581).

[50] *In Isaiam* 5, 6 (*PG* 70, 1400); cf. du Manoir, *Dogme et spiritualité*, pp. 89–90.

[51] Cf. *ibid.* For Cyril's understanding of providence and predestination cf. du Manoir, *Dogme et spiritualité*, p. 86 ff.

and multiply and exercise complete dominion" over the earth (Gn 1: 28). But "we have fallen from God's free gift (χάριτος) in Adam."[52]

In the context of Adam's holiness Cyril bids us "count the whole of humanity as if it were in him."[53] Through the transgression of Adam "the heart of all men was soiled."[54] The image of Adam which humanity bore includes subjection to sin;[55] it is the reverse of holiness.[56] It was "man's nature" that "sold the gift" which is resemblance to God through sanctification, and consequently was condemned to death and enslaved to sin.[57] But perhaps the most expressive proof that human nature lost holiness is the fact that human nature lost the Spirit of holiness. Man "was sanctified when made partaker of the Holy Spirit"; but the Spirit "he cast from himself through sin; for God said, 'My Spirit shall not remain in these men, because they are flesh' (Gn 6:3), that is, they are carnal-minded and only that."[58]

It is a curious feature of his thought that Cyril more than once relegates the definitive departure of the Spirit from humankind to a relatively advanced period in the story of sin:

In consequence of the transgression in Adam, as in the first fruits of the race, God's face was turned from human nature. Besides, human nature was turned out of paradise. Once blessed by its Maker, now it lay accursed. But when the human race had multiplied apace and sin was universal despot, then departed too the Holy Spirit of God breathed into us in the beginning, and the beauty of the image was falsified.[59]

When the human race was unfolding beyond number, and sin, versatile scavenger of each individual soul, was universal master of men, human nature was stripped bare of the ancient grace; the Spirit took His leave totally and rational man dropped to the depths of irrationality, ignorant of his very Creator.[60]

[52] In Hebraeos, Heb 2:7–8 (Pusey, In Ioannem 3, 383; cf. 382).

[53] De adoratione 2 (PG 68, 244).

[54] In psalmos, Ps 50:12 (PG 69, 1100).

[55] Cf. In Ioannem 11, 2 (Pusey 2, 657).

[56] Cf. ibid. 11, 11 (Pusey 2, 730); Adversus Nestorii blasphemias 3, 2 (ACO 1, 1, 6, 60; PG 76, 128–29).

[57] Cf. De sancta et consubstantiali trinitate dial. 6 (PG 75, 1008); ibid. (PG 75, 1013); ibid. 7 (PG 75, 1088).

[58] De dogmatum solutione 2 (Pusey, In Ioannem 3, 553–54). On God's aversion from humanity cf. In Romanos, Rom 5:12 (Pusey, In Ioannem 3, 182): Adam was "the cause of heaven's wrath and aversion for his progeny"; In psalmos, Ps 68:18 (PG 69, 1168): "Because of the transgression in Adam the Father's face was turned from human nature. . . . But God's aversion is divine dereliction."

[59] In psalmos, Ps 50:13 (PG 69, 1100).

[60] In Ioannem 2, 1 (Pusey 1, 183).

... degenerating to disobedience [the first man] descended to the mother-earth of his making, and, mastered now by corruption and death, transmitted the penalty to the entire race. But with human wickedness growing by leaps and bounds, and our understanding constantly deteriorating, sin was king, and so the nature of man was for the future stripped of the Holy Spirit dwelling within.[61]
... turned to sin from that ancient deception, then little by little advancing far in sin as time went on, [man] suffered, together with his other gifts, the loss of the Spirit as well, and for that reason became thenceforth not merely subject to corruption but prone to every sin.[62]
... [human nature] lost little by little the very gifts calculated to win for it reverence and the perfection of propriety. For instance, human nature sold incorruptibility in Adam. ... And after this it was deprived of the Spirit; for, when God saw the minds of men solely and deliberately focused on the unholy, loathsome passions of the flesh, He said, "My Spirit shall not remain in these men, because they are flesh."[63]

In Adam all men lost incorruptibility. Φθορά entered in, that is, subjection to bodily death, and a flesh that was the root of tyrannous concupiscence; for "the transgression in Adam" meant "the return of man's nature to its own earth,"[64] and "we were followers not merely of death but of all the passions of the flesh—and this happened to us in the first man because of the transgression and God's curse."[65] The original condemnation extended to all men; and so even those who did not sin, "that is, at the time when our first father fell from the command given

[61] *Ibid.* (Pusey 1, 184). In support of his thesis Cyril quotes Wis 1:4-5 as follows: "The holy Spirit of wisdom will flee from guile ... and will not dwell in a body involved in sin."
[62] *Ibid.* 5, 2 (Pusey 1, 691). Cf. *In Romanos*, Rom 9:14-24 (Pusey, *In Ioannem* 3, 232): "the whole earth had strayed" (apparently around the time of Abraham); some adored creatures, others worshiped as they pleased.
[63] *Glaphyra in Genesim* 2 (*PG* 69, 77). Cyril's position is enigmatic. The thesis, based on Gn 6:3, that the Spirit deserted humanity only after sin had multiplied beyond measure, does not square with Cyril's doctrine that "human nature sold incorruptibility in Adam" (*ibid.*) and that in consequence of Adam's sin "man's nature was cast out of the paradise of delight and instantly transformed to ugliness"; *De adoratione* 1 (*PG* 68, 149). I do not see how it can be reconciled with human nature's loss, in Adam, of that resemblance to God which is achieved through sanctification; cf. *De sancta et consubstantiali trinitate* dial. 6 (*PG* 75, 1008).
[64] *In Ioannem* 9, 1 (Pusey 2, 488); cf. *ibid.* 12 (Pusey 3, 106); *In epistolam 1 ad Corinthios* 7 (Pusey, *In Ioannem* 3, 315). Note that the soul was "preserved in immortality"; *In Ioannem* 1, 9 (Pusey 1, 139).
[65] *In Ioannem* 9, 1 (Pusey 2, 483).

him," even they bore the image of Adam: death and corruption, a flesh that lusts and a mind earth-bound.[66]

Accepting the fact of universal death and sinfulness as nature's heritage from Adam, Cyril recognizes the difficulty inherent in the how. How was it that Adam was able to transmit to us the death inflicted on him for his transgression? More vital still, how is it that, because of Adam's sin, his descendants "have been made sinners"? Cyril's most thorough and penetrating treatment of death's transmission is contained in the following passage:

> We must inquire how it is that our first father Adam transmitted to us the punishment laid on him for his transgression. He heard the words, "Earth thou art and into earth shalt thou return" (Gn 3:19), and the incorruptible became corruptible and bound with the chains of death. But because he begot children after falling to death's estate, we his progeny have become corruptible, since we are born of a corruptible father. So it is that we too are heirs of the curse in Adam; for surely we have not been visited with punishment as though we disobeyed with him the divine command which he received, but because . . . become mortal he transmitted the curse to the seed he fathered. We are mortal because mortal-sprung.[67]

And yet, it is not simply the problem of inherited death which causes Cyril concern; he faces squarely the mystery of hereditary sin. In his own *locus classicus* he anticipates the logical objection. Someone, he reasons, may object: Granted that Adam did sin, that for his sin he was condemned to corruption and death; how is it that "the many have been made sinners" because of him? What have his sins to do with us? How is it that we, who did not even exist at the time, have been sentenced with him? Is not this a clear case of the children dying for their fathers? But are we not rather assured that "the soul that sinneth, the same shall die" (Dt 24:16; Ez 18:4, 20)?

---

[66] Cf. *ibid.* 11, 11 (Pusey 2, 730); also *Adversus Nestorii blasphemias* 3, 2 (*ACO* 1, 1, 6, 60; *PG* 76, 128); *De recta fide, ad dominas* 134 (*ACO* 1, 1, 5, 95; *PG* 76, 1281).

[67] *De dogmatum solutione* 6 (Pusey, *In Ioannem* 3, 560). Such too, I believe, is Cyril's meaning when he says that Adam sent the power of the curse hurtling φυσικῶς into the entire race, like some inheritance; cf. *Glaphyra in Genesim* 1 (*PG* 69, 29). Cf., however, *In Romanos*, Rom 5:12 ff. (Pusey, *In Ioannem* 3, 182-83): because we have imitated the transgression in Adam through actual sin, the same punishment has been inflicted on us. But Cyril admits that even they who did not transgress the law like Adam—because there was no law—suffered corruption as branches with their root in Adam.

Yes, "the soul that sinneth, the same shall die." But we have become sinners through the disobedience of Adam in this way. Adam, you see, had been made for incorruption and life. Moreover, the life he led in the paradise of delight was suited to saints; his mind was ever absorbed by the vision of God; his body was perfectly at peace, all base lust at rest; for unbecoming emotions did not disturb him. But when he fell subject to sin and sank down to corruption, from that time forth impure lusts invaded the nature of the flesh and the law of sin blossomed which rages in our members. Human nature has, therefore, contracted the malady of sin through the disobedience of one man, Adam. It is in this way that the many have been made sinners—not as though they had transgressed with Adam (for they did not yet exist), but because they are of his nature, the nature that fell beneath the law of sin. . . . Human nature grew ill with corruption in Adam because of the act of disobedience, and so the passions entered in. . . .[68]

The passage is significant as much for its omissions as for its assertions. As is obvious, the fact of a common punishment does not here lead Cyril, as it does Augustine, to the notion of a common guilt in Adam. In characterizing the state of fallen nature, Cyril prefers to speak of an organic rather than a juridic solidarity. We inherit the curse leveled at Adam inasmuch as we receive from Adam his nature in the condition created for it by sin: a condition of mortality, concupiscence, struggle against carnal stirrings that can be overcome only by heroic human effort seconded by the Spirit of God.[69]

[68] *In Romanos*, Rom 5:18–19 (Pusey, *In Ioannem* 3, 186–87).

[69] Cf. Gaudel, *art. cit.*, col. 404. For a rounded view of Cyril's thought on inherited sin the corpus of his doctrine (not merely isolated passages) must be studied—especially, I suggest, his total conception of φθορά. Moreover, it would be unfair to conclude that Cyril knows nothing of race solidarity in Adam's sin or that he restricts the term "sin" always and everywhere to personal transgressions or to tyrannizing concupiscence. In this connection the consistent use of the phrase, "the transgression in Adam," is significant; cf., e.g., *In Ioannem* 1, 9 (Pusey 1, 123); *ibid.* 12 (Pusey 3, 115); *In Abacuc* 2 (Pusey 2, 125–26). But even more meaningful is the declaration that "the whole of human nature became guilty in him who was first formed"; *In Lucam* hom. 42 (*CSCO* 70, 113; Lat. tr. 140, 75). "We have been made partakers of the transgression in Adam"; *De adoratione* 11 (*PG* 68, 757). "We sinned in the first Adam, trampling God's command underfoot"; *In Ioannem* 11, 12 (Pusey 3, 36). According to M. Jugie, "Le dogme du péché originel dans l'église grecque," *Revue augustinienne* 16 (1910) 163 ff., the Eastern Fathers, with rare exceptions, taught the doctrine of original sin. Attracted more by its penal consequences for the race, however, they evince little preoccupation with the question, in what precisely the fault charged to human nature consists: wherein lies the sin? The few who put the problem to themselves resolve it only in passing and without plumbing its depths. Cyril,

Finally, sonship. Again, if Janssens is correct in his exegesis of Cyril, human nature could not have forfeited divine adoption in Adam, because Adam never possessed it. What human nature did lose in its root was the supernatural kinship which is the effect of the indwelling Spirit. Men remained merely τέκνα; they could still call God Father by title of creation, of existence.

Was the divine image *lost* to humankind through Adam's sin? The logical inference from Cyril's doctrine is a set of distinctions. Those aspects of the image which are part and parcel of man's essential structure—basic rationality and psychological freedom—were not lost. Those facets of the image which owe their existence to the indwelling of the Spirit—holiness, incorruptibility, kinship with God—were lost. That phase of the image which neither flows necessarily from man's essence nor (apparently) is a formal effect of the Spirit's inhabitation—dominion —was at least seriously diminished. Lost, too, was that perfection of rationality which is undistracted absorption in the divine, and that perfection of freedom which means that man's will and God's will are one will.

But Cyril's terminology plays havoc with so simple a construction. Thus, he remarks that, when the Spirit departed from humanity, the beauty of the image παρεχαράττετο: it was falsified, marked with a false stamp—like a counterfeit coin.[70] Again, the beauty of the image παρεσημαίνετο: it was marked falsely—like a counterfeit seal.[71] Again, when man disobeyed, God took from him the grace of immortality, "the likeness to God was falsified (παρεχαράττετο) through the invasion of sin, and [God's] features (χαρακτῆρες) were no longer limpid (λαμπροί) in him but rather indistinct (ἀμυδρότεροι) and darkened (ἐσκοτισμένοι) because of the transgression."[72] In similar vein, "when sin stole in, the distinctive

like Chrysostom, "does not seem to have settled the question clearly, but it can be said that in his eyes the privation of grace holds the first place among the consequences of Adam's sin. . . . The loss of preternatural gifts is related to the loss of divine grace as effect to cause, but St. Cyril does not say expressly that it is only the latter which constitutes original sin properly so called"; *ibid.*, pp. 168–69.

[70] *In psalmos*, Ps 50:13 (*PG* 69, 1100); here the Spirit departs altogether after sin has multiplied, and so the image is falsified.

[71] *De sancta et consubstantiali trinitate* dial. 6 (*PG* 75, 1013); cf. *ibid.*, dial. 7 (*PG* 75, 1113): man had become παράσημον, i.e., spurious, falsely stamped; and ἀκαλλές, ugly.

[72] *In Ioannem* 2, 1 (Pusey 1, 183). Cyril goes on to describe the subsequent unfolding of sin and the total departure of the Spirit, so that "man dropped to the depths of irrationality, ignorant of his very Creator." The Savior makes God's features shine out (ἀναλάμψαι) as they had done before.

features of our likeness to God no longer remained limpid (λαμπροί) in us."[73] On another occasion it is a question of mutilation resulting in ugliness (λελωβημένης εἰς τὸ ἀκαλλές).[74] Even more ambiguously, Cyril maintains that sin ἠφάνισε the beauty of the image;[75] an unfortunate verb, because ἀφανίζειν runs the gamut from "disguise" and "hide from sight," through "obscure" and "mar," to "obliterate," "do away with," "destroy utterly."[76]

A possible explanation, if not a solution, of the enigma is that, in Cyril's eyes, such a problem is insignificant. He has little concern for the precise sense in which God's features fail to shine forth in men—that is, whether it is because they are no longer there at all, or because they have been covered over, obscured. Only the basic fact and the basic reason are of interest to him: sinful man does not image God as he ought, and the cause is sin.

I would suggest, however, that Cyril is heir here to disparate traditions. One tradition states, simply and unconditionally, that man's resemblance to God (at least in its higher manifestations) was lost through sin. That tradition is represented by Irenaeus, whose recapitulation theory involves the restoration in Christ of a likeness lost in Adam.[77] "In times past it was indeed said that man had been made in God's image (εἰκόνα), but it was not shown; for the Word was as yet invisible, and it was in His image that man had been made. That is why he lost the likeness (ὁμοίωσιν) so easily. But when the Word of God was made flesh, He confirmed both; for He actually showed the image, becoming what His image was, and He established the likeness firmly, making man quite like the invisible Father through the visible Word."[78] More simply, "the Son of God . . . received from the Father dominion over our life and, having received it, brought it down to us, to those who are far from Him, when 'He was seen on earth and conversed with men,' joining and uniting the Spirit of God the Father with what God had fashioned, so

---

[73] De dogmatum solutione 3 (Pusey, In Ioannem 3, 556).

[74] De sancta et consubstantiali trinitate dial. 3 (PG 75, 805; cf. 808).

[75] Responsiones ad Tiberium 8 (Pusey 3, 590). He adds that "Satan filled the radiant (λαμπρόν) face of humanity with sordidness (ῥυποῦ)," and that through Christ "the distinctive marks of His divine nature are conspicuous (ἐμπρέπειν) in us," and "the beauty of the most excellent image shines forth (ἐκφαίνεται) in us."

[76] Cf. Liddell-Scott, s.v.

[77] Cf. Slomkowski, op. cit., p. 42; Aubineau, art. cit., p. 52.

[78] Irenaeus, Adversus haereses 5, 16, 1 (Harvey 2, 268). What I have translated "established firmly" is κατέστησε in the Greek, "restituit" in the Latin version.

that man became according to the image and likeness of God."[79] It is substantially this tradition, without its nuances, that Didymus of Alexandria recalls two centuries later when he teaches that through baptism we put on Christ "and we recover God's image and likeness of which Scripture speaks—which we received from God's inbreathing and lost through the sin."[80]

The other tradition states just as emphatically that the image of God in man can be obscured but cannot be lost. That tradition is represented by Origen: "The painter of [the image of the heavenly] is the Son of God. And because the painter is so remarkable, His image can be obscured by carelessness, it cannot be destroyed by malice; for it remains always the image of God, even though you may put over it the image of the earthy."[81] Origen argues that, "even if the mind through carelessness should fall away from the pure and perfect reception of God into itself, it nevertheless always possesses within it some seeds as it were of restoration and recall to a better state, which become operative whenever the inner man, who is also termed the rational man, is recalled into the image and likeness of God who created him."[82]

[79] Irenaeus, *Demonstratio apostolicae praedicationis* 97 (*PO* 12, 729; tr. J. P. Smith, *ACW* 16, 107–8). For a detailed study of the image and its fate as seen by Irenaeus, cf. Struker, *op. cit.*, pp. 76–128.

[80] Didymus, *De trinitate* 2, 12 (*PG* 39, 680).

[81] Origen, *In Genesim homiliae* 13, 4 (*GCS* 29, 119). Origen does use the expression, "abiecta imagine Dei"; *In Leviticum homiliae* 4, 3 (*GCS* 29, 318); but, as Bernard points out (*op. cit.*, p. 52), "apart from the fact that we do not know what Greek word Rufinus has rendered by *abiecta*, the whole context concerns a denial, an infidelity, a perverted use, not a rejection which could effectively remove the image of God from the soul." For a detailed analysis of Origen's mind, and a reconciliation of apparently conflicting texts, cf. Crouzel, *op. cit.*, pp. 181–215.

[82] Origen, *De principiis* 4, 4, 9 (*GCS* 22, 363; tr. Butterworth, *op. cit.*, p. 327).— Although Eastern theology before and after Clement of Alexandria linked the problem of divine resemblance intimately with Adam, i.e., Christ restored a resemblance which was lost or obscured in Adam, such a conception is completely foreign to the dimensions of Clement's thought; cf. Mayer, *op. cit.*, pp. 76–77. He lists neither ὁμοίωσις θεοῦ nor τὸ πνεῦμα among the possessions of Adam. The recapitulation theory of his contemporary, Irenaeus, is not Clement's ἀποκατάστασις; his anthropology is centered not in a second Adam but exclusively in a God-Man. Cf. also C. Bigg, *op. cit.*, p. 106: "The idea of the 'Recapitulation' of all men in Christ as the second Adam, so fruitful in the brooding soul of Irenaeus, is strange to [Clement]. He looks upon Redemption, not as the restitution of that which was lost at the Fall, but as the crown and consummation of the destiny of Man, leading to a righteousness such as Adam never knew, and to heights of glory and power as yet unscaled and undreamed."

Still more pertinent, in the light of Cyril's vacillation, is the fact that both traditions appear at times in one and the same writer. Athanasius, for example, seems to hover uncertainly between a κατ' εἰκόνα that is simply tarnished, covered over,[83] and a κατ' εἰκόνα that is genuinely destroyed.[84] Despite his wavering terminology, however, this much may be said: "The κατ' εἰκόνα is equivalently divided into two. As grace of union with God, it is lost, then created anew; but as ordination of the soul to God, witness to a calling which abides, it subsists, though neutralized, beneath the blemishes."[85]

In Gregory of Nyssa, too, there are two sets of conflicting texts. One series of texts speaks of the "loss" of the image,[86] the loss of those gifts (e.g., immortality, ἀπάθεια, purity, virtues, estrangement from all evil) which concretely constitute the image.[87] In another series of texts the image is "blurred," "overlaid," obscured but not lost. "If by careful and diligent living you wash off once more the filth that has been spread over your heart, the godlike beauty will shine out in you."[88] Tempted to explain this fluctuation by a residue of Neoplatonism, if not in Gregory's thinking, at least in his pictures and representations, Leys finds it more probable that there is in Gregory, as in Origen, "the feeling that the soul once stamped with the divine image can never completely lose its trace." He sees in Gregory an incipient, if hidden and confused, doctrine of the "character," with the author "portraying not the presence of grace but the fact of being destined for it, not actual sanctification but the sacral character of the soul which still belongs to God, though no longer linked to Him by love."[89]

---

[83] This especially in the *Contra gentes*; cf. 8 (*PG* 25, 16); 34 (*PG* 25, 68–69).

[84] This especially in the *De incarnatione Verbi*; cf. 6 (*PG* 25, 105–8). Cf. *ibid.* 14 (*PG* 25, 120) the example of a painting (wood carving?) where the representation has been obliterated by filth. But here a cleaning process is considered insufficient; the model must be present once more; hence the Incarnation. The Word, however, is not merely model of the restoration; He is its agent as well, because the κατ' εἰκόνα is more participation than resemblance; cf. *ibid.* 7 (*PG* 25, 108–9). The analysis of Bernard, *op. cit.*, pp. 49–54, 62–70, is rewarding reading.

[85] Bernard, *op. cit.*, p. 69.

[86] Cf., e.g., Gregory of Nyssa, *De virginitate* 12 (*Gregorii Nysseni opera* 8/1, 299).

[87] Cf. Gregory of Nyssa, *In Canticum canticorum* hom. 2 (*PG* 44, 800).

[88] Gregory of Nyssa, *De beatitudinibus* 6 (*PG* 44, 1272); cf. fuller documentation in Leys, *op. cit.*, pp. 111–12.

[89] Leys, *op. cit.*, p. 114. Note in Gregory's *De opificio hominis* 5 (*PG* 44, 137) the same example of a painter which we have seen in Origen, *In Genesim homiliae* 13, 4 (*GCS* 29, 119–20). Gregory, ardent admirer of Origen, may have known this text.

It is perhaps this twin tradition in Cyril's background[90] which lies at the root of his oscillation between a destroyed and a disfigured image.[91] And the root of the twin tradition itself may well be the conviction of the soul's supernatural finality, its Godwardness, even when enslaved to sin. It is a conviction which, we have seen, is not at all foreign to the perspectives of Cyril.

Two further clues to the state of the image after Adam's sin emerge from Cyril's portrait of pre-Christian sinfulness and sanctity. The first clue comes from his consistently dismal picture of a world torn from God. Sin was sovereign of all earth; no one could escape its tyranny; it led everyone's will to all manner of wickedness.[92] So shamefully did sin maltreat the whole race that it seemed as though no one did good (cf. Ps 13:3).[93] Our nature was separated from God,[94] and men were the playthings of concupiscence.[95] Soon after Adam's sin, even that "natural law" which persuades man to know the true God "perished utterly."[96] At the time of Moses, knowledge of God was limited to the land of the Jews.[97] As for the Gentiles, they had neither knowledge of God nor good works.[98]

The second clue is furnished by Cyril's doctrine on the grace of the

[90] The two traditions crop up in Latin theology too. Compare, e.g., the loss of the likeness in Tertullian, *De baptismo* 5 (*CSEL* 20, 206), with Augustine's remarks in *Retractationes* 2, 50 (*CSEL* 36, 160): ". . .what I said [*De Genesi ad litteram* 6, 27–28; *CSEL* 28/1, 199], i.e., 'by sin Adam lost the image of God according to which he was made,' is not to be taken in the sense that no image remained in him, but that it was so misshapen that it needed a refashioning."

[91] In *De sancta et consubstantiali trinitate* dial. 3 (*PG* 75, 805–8) Cyril develops the example of an excellent coppersmith who has fashioned a statue. Some envious fellow has lifted the statue from its base with a lever; it has crashed with a loud, heavy sound; and so it has been mutilated, deformed. Then the coppersmith, finding this state of things intolerable, decides to refashion his work of art to its original form by removing the mutilation. He will not, however, be acting properly if he forgets about the original form and remodels the masterpiece to a form quite different; rather will he once more impress its own form, its original image, on the work of art. Then Cyril applies the example to the reformation of man by God to the original image: formation to Christ is reformation to God the Father.

[92] Cf. *Homiliae paschales* 29, 2 (*PG* 77, 964).

[93] Cf. *ibid.* 7, 2 (*PG* 77, 549).

[94] Cf. *De adoratione* 15 (*PG* 68, 1008).

[95] Cf. *Homiliae paschales* 19, 2 (*PG* 77, 825–29).

[96] *Ibid.* 9, 4 (*PG* 77, 589).

[97] Cf. *In Hebraeos*, Heb 2:17 (Pusey, *In Ioannem* 3, 395).

[98] Cf. *Homiliae diversae* 17 (*PG* 77, 1097). This is one of the homilies which demand further investigation before they can be confidently ascribed to Cyril; cf. du Manoir, *Dogme et spiritualité*, p. 58.

just in the Old Law. He admits that "it is by the one Holy Spirit that God sanctifies those who preceded us and sanctifies us."[99] But it is in his exegesis of Jn 7:39 that he confronts the problem frankly and with theological sensitivity.[100] Anyone, he reflects, who gives thought to the prophets "speaking in the Spirit God's mysteries about Christ" will wonder how it could be that before Christ "the Spirit was not yet." In the face of Scripture's own testimony and the very fact of prophecy, it would be irrational to believe that the minds of the prophets were destitute of the Spirit, unreasonable to deny that they were Spirit-borne ($\pi\nu\epsilon\nu\mu\alpha\tau\delta\phi\rho\rho\iota$). What, then, is John's meaning? After a backward glance at human history from Adam to Christ, Cyril gives his answer:

... in the holy prophets there was, as it were, some abundant illumination ($\tilde{\epsilon}\lambda\lambda\alpha\mu\psi\iota\nu$) of the Spirit, a torch-carrying, which could educate them to a perception of the future and a knowledge of the hidden. But in those who believe in Christ there is not merely an enlightenment from the Spirit; we believe confidently that the Spirit Himself dwells in them and makes His home in them ($\kappa\alpha\tau\iota\kappa\epsilon\hat{\iota}\nu$ ... $\kappa\alpha\iota$ $\dot{\epsilon}\nu\alpha\nu\lambda\dot{\iota}\zeta\epsilon\sigma\theta\alpha\iota$). In consequence of this, we are justifiably called temples of God, whereas no one of the holy prophets has ever been called God's temple.[101]

That is why John the Baptist, despite his remarkable virtue ($\dot{\alpha}\rho\epsilon\tau\dot{\eta}$), despite his incomparable justice ($\delta\iota\kappa\alpha\iota\sigma\dot{\nu}\nu\eta$), despite his perfection among men ($\tau\dot{\epsilon}\lambda\epsilon\iota\sigma$ ... $\dot{\epsilon}\nu$ $\dot{\alpha}\nu\theta\rho\dot{\omega}\pi\iota\sigma$), begged baptism of Christ—a confession that the Christian just baptized, and not yet distinguished in activity, is superior to John—by this title alone, that the Baptist was born of woman and the baptized is born of God.[102]

To return to the subject of discussion: The Spirit was in the prophets for the requirements of prophecy, but now He dwells in ($\dot{\epsilon}\nu\iota\kappa\dot{\iota}\zeta\epsilon\tau\alpha\iota$) the faithful through Christ—and first of all in Him, when He became man. . . . When, therefore, the sacred evangelist says, "The Spirit was not yet, because Jesus had not yet been glorified," let us surmise that he means the complete and perfect indwelling ($\tau\dot{\eta}\nu$ $\dot{\delta}\lambda\sigma\sigma\chi\epsilon\rho\hat{\eta}$ $\kappa\alpha\iota$ $\dot{\delta}\lambda\dot{\delta}\kappa\lambda\eta\rho\sigma\nu$ $\kappa\alpha\tau\sigma\dot{\iota}\kappa\eta\sigma\iota\nu$) of the Holy Spirit in men.[103]

[99] Glaphyra in Exodum 2 (PG 69, 464). Cf. also Thesaurus 11 (PG 75, 175-76): the saints of the Old Testament were conformed to the image of God's Son.
[100] Cf. In Ioannem 5, 2 (Pusey 1, 690-98). We saw Cyril's solution in brief when we dealt with divine adoption.
[101] Ibid. (Pusey 1, 696).
[102] Cf. ibid. (Pusey 1, 696-97).
[103] Ibid. (Pusey 1, 697-98).

And such, for Cyril, is the case with all those who have achieved the justice of the Law: however superior they may be to us in the practice of virtue, we have been raised to a loftier level, established in a higher order of things, through Christ.[104] Israel's adoption was no more than type and external form, like Israel's circumcision in flesh; it was not the reality, which is given only through the indwelling Spirit of the Word enfleshed.[105]

So, then, we must draw the conclusion—though Cyril does not—that the image of God is to be found in Old Testament times, but on a distinctly low level at best: in all men, basic rationality and psychological freedom; in the just, a dynamic imitation of God by the practice of virtue, and a sonship which is simply type and figure. We do not discover the ontological holiness which is oneness with the indwelling Spirit, the incorruptibility which is the effect of the Spirit's self-communication, the sonship which is the gift exclusively of the Spirit of adoption. May we not discern here some justification for vacillation in terminology between an image lost and an image obscured, disfigured, falsified?

[104] Cf. *In Matthaeum*, Mt 11:11 (*PG* 72, 400). Virtue was not perfect in the Old Testament; cf. *De adoratione* 8 (*PG* 68, 568). Nevertheless, there were religious, God-fearing individuals, e.g., Abel, Enoch, and Noah; cf. *Homiliae diversae* 17 (*PG* 77, 1097).

[105] Cf. *In Ioannem* 1, 9 (Pusey 1, 135). Philips, *art. cit.*, pp. 554-55, has observed that "the personal views of St. Cyril on the grace of the ancients have never become part of the common property of popular theology. But his way of seeing things, the realism of his interpretation of the sources, his concern to grasp the data of revelation in their proper sense—particularly with reference to the diffusion of the life of the Trinity through the Incarnation of the Word —all this commands respect and attention. This method alone can preserve us from the temptation to adopt facile solutions which are more verbal than real. A superficial clarity runs the risk of sacrificing more than one element in the complex wealth that is God's message. And we shall no longer understand the enthusiasm of the apostles and the first Christians when confronted with the staggering newness of the personal presence of the Word and the Spirit breaking right into human history. Moreover, St. Cyril is far from being the only one to develop his 'opinion'. . . ."

# CHAPTER 11

# CHRIST

As soon as Adam fell—in fact, before Adam's fall—God had determined the measures He would take to mend it.[1] In that divine decree, as Cyril sees it, the central themes were image and Incarnation. Redemption is recapitulation (ἀνακεφαλαίωσις), and recapitulation means "restoration to original state."[2] God "hastened to link His fugitive flock on earth to the flocks above, and decided to refashion humanity to the original image through the Spirit; for otherwise the divine features could not shine out in humanity as they had done before."[3]

This recapitulation was achieved radically in the person of the Word Incarnate. As all men were in God's Son when He took flesh,[4] so all human nature rose with Him from the grave[5] and ascended with Him into heaven.[6] Central to this process was Christ's redemptive sacrifice;[7] for man's restoration, like man's fall, was accomplished "through the wood."[8] "After the death of Emmanuel according to the flesh, another seed sprang up immediately to Adam, enriched within with the supreme beauty of the divine image.... When, like some grain, after the manner of an ear of corn, He fell into the ground, He sprang up one of many (πολλοστός); for human nature was refashioned in Him to the original image according to which the first man had been made."[9]

Concretely and individually, the image of God is recovered in baptism, with its attendant renunciation of Satan, when the convert, facing the West, cries aloud: "I bid you adieu, Satan, and all your works, and all your angels, and all your pomp, and all service of you." For, "if . . . you have been purified and have forgotten your past misdeeds and have recovered the natural (φυσικόν) beauty of the soul, your creation to

[1] Cf. *In Isaiam* 3, 5 (*PG* 70, 832); *In Ionam* (Pusey 1, 565–66); *In Aggaeum* (Pusey 2, 281).

[2] *In Ioannem* 9, 1 (Pusey 2, 481); cf. *De adoratione* 2 (*PG* 68, 248); *In Isaiam* 4, 5 (*PG* 70, 1121–24).

[3] *In Ioannem* 2, 1 (Pusey 1, 183).

[4] Cf. *ibid.* (Pusey 1, 185).

[5] Cf. *ibid.*; also *Thesaurus* 23 (*PG* 75, 385); *Glaphyra in Genesim* 5 (*PG* 69, 233).

[6] Cf. *Thesaurus* 20 (*PG* 75, 332).

[7] Cf. *Quod unus sit Christus* (*PG* 75, 1337).

[8] Cf. *In Ioannem* 12 (Pusey 3, 85).

[9] *Glaphyra in Genesim* 1 (*PG* 69, 44).

God's image, you will have the Beloved of God for your lover."[10] Baptism is so significant for the recovery of the image because it is in baptism that we receive the Spirit of Christ;[11] and "quite clearly it is impossible for him who does not somehow (πως) partake of His nature to have the likeness to God."[12] At any rate, "participation in the Spirit bestows on man perfection (τελείωσιν) in imaging the divine essence";[13] for "we who have been made to the image of the Creator obviously preserve this best of all when, become partakers of His divinity through the Holy Spirit indwelling in us, we are formed to the divine nature. And so they who have not yet partaken of Him have not yet been made conformed to the image of the Son."[14] The Spirit, stamped on our souls, dwelling within us, deifies us through His very self;[15] for He "is able of His nature and of His power to transform [man] in fair fashion to the supramundane image by remodeling him to His own likeness."[16]

It will be of interest, by way of conclusion, to indicate the impact of the Incarnation on the various aspects of the divine image: mind, will, dominion, sanctification, incorruptibility, and adoption.

First, mind. In Cyril's view, the image of God involves a created illumination in us which makes us image Him who is Light; for the Son, the Father's exact Image, "has been stamped upon us in making us conformed to Him and in engraving, like a divine image, on those who believe in Him the illumination (φωτισμόν) that comes through His own Spirit, that they may be called, like Him, gods and sons of God."[17] The light (φῶς) from the Son (cf. Ps 4:7) is "the grace which passes through the Spirit to the creature, the grace through which we are re-fashioned to God by faith, recovering conformity to the Son as by some

[10] *In psalmos*, Ps 44:12–13 (*PG* 69, 1044); here "natural" seems equivalent to "original." Cf. also *In Ioannem* 2, 1 (Pusey 1, 219): "the spirit of man is sanctified by the Spirit, and the body by sanctified water"; *Homiliae paschales* 10, 1 (*PG* 77, 612): the image is restored through faith and baptism; *Glaphyra in Exodum* 2 (*PG* 69, 441): conformity with Christ is achieved in baptism, where we die spiritually in order to gain resurrection too (cf. Rom 6:4–5). Cf. *Contra Iulianum* 7 (*PG* 76, 880).

[11] Cf. *In Romanos*, Rom 1:3–4 (Pusey, *In Ioannem* 3, 175–76).

[12] *Thesaurus* 13 (*PG* 75, 228).

[13] *Ibid.*; cf. *De sancta et consubstantiali trinitate* dial. 7 (*PG* 75, 1112). In fact, "all perfection (τελειότης) comes to creatures through the Spirit"; *Thesaurus* 34 (*PG* 75, 584).

[14] *Thesaurus* 13 (*PG* 75, 225).

[15] Cf. *De sancta et consubstantiali trinitate* dial. 7 (*PG* 75, 1088–89).

[16] *Ibid* (*PG* 75, 1113).

[17] *In Ioannem* 1, 8 (Pusey 1, 103).

seal through Him who is the Father's Image, in order that our creation to the likeness and image of the Creator may be nicely preserved in us."[18]

For Cyril, it is obviously faith that is the perfection of light in man here below; for it is faith that conforms man's intelligence to divine Wisdom, to Christ.[19] In sum, likeness to God is restored through faith; it is more perfect, the more perfect our faith; it is made abortive through loss of faith. "The fruit and fetus of the mind is faith ($\pi \iota \sigma \tau \iota s$) in Christ, which refashions us to Him through perfect knowledge and shapes us to the figure ($\tau \iota \pi o \nu$) of God. . . . So then, perfection of knowledge and integrity of faith will make the Savior's semblance ($\mu \acute{o} \rho \phi \omega \sigma \iota \nu$) reside in the souls of all of us, and this will be like some divine seed in us."[20] On the other hand, in those who sin against faith, God's "features do not shine forth clearly ($\dot{\nu} \gamma \iota \tilde{\omega} s$)." In that case "another spiritual travail and suprasensible regeneration" is necessary, "that they may be formed once more to Christ inasmuch as the Holy Spirit makes the divine image gleam in them through sanctification."[21] In Cyril's theology, faith, the perfection of knowledge, is at once a principle and a facet of human resemblance to the divine. Divine light effects likeness to God and it is itself participation in divinity.

A second aspect of the image resides in the will, in human liberty. Here, too, the Incarnation was revolutionary. Christ removed Satan's yoke of sin, made men "free ($\dot{\epsilon} \lambda \epsilon \nu \theta \acute{\epsilon} \rho o \nu s$) again," and so restored that facet of freedom which is the unshackled power to do good.[22] This is Christian liberty; this is proper godlikeness.

Third, dominion. Cyril seems to believe that the Word enfleshed recovered for human nature the sovereignty over creation which Adam lost for it. In a context of dominion we have his stated opinion that through Christ we have regained the gifts given our nature in the begin-

[18] *Ibid.* 3, 5 (Pusey 1, 444); cf. *In Isaiam* 1, 5 (*PG* 70, 236), where the "light" of Ps 4:7 is the Holy Spirit, "through whom we have been sealed, refashioned to the first image through sanctification."

[19] Cf. *In Isaiam* 5, 1 (*PG* 70, 1188–89); also *Homiliae paschales* 5, 2 (*PG* 77, 476): one who is the image of God should "be passionately in love with divine learning and consider the words of wisdom an admirable thing." Cf. *In Ioannem* 9 (Pusey 2, 427): a better $\theta \epsilon o \pi \tau \iota a$ came with Christ than was given to the ancients; for in the Son we see the Father.

[20] *De adoratione* 8 (*PG* 68, 545–48); cf. *In Ioannem* 10, 2 (Pusey 2, 597). Christ brought the whole world to a knowledge of God; cf. *In psalmos*, Ps 97:1 (*PG* 69, 1253); *In Amos* 3 (Pusey 1, 502).

[21] *Responsiones ad Tiberium* 10 (Pusey 3, 593). Loss of faith means loss of divine beauty; cf. *In psalmos*, Ps 41:6 (*PG* 69, 1005); *ibid.*, Ps 45:6 (*PG* 69, 1049).

[22] Cf. *In Isaiam* 1, 5 (*PG* 70, 249).

ning; through Christ we possess them securely.[23] But Cyril is acutely aware of the sentence in Hebrews: "now we do not see as yet all things subject to [man]" (Heb 2:8). And so he concludes that man's empire will be actualized in the next life; the world to come has not been subjected to angels but has been given to men.[24]

Fourth, holiness. In Christ we have returned "through sanctification (ἁγιασμοῦ) to our nature's original beauty," to the divine image.[25]

When it pleased God the Father to recapitulate (ἀνακεφαλαιώσασθαι) all things in Christ and to refashion to its primal state what had been made, He sent us His only-begotten from heaven. . . . Then it was that He laid hold of prostrate humanity and, freeing us from the bitterness of sin, brought us back through sanctification (ἁγιασμοῦ) to kingly honor and virtue's mildness. And to those who believe He gave that primeval dwelling place, in the person of the robber who hung with Him, as in the first fruits and first beginnings.[26]

As at creation, so in recapitulation, ἁγιασμός is an ontological thing and it has a dynamic aspect. On the one hand, it is through participation of the Spirit that we are reformed "to justice and holiness and to the first image,"[27] that "we are rich with the presence of Christ Himself within us."[28] For the Spirit "instils in us His own proper sanctification, refashions to His own life the nature that fell subject to corruption, and thus restores to God and to God's semblance what had been deprived of this glory."[29] Participation in holiness *is* likeness to God.[30] On the other hand, the ontological is prelude to the dynamic. In imaging Christ we are transformed to a new life, a holy life.[31] Kinship with Christ means having the mind of God; it means likeness to Christ in action.[32] God's

---

[23] Cf. *In Hebraeos*, Heb 2:7-8 (Pusey, *In Ioannem* 3, 384).

[24] Cf. *ibid.* (Pusey, *In Ioannem* 3, 383).

[25] *In Isaiam* 4, 1 (*PG* 70, 892). Cf. *De dogmatum solutione* 2 (Pusey, *In Ioannem* 3, 554): The restoration took place in the apostles as the first fruits, when Christ breathed upon them (cf. Jn 20:22) and restored man's nature "to the sanctification given us in the beginning at our original creation."

[26] *De adoratione* 2 (*PG* 68, 244-45); cf. also *In Isaiam* 1, 5 (*PG* 70, 236); *De sancta et consubstantiali trinitate* dial. 6 (*PG* 75, 1013); *De dogmatum solutione* 3 (Pusey, *In Ioannem* 3, 556); *Responsiones ad Tiberium* 8 (Pusey, *In Ioannem* 3, 590).

[27] *In Ioannem* 11, 10 (Pusey 2, 753).

[28] *De recta fide, ad Theodosium* 36 (*ACO* 1, 1, 1, 66; *PG* 76, 1188).

[29] *In Ioannem* 11, 11 (Pusey 2, 731).

[30] Cf. *In epistolam 2 ad Corinthios* 1, 2 (Pusey, *In Ioannem* 3, 326).

[31] Cf. *In Isaiam* 5, 2 (*PG* 70, 1197-1200); also *Contra Iulianum* 2 (*PG* 76, 593).

[32] Cf. *In Ioannem* 5, 5 (Pusey 2, 72); *ibid.* (Pusey 2, 81-82); *ibid.* 6 (Pusey 2, 94 ff., 101-2); *ibid.* 11, 9 (Pusey 2, 714).

image in man involves "splendid and virtuous living,"[33] deliberate choice of the good,[34] an imaging of God's innate goodness.[35]

Fifth, incorruptibility. Cyril declares that God

devised as it were a second root of our race, to raise us up to our former incorruptibility (ἀφθαρσίαν), in order that, just as the image of the first man, the man from the earth, engraved on us the necessity of dying and involved us in the meshes of corruption (φθορᾶς), so conversely the second beginning, the one after him, that is, Christ, and the likeness (ὁμοίωσις) to Him through the Spirit, would stamp us with indestructibility (τὸ ἀνώλεθρον).[36]

It is not simply death that has met defeat. The image of Christ means "freedom from passions" as well; Christ remodeled the flesh "so that it would be stirred to do God's pleasure rather than self-will."[37] Both aspects of incorruptibility, that is, unending life and liberation from passion, emerge from a passage in whose context Cyril has maintained that the most remarkable aspect of the divine image is τὸ ἄφθαρτον καὶ ἀνώλεθρον.[38] In his interpretation of Jn 14:19–20 we read:

[Christ] says: "I live, seeing that I am Life by nature, and I have shown that my temple is alive. But when you, though of a corruptible nature, shall see yourselves alive, like as I am, then you will know, and very clearly, that being Life by nature I have linked you through myself to God the Father, who is Himself Life by nature, making you as it were sharers and partakers of His incorruptibility.... I have made you sharers of the divine nature, settling my Spirit in you." For Christ is in us through the Spirit, restoring to incorruptibility what is naturally corruptible, and changing it from death to deathlessness. [The transgression in Adam and the refusal to obey meant the return of human nature to its own earth.] But when God sent His Spirit and made us partakers of His own nature and through Him the face of the earth was renewed, we were transformed to newness of life, casting off the corruption that stemmed from sin and laying hold hereafter of eternal life through the grace of our Lord Jesus Christ and His love for men....[39]

---

[33] *Ibid.* 11, 9 (Pusey 2, 716); cf. *Responsiones ad Tiberium* 14 (Pusey, *In Ioannem* 3, 599–600).

[34] Cf. *De sancta et consubstantiali trinitate* dial. 1 (*PG* 75, 673–76).

[35] Cf. *Homiliae paschales* 27, 3 (*PG* 77, 936).

[36] *Glaphyra in Genesim* 1 (*PG* 69, 28); cf. *In Ioannem* 12, 1 (Pusey 3, 134–36); *Contra Iulianum* 8 (*PG* 76, 928).

[37] *In Ioannem* 9, 1 (Pusey 2, 483).

[38] Cf. *ibid.* (Pusey 2, 484).

[39] *Ibid.* (Pusey 2, 487–88); cf. *Thesaurus* 33 (*PG* 75, 572); note *In Ioannem* 12 (Pusey 3, 106): death is now a sleep full of hope, as Christ's was.

The definitive imaging of an incorruptible Christ will come at the resurrection, when our bodies are transformed to the likeness of His glorified body.[40]

Finally, sonship. Cyril asserts that sonship is the reason for the Incarnation;[41] the Son took the form of a slave, to make the slave a son.[42] Through participation in the Spirit, through sanctification, we are fashioned to a sonship such as was not fitting under the Law,[43] a divine adoption which is a new birth[44] after the likeness of Him who is firstborn.[45] For "the Son fashions us to, as it were, His own glory and stamps and, as it were, engraves the distinctive marks of His own form on the souls of the recipients."[46] He is the archetype; we are the images.[47] The consequence, the implication, of so intimate a relationship is that our brotherhood with Christ is not merely a thing of the flesh; it is divine, suprasensible.[48] In a terse line, the image of Christ is stamped on us "through the vocation to adoptive sonship (υἱοθεσίαν)."[49]

Such is recapitulation in the concrete—the image of God restored, even enhanced, by the Incarnation. In the light of the above, it is hardly surprising to find Cyril saying that "the new covenant" which God promised through Jeremiah (cf. Jer 31:31), "that is to say, Christ's own utterances, were a summons through faith to divine adoption, to glory, to incorruptibility, to endless life, to participation in God through the Spirit, to the kingdom of heaven."[50]

[40] Cf. *In epistolam 2 ad Corinthios* 2, 1 (Pusey, *In Ioannem* 3, 339); *De dogmatum solutione* 3 (Pusey, *In Ioannem* 3, 556-57); *De recta fide, ad dominas* 134 (*ACO* 1, 1, 5, 95; *PG* 76, 1281-84).

[41] Cf. *In Ioannem* 9, 1 (Pusey 2, 482).

[42] Cf. *ibid.* 12, 1 (Pusey 3, 122).

[43] Cf. *In Isaiam* 4, 2 (*PG* 70, 936). In fact, as we have seen in the chapter on sonship, the Spirit of adoption was not given even to Adam, in Cyril's view.

[44] Cf. *In Ioannem* 2, 1 (Pusey 1, 219).

[45] Cf. *Thesaurus* 25 (*PG* 75, 412-13).

[46] *De sancta et consubstantiali trinitate* dial. 3 (*PG* 75, 837).

[47] Cf. *ibid.*, dial. 4 (*PG* 75, 889).

[48] Cf. *Adversus Nestorii blasphemias* 3, 2 (*ACO* 1, 1, 6, 59-60; *PG* 76, 128-29); *Contra Iulianum* 9 (*PG* 76, 948).

[49] *In Ioannem* 1, 9 (Pusey 1, 133); cf. *De dogmatum solutione* 4 (Pusey, *In Ioannem* 3, 558).

[50] *In Oseam* 4 (Pusey 1, 144-45).

# INDEX

## SCRIPTURAL REFERENCES

φθορά, 84, 89, 91, 93–100, 102, 103, 106, 146, 150, 152, 164
φρόνημα, 60
φρόνησις, 35, 36
φυσικός, 10, 11, 30, 37, 47, 60, 160
φυσικῶς, 20, 55, 117, 120, 151
φύσις, 31, 35–37, 54, 105, 106, 125

φῶς, 35, 161
χαρακτήρ, 49, 65, 71, 106, 153
χάρις, 11, 35, 37, 55, 56, 86, 94, 102, 105, 106, 120, 125, 134, 149
χριστιανός, 32
ψυχή, 20, 41, 98
ψυχικός, 98

**In Gen. Glaphyra**
**1.** 38, 45, 51–52, 55, 73, 96, 141, 142, 143, 151, 160, 164
**2.** 142, 150
**3.** 51, 128
**5.** 38, 66, 160
**6.** 95

**In Ex. Glaphyra**
**1.** 85, 126, 129, 147-48
**2.** 51, 66, 76, 126, 158, 161

**In Lev. Glaph.** 126, 128, 132

**In Num. Glaph.** 128

**In Deut. Glaph.** 98

**Exp. in psalmos. x**
**Ps 2:8.** 110
**6:3.** 97, 143
**18:2–3.** 38
**18:8.** 37
**32:9.** 21
**37:7.** 38
**41:6.** 162
**44:3.** 147
**44:12–13.** 160–61
**45:6.** 162
**50:12.** 149
**50:13.** 149, 153
**50:14.** 98
**67:29.** 97
**68:18.** 149
**88:11.** 51
**95:5.** 38
**97:1.** 162
**103:25.** 34
**113:16.** 8

**Comment. in Cant.** 20

**Comment. in Is.**
**1, 1.** 46
**1, 2.** 52, 53, 55
**1, 3.** 38, 129
**1, 5.** 48, 73, 145, 148, 162, 163
**1, 6.** 69
**2, 1.** 51, 147
**2, 3.** 38, 129
**2, 4.** 129

**2, 5.** 37, 38, 129
**3, 1.** 51, 128, 131–32
**3, 3.** 38
**3, 4.** 38, 54
**3, 5.** 38, 51, 160
**4, 1.** 38, 66–67, 114, 163
**4, 2.** 21, 70–71, 116, 165
**4, 3.** 38, 51
**4, 4.** 38
**4, 5.** 23, 38, 160
**5, 1.** 38, 39, 67, 162
**5, 2.** 69, 95, 163
**5, 6.** 38, 127, 148

**Comment. in Os.**
**1.** 38, 126
**3.** 129
**4.** 165
**6.** 134
**7.** 38

**Comment. in Ioel.**
**1.** 69, 129
**2.** 69, 115, 132–33

**Comment. in Amos**
**1.** 38
**3.** 8, 162
**4.** 54

**Comment. in Ion.** 52, 66, 160

**Comment. in Mich.**
**3.** 38, 129

**Comment. in Nah.**
**1.** 129

**Comment. in Abac.**
**2.** 85, 152

**Comment. in Soph.**
**1.** 69
**2.** 97

**Comment. in Ag.** 8, 160

**Comment. in Zach.**
**2.** 126
**3.** 129
**6.** 69

**Comment. in Mal.**
**1.** 38, 128, 129, 134

Alès, A. d', 18
Altaner, B., 15, 16, 51, 59, 60, 125
Andriessen, P., 16
Asselin, D. T., 64
Aubineau, M., 101–2, 154
Aulén, G., 103

Bardenhewer, O., x, 6, 14, 15, 16
Bardy, G., 60
Bender, L., 136
Bernard, R., viii, 3, 13, 14, 28, 29, 79–80, 81, 125, 155, 156
Bigg, C., 40, 155
Billot, L., 47
Bonsirven, J., 136
Bouyer, L., 102–3
Budge, E. A. W., 13–14
Butterworth, G. W., 41–42, 155

Camelot, Th., 3, 80, 81
Cavarnos, J. P., 43
Cayré, F., 60, 61
Chabot, I. B., xi
Chadwick, H., 28, 42
Charlier, N., x
Cherniss, H., 31, 139
Clamer, A., 9, 63–64
Cortellezzi, G., 136
Crespy, G., 24
Crouzel, H., viii, 3, 13, 28, 79, 155

Daniélou, J., 31, 83, 103–4, 139
des Places, E., 6
Devreesse, R., x, 62
Diekamp, F., 4
Dillmann, A., 9
Dölger, F. J., 127
Dörr, F., 6
Dubarle, A. M., xiii
du Manoir, H., viii, x, xii, 8, 47, 61, 62, 67, 74, 92, 95, 107, 113, 148, 157

Eberle, A., 130
Ehrhard, A., 62
Epstein, I., 128

Fitzsimons, J., 136

Gaïth, J., 43
Galtier, P., 74
Gaudel, A., 147, 152
Geffcken, J., 16
Giet, S., 6
Gilson, E., 33
Gross, J., viii, 1, 2, 3, 5, 8, 17, 18, 25, 28, 30, 31, 44, 60, 63, 92, 101, 102, 125
Gunkel, H., 8, 24

Harnack, A., 2, 16
Hebert, A. G., 103
Heinisch, P., 8
Hilt, Fr., 4
Hislop, I., 2
Hochban, J., 2
Huser, R. J., 127

Jaeger, W., 57
Janssens, L., 107, 109–10, 111, 113, 115, 116–17, 118–20, 125, 147, 153
Jeiler, I., 15
Jouassard, G., x, 69
Jugie, M., 51, 152–53

Kerrigan, A., 2
Kittel, G., 8, 136
Klebba, E., 2, 15, 17

La Barre, A. de, 3, 40
Langevin, G., 99
Laplace, J., 31
Lawson, J., 102
Le Bachelet, X., 44
Lebreton, J., 121
Leys, R., viii, 4, 5, 14, 30–31, 32, 58, 82, 104, 139, 156

McClear, E. V., 139
McKenzie, J. L., 62
Mahé, J., viii, x, 67, 71, 74, 75, 113
Malevez, L., 109
Martini, C., 58
Mayer, A., viii, 102, 124, 155
Meecham, H. G., 16, 136
Merki, H., viii, 4–5, 79
Michaud, E., 113

184 INDEX

Cleopatra (queen): 128

Clytemnestra: 136

*Cohortatio ad gentiles:* 1, 15–16

concupiscence: and corruption, 98, 99; *see* passions

conformity: to Christ: by Incarnation, 23; recovery of, 161–62; by sanctification, 66–67, 112; by virtue, 76; to God: in tenor of life, 47

consecration to God: 67–69, 76

consubstantiality: of Christ with Father, 108; of Christ with men, 108; of men, 108

contemplation of God: by Adam, 141, 144; in Athanasius, 29, 80–81, 103; of Father in Son, 162; image, 29; incorruptibility, 103; lost for human nature, 148; mind created for, 31; participation of God, 30; sacrifice of self by, 69; sanctification, 69

corruptibility: body, 85–88, 96, 97, 99; concupiscence, root of, 98–100; all creation, 85; deprivation of God's life, 96, 103–4; law of nature, 85; man, 85; moral implications in Cyril, 94–100; *see* incorruptibility

creation: by Father through Son in Spirit, 51–52; sonship, 114; of world and of man, 51–52; *see* double creation

Cyprian: 19

Cyril of Alexandria: use of analogy, 47; contemplation of God, 69; grace, necessity of, 46; image-theology, prior studies, viii–ix; image in body, defect in presentation, 100–101; general theory of image, 9–11; image and likeness identical, 7–9, 93; loss of image, 22; man as image of Christ, 23; incorruptibility, holistic outlook, 99–100; moral implications of incorruptibility, 94–100; laws of nature, 38; man, definition, 19–21, 33–34; Mary, psychology and theology, 130; natural, ambiguous use, 54–55; natural law, 37–38; participation, importance of, 10–11, 79; rational faculty, location, 34; on sanctification, 67–70; on adoptive sonship, 107–20; woman, psychology, 126–30, 136;

woman, theology, 130–37; works, authenticity, dating, editions, x–xii; *see under individual topics*

Cyril of Jerusalem: 5, 17, 32, 44

Cyrus: 68

Damasus: 58

Daniel: 62

David: 55–56, 95

*De anima et corpore deque passione domini:* 13–14

death: inherited, 151; law of nature, 85; separation from God, 95, 103–4; includes sin in Athanasius, 103; tyrannizing, 94; *see* mortality

dedication to God: 67–69, 76

*De hominis structura:* 5–6, 14, 138

*De incarnatione domini:* 62

Demiurge: 89

*dᵉmût:* 1, 8–9, 64

*De resurrectione:* 15

desire: *see* appetite

determinism: 40, 46, 50; *see* freedom

Diadochus: 5–6

Didymus: divinization, 125; freedom, 43–44, 45; image and likeness identical, 5; loss and recovery of image, 155; sin, 155; sonship, 124, 125

Diodore: 59–60, 61, 62, 139

Diogenes of Apollonia: 127

*Diognetus, Letter to:* 16–17

divine nature: image of, 120–24; participation in, 70, 71

divinization: adoption, 124–25; in Greek Fathers, viii; and incorruptibility, 90, 101–3; physical concept of, 92; of whole man, 96; by Word, 29; *see* progressive assimilation

dominion: of God, 52, 54, 61, 63; of Adam, 52, 53, 59, 60–61, 63, 141; of woman, 58, 59, 61, 62, 139; over irrational creation, 52–63; over passions, 58–63; impact of Christ, 56–57, 162–63; impact of sin, 56–57, 61–62, 145, 148–49; as aspect of image in Alexandrian tradition, 57–58; Antiochene exegesis, 59–63; Latin writers, 58–59; contemporary exegesis, 63–64; Cyril, 52–57, 63

double creation: 12, 13, 31, 139

Greek thought: concept of reason, 30; fatalism, 46

Greek Fathers: divinization, viii, 101-3; incorruptibility, 101-4; nature and grace, 31; Spirit's role in sanctification, 73-75; *see* Alexandrian tradition; Antiochene tradition; *and under individual authors*

Gregory of Elvira: 6, 32

Gregory of Nazianzus: 3, 14, 30; *see* Cappadocians

Gregory of Nyssa: breath of God, 30; consubstantiality of men, 108-9; contemplation, 30-31; divinization, 103-4; dominion, 57-58; double creation, 31, 139; freedom, 31, 43, 58; ideal reality of human nature, 108-9; image and likeness, distinct or identical, 4-5; image static-ontic, likeness dynamic, 4-5; immortality, 103-4; *In verba: Faciamus hominem*, 5-6; location, 14; loss, 31, 156; nature and grace, 4, 5, 30-32, 103-4; Platonism, 108-9; reason, 5, 14, 30-31, 39, 58; sanctification, 82-83; sin, 156; woman, 138-39; *see* Cappadocians

Haggai: 68

Hebrew conception of image: 24, 64

Hilary of Poitiers: 6, 18-19, 32

Hippocrates: 127

Hippolytus: 6

holiness: in God, 65, 66, 70, 74, 76; of Father, 74; of Christ, 75; of Spirit, 72; human and divine, analogy, 74; Adam, ontological and dynamic, 65-66, 141-42; of man, 74; natural appetite for, 48-50; ontological and dynamic, 74-77; primitive state and Christian era, 115; union with God, 72; virtuous living, 74-77; impact of Incarnation, 163-64; impact of sin, 146-47, 149-52; *see* sanctification; virtue

Illumination: of men by Spirit of Christ, 161-62; of men by Word, 34-38; of prophets by Spirit, 115, 158; *see* light

image: of divine nature, 23, 120-24; of all three Persons, 23, 120-24; of Son, 23, 122-24; of Christ, 17, 23; of earthly and heavenly man, 72, 96, 105, 112; analogy, application to, 47; anthropomorphism, 12-24; carriage of body, 57; contemplation of God, 29; dominion, 51-64; as dynamic and static, 4-5, 47; faith, 39, 161, 162; freedom, 40-50; and gnostic, 57, 78, 124; essential holiness, 6; justice, 22, 27, 60, 66-67, 75, 77, 78, 79, 84; location of, 12-24, 57, 65; lost and/or obscured, 22, 153-59; moral, 9-10; natural and supernatural, 2, 4-5, 28, 31, 34-39, 47, 49-50; by nature and participation, 9-11; ontological and dynamic, 47, 75-77, 79-83; purification, 83; reason, 25-39; recovered radically in Incarnation, individually in baptism, 43, 160-65; sonship, 114; fashioned through virtue, 65, 74-77, 82; will, predisposition to virtue, 48-50; woman, 133-39; impact of Incarnation, 161-65; impact of sin, 22, 31, 74-77, 143-59; Gnosticism, 1-2, 15, 40; Hebrew conception, 24, 64; in Old Testament, 159; New Testament texts, 23; patristic conception, significance, viii; Cyril, general theory, 9-11; *see* image and likeness; imitation; *and under individual topics*

image and likeness, relationship between: writers of first two centuries, 1-2; Alexandrian tradition, 2-7; Antiochenes and others, 5-6; Latin writers, 6, 9; modern exegesis, 8-9; Cyril, 7-9

imitation: of God, 78, 79; creatures have light by, 35; and sonship, 105-6, 112, 119, 120

immortality: angel, 86; body, 90 ff.; God, 85-86; soul, 86; *see* incorruptibility

imperishability: *see* immortality; incorruptibility

Incarnation: brotherhood of Christ and men, 110; as exchange, 107-8; impact on image, 161-65; inclusion of all men in Christ, 92, 108; impact on holiness, 163-64; on incorruptibility, 89, 90,

life: breath of (Gn 2:7), 49, 52, 55, 84; in Christ, 95; God's in man, 102–4; natural, by participation in Word, 88–89

light: Word by nature, creatures by participation, 34–38; see illumination

location of image: body, 12–24, 57, 65; carriage of man, 16–17, 19; soul, 12–24; total being of man, 15, 17–18, 24, 58; Alexandrian tradition, 12–15, 18; non-Alexandrian Greek literature, 15–18; first two centuries, 15–17; Cyril, 19–24; Latin writers, 18–19; modern exegesis, 24

Logos: see Word

Logosophy: 90

lordship: see dominion

loss of image through sin: 22, 31, 143–59

Lot: 126

Male: immediacy of resemblance to God, 134–35; superior to woman, 128–29, 137–38

man: brother of Christ, 110, 112; consubstantiality with Christ, 108; with all men, 108; corruptibility, 85; creation of, 51–52; definition, in Cyril, 19–20, 33–34; in Gregory of Nyssa, 32; Hebrew concept of, 24, 64; image of Father, 10–11; of Trinity, 120–24; proclivity to justice, 48–50; illumination by Word, 161–62; by Spirit of Christ, 161–62; participation in Word, 88–89; light by participation, 34–38; essentially mortal, 85; reason as prerogative of, 34; sonship, see sonship, adoptive; see under individual topics

marriage: 98, 134

Mary: Mother of God, 130–31; Cyril's psychology and theology of, 130; destruction of Eve's curse, 131

Mary Magdalene: 132

Medes: 68

mediation of Christ and Moses: 117

Melito: 13, 16

merit: and freedom, 42, 43, 45

Methodius: 5, 17, 32, 44

mind: created for contemplation of God, 31; has seeds of all virtue, 39; see reason

mortality: essential to man, 85; meaning of, 85; see corruptibility; death; immortality

Moses, mediation of: 117

Natural: ambiguous in Cyril, 54–55; contrasted with given, 55, 85–86; equivalent to original, 30, 50; and inseparable, 86–87; law, 37–38

nature: essential properties, 35–36; laws of, 38, 85

nature and grace: dominion, 54–57, 63; faith, 39; incorruptibility, 100, 102, 103; kinship with Christ, 111, 113, 117, 118, 120; knowledge, 81; light, 37; participation in Logos, 89–90; reason, 30–32, 34–39; sanctification, 70 ff.; sonship, 105–7; virtue, innate orientation to, 48–50; woman, 136–37

Neoplatonism: 156

Nestorius: 66, 112, 113, 130

New Testament: adoptive sonship in, 115–18; image texts, 23; Spirit in, 115–18

Niobe: 136

Noah: 61–62, 159

Old Testament: concept of man, 24, 64; sonship, 115–18, 158–59; Spirit, possession of, 115–18, 157–59; theophanies, 16; virtue in, 157–59

oneness: physical and mystical with Christ, 93–94; with God, 103–4; necessity of grace for, 46; with Word, through Eucharist, 113

operations of God ad extra: common to all three Persons, 51

Oracula Sibyllina: 1, 15, 25, 32

Oriental Church: interpretation of Gn 1:26, 22

Origen: dominion, 57–58; double creation, 13; freedom, 40, 41–43; image and likeness distinct, 3; location of image, 13; loss of image, 155, 156; nature and grace, 31; participation, 79; progres-

Made in the USA
Lexington, KY
28 March 2018